INTERVENTIONS: NEW STUDIES
IN MEDIEVAL CULTURE

Ethan Knapp, Series Editor

CHALLENGING COMMUNION

The Eucharist and Middle English Literature

∼

JENNIFER GARRISON

THE OHIO STATE UNIVERSITY PRESS
COLUMBUS

Copyright © 2017 by The Ohio State University.
All rights reserved.

Library of Congress Cataloging-in-Publication Data
Names: Garrison, Jennifer (Professor of English), author.
Title: Challenging communion : the Eucharist and Middle English literature / Jennifer Garrison.
Other titles: Interventions (Columbus, Ohio)
Description: Columbus : The Ohio State University Press, [2017] | Series: Interventions: new studies in medieval culture | Includes bibliographical references and index.
Identifiers: LCCN 2016043572 | ISBN 9780814213230 (cloth ; alk. paper) | ISBN 0814213235 (cloth ; alk. paper)
Subjects: LCSH: Lord's Supper in literature. | English literature—Middle English, 1100–1500—History and criticism.
Classification: LCC PR275.L6 G37 2017 | DDC 820.9/38230902—dc23
LC record available at https://lccn.loc.gov/2016043572

Cover design by Larry Nozik
Text design by Juliet Williams
Type set in Adobe Minion Pro

∞ The paper used in this publication meets the minimum requirements of the American National Standard for Information Sciences—Permanence of Paper for Printed Library Materials. ANSI Z39.48–1992.

9 8 7 6 5 4 3 2 1

To Mary Kate and Shannon

CONTENTS

Acknowledgments ix

INTRODUCTION Eucharistic Poetics and Christian Community 1

CHAPTER 1 Resisting the Fantasy of Identification in Robert Mannyng's *Handlyng Synne* 19

CHAPTER 2 Devotional Submission and the *Pearl*-Poet 51

CHAPTER 3 Christ's Allegorical Bodies and the Failure of Community in *Piers Plowman* 81

CHAPTER 4 Julian of Norwich's Allegory and the Mediation of Salvation 105

CHAPTER 5 The Willful Surrender of Eucharistic Reading in Nicholas Love and Margery Kempe 132

CHAPTER 6 John Lydgate and the Eucharistic Poetic Tradition: The Making of Community 159

CONCLUSION 182

Bibliography 187
Index 203

ACKNOWLEDGMENTS

I would first like to express my thanks to Larry Scanlon for his unflagging support of this project in its early stages; I am grateful for his challenging critiques and his continued encouragement. Thanks also to Christine Chism, Stacy Klein, and Claire Waters for their thorough and insightful feedback. The members of the Rutgers Medieval and Renaissance Colloquium consistently offered me support and constructive feedback during this early stage. I would also like to offer my gratitude for financial support from the Social Sciences and Humanities Research Council of Canada as well as the Graduate School of Rutgers University during this initial stage of research.

I owe thanks to St. Mary's University for supporting this research through two internal research grants and to my St. Mary's faculty colleagues, particularly Luke Bresky and Tara Hyland-Russell, for their encouragement. I also had the good fortune to have Chelsea Glover as my research assistant for one all-too-brief but enormously helpful semester.

Many people generously offered their feedback on various parts of this work at different stages, and their insights have been invaluable in transforming my thinking on both my own writing and on the field of medieval studies, more broadly. Many thanks to Stephen Barney, Andrew Cole, Darryl Ellison, Susanna Fein, Angela Florschuetz, Shannon Gayk, Mary Kate Hurley, Jacqueline Jenkins, Susie Nakley, David Raybin, Ellen Rentz, Colleen Rosenfeld, Fiona Somerset, Paul Szarmach, and Lawrence Warner. I am indebted to the two anonymous readers of this manuscript whose feedback has tremendously improved this book. Thanks to Eugene O'Connor and the editorial staff of Ohio State University Press for shepherding this book through the publishing process.

I would like to thank the University of Chicago Press, Penn State University Press, and Brepols for permission to adapt material from earlier published essays. Chapter 1 is a revised version of "Mediated Piety: Eucharistic Theology and Lay Devotion in Robert Mannyng's Handlyng Synne" in *Speculum* 85 (2010): 894–922, reprinted by permission of the University of Chicago Press. Chapter 2 is a revised and expanded version of "Liturgy and Loss: Pearl and the Ritual Reform of the Aristocratic Subject" in *Chaucer Review* 44.3 (2010): 294–322 (copyright © 2010 *Chaucer Review*). This article is used by permission of The Pennsylvania State University Press. Chapter 3 is a slightly revised version of "Failed Signification: Corpus Christi and Corpus Mysticum in *Piers Plowman*" in *Yearbook of Langland Studies* 23 (2009): 97–123, reprinted by permission of Brepols Publishing. Some of the theological background material from these articles also appears in the introductory chapter.

Finally, I am thankful for the continued support of my family and friends. My husband, Jesse, has always believed in me and encouraged my academic career even when I've asked him to move to other countries; I will be eternally grateful for his love and support. My beloved children, Omar and Ivy, came into the world during the process of writing this book and, while I'm fairly certain that they slowed down rather than helped with the writing, I thank them for their overwhelming love and for being the fabulous joy-filled people that they are. Finally, I dedicate this book to Shannon Swekla and Mary Kate Hurley, two intelligent and compassionate women who have believed in me, danced with me, and kept me sane over the years: thank you.

INTRODUCTION

Eucharistic Poetics and Christian Community

*I*n late medieval England, cultural expectations of the Eucharist were fantastically high and astoundingly numerous.[1] According to both popular wisdom and ecclesiastical authorities, ingesting the Eucharist could grant believers everything from personal fulfillment and complete identification with the suffering body of Christ to salvation and the unification of fractured communities. At first glance, these eucharistic promises of fulfillment and completeness seem to require little to no intellectual labor on the part of believers. Take, for instance, a particularly vivid example from a fourteenth-century verse sermon on the feast of Corpus Christi. In the central exemplum of the poem, an unbelieving Jew attends a Mass during which he sees each individual Christian literally eat the entire bleeding body of the infant Christ. As he describes the event afterward to his Christian travel companion, "I sauh wiþ myn eȝen two / Where þou and oþur mo, / Vche of ow heold a child blodie, / And siþen ȝe eten hit, I nul not lye."[2] Confronted with this horrifying proof of Christ's physical presence in the consecrated host, the Jew converts to Christianity not simply because of the self-evident truth of the doctrine of transubstantiation but also because "leuere ichaue cristned

---

1. For an overview of the Eucharist's role in late medieval religious culture, see Miri Rubin, *Corpus Christi: The Eucharist in Late Medieval Culture* (Cambridge: Cambridge UP, 1991).

2. Carl Horstmann, ed., "On the Feast of Corpus Christi," in *The Minor Poems of Vernon MS*, Part 1, (London: Kegan Paul, 1892), lines 175–78.

• 1 •

ben / þen euere seo such a siht a3en."³ The Jewish man is content to engage in the cannibalism of eating Christ's flesh during the Mass, provided he, like the Christians, does not have to think about how it works. The sermon then goes on to detail how eucharistic reception unites the Christian community, deters sinful behavior, and limits time in purgatory. As gruesome and somewhat absurd as this exemplum is, the promise that it makes believers is one that would have been quite familiar to medieval audiences: a belief in the Eucharist will help each believer to reach a largely unthinking but highly beneficial union between Christ and oneself. Despite the various physical and conceptual boundaries between the believer and the Eucharist—from altar screens to infrequent eucharistic reception to a doctrine of transubstantiation that defied human logic—the desire for direct contact with Christ's body in the host became increasingly fervent in the late Middle Ages; this desire stemmed at least in part from simplistic eucharistic promises of spiritual completeness.

However, contrary to our generally accepted scholarly assumptions, many mainstream believers—clerical and lay believers who regarded themselves as orthodox—doubted these promises. In this book, I identify a pervasive Middle English literary tradition that rejects simplistic notions of eucharistic promise. Writers of Middle English often take advantage of the ways in which eucharistic theology itself contests the boundaries between the material and the spiritual, and these writers challenge the eucharistic ideal of union between Christ and the community of believers. By troubling the definitions of literal and figurative, they respond to and reformulate eucharistic theology in politically challenging and poetically complex ways. I argue that Middle English texts often reject simple eucharistic promises in order to offer what they regard as a better version of the Eucharist, one that is intellectually and spiritually demanding and that invites readers to transform themselves and their communities.

Over the course of this book, I argue that writers of Middle English engage in what I term "eucharistic poetics," formal literary techniques, including but not limited to figuration and allegory, that emphasize both communion with and alienation from Christ in order to encourage readers to contemplate and question not only their own personal connection with the divine but also the necessity of the institutional church as mediator between Christ and humanity. For Middle English writers, as for many medieval theologians, the Eucharist is a sign that paradoxically both signifies and contains the physical body of Christ. Vernacular writers from William Langland to Margery Kempe take advantage of this paradox, exploring the difficulty of a direct encounter with

---

3. Ibid., lines 201–2.

a physical body that is always expressed in signs, whose very identity is itself linguistic and textual: the Word made flesh.

In much of Middle English literature, the Eucharist and the poetic become mutually defining; both gain their meaning from simultaneously enabling and frustrating access to transcendence. Middle English writers draw on the Eucharist to reimagine the function of poetic language; both the Eucharist and poetic language promise an abundance of meaning beyond the literal sign, an abundance that can never be fully realized. From the *Pearl*-dreamer's frustrated encounter with the irreducibly allegorical Lamb to Julian of Norwich's failed attempts to understand Christ's suffering through metaphorical "likenesses," vernacular texts encourage their readers to desire communion with Christ's body but simultaneously depict that body as ultimately inaccessible. For many writers of Middle English, through this dynamic of inviting and refusing interpretation, the sacrament of the Eucharist provides a model for devotional reading practices as always predicated on distance, mediation, and the refusal of total access to transcendent meaning.

Eucharistic poetics centers on the self-conscious use of literary language—language that is figurative, semantically dense, or gestures toward a literary tradition—to explore the reader's ability to access transcendence through a textual, material object. Recently, scholars of Early Modern literature have shown how poets such as John Donne and George Herbert draw on the Eucharist in an effort to produce poetry that replaced the medieval Eucharist's unification of sign and meaning, materiality and divinity.[4] However, medieval poets, unlike their successors, do not necessarily regard their own time period as possessing a plenitude of meaning deriving from the Mass. Rather, Middle English writers often engage with the Eucharist precisely to foreground the important spiritual work of frustrated meaning, meaning that is only partially understood whether through sacrament or language. In Middle English texts, the Eucharist is often vital to poetic meaning because it simultaneously invites the reader's engagement and proclaims its own opacity. For Middle English writers, as for most Latin theologians, this opacity stems from the ways in which a belief in the material presence of Christ both challenged and supported belief in the Eucharist as a sign of the Christian community of believers.

The Eucharist was often a symbol of both the human community's connection with the divine and the necessity of individual believers' submission before the institutional church. Though this sense of distance from the divine was often theologically and poetically productive, it stemmed in large part

---

4. Ryan Netzley, *Reading, Desire, and the Eucharist in Early Modern Religious Poetry* (Toronto: University of Toronto Press, 2011); Regina M. Schwartz, *Sacramental Poetics at the Dawn of Secularism: When God Left the World* (Stanford: Stanford UP, 2008).

from the social and political restrictions the ecclesiastical hierarchy placed on individual believers, especially the medieval laity. During the period of time covered by this study—beginning with the surge of vernacular pastoral literature in the late thirteenth century and extending roughly to the end of the fifteenth century—the relationship between readers and Christ's body in the Eucharist became increasingly politically fraught. According to the ecclesiastical hierarchy, the relationship between individual believer and the body of Christ required church mediation; only priests could make Christ's body present through the miracle of transubstantiation. By the beginning of the fifteenth century, following Parliament's 1401 *De Heretico Comburendo* and Archbishop Arundel's 1409 *Constitutions,* which authorized the burning of heretics and banned vernacular theology respectively, those who questioned the literal, physical presence of Christ's body in the altar bread faced the very real threats of persecution and execution.[5] The relationship between community, identity, and the Eucharist was not merely of poetic or theological importance; how the Christian community imagined the Eucharist had the power to transform the very nature of that community.

I have titled this book *Challenging Communion* because Middle English texts challenge the received ideas surrounding the Eucharist in at least three important ways. First, taking "communion" as a synonym for "Eucharist," Middle English texts challenge mainstream believers' preconceived beliefs about the simplistic nature and effects of the sacrament itself. Second, they question the ideal of a simple identification, or communion, between Christ and individual believers, between Christ and the Christian community, and between members of the earthly human community. Finally, and perhaps most significantly, Middle English texts often present the Eucharist itself as intellectually and spiritually demanding because it invites believers to transform their individual and community identities. On all three levels, these texts examine the power of the Eucharist through textual representation in order to show and celebrate the ways in which the Eucharist is a challenging communion.

DEFINING EUCHARISTIC POETICS

As a divinely inscribed material object, the transubstantiated altar bread was central to how late medieval writers imagined the written text as well as figu-

---

5. The landmark work on the *Constitutions* and their effect on Middle English writing is Nicholas Watson, "Censorship and Cultural Change in Late-Medieval England: Vernacular Theology, the Oxford Translation Debate, and Arundel's Constitutions of 1409," *Speculum* 70 (1995): 822–64. See also, Vincent Gillespie and Kantik Ghosh, eds., *After Arundel: Religious Writing in Fifteenth-Century England* (Turnhout, BE: Brepols, 2011).

rative and poetic language. In this study, I focus predominately on a broad range of nondramatic literature—penitential manuals, dream visions, religious allegories, mystical literature, devotional treatises, and lyrics—that presents itself as, for lack of a better term, nonheterodox. Though there is extensive scholarship on Lollard texts that explicitly reject transubstantiation, there has been no recognition of the way in which belief in transubstantiation enables writers to focus on the power of the Eucharist as a textual object.[6] In fact, considering the cultural importance of the Eucharist, there has been surprisingly little literary scholarship on this central symbol outside of the context of heresy.[7] An important exception to this general rule is the scholarship on medieval drama. Sarah Beckwith, drawing on the work of Mervyn James and Miri Rubin on Corpus Christi celebrations, has persuasively shown the importance of the Eucharist to medieval drama, particularly the York Corpus Christi plays.[8] According to Beckwith, these plays rely on an understanding of the Christian community as enacting the body of Christ, the body that Christians also worship in the consecrated host. Through performance, the plays reinterpret the nature of sacramentality itself, moving "the sacraments away from the possession *of* the church and toward the relations performed

---

6. Over the past few decades, studies of heretical literature, particularly Lollard literature, have become central to medieval literary studies, and a central defining feature of such literature is often a rejection of the Eucharist. A few of the most influential works in the expanding field of Lollard studies include the following: Margaret Aston, *Lollards and Reformers: Images and Literacy in Late Medieval Religion* (London: Hambledon, 1984); Andrew Cole, *Literature and Heresy in the Age of Chaucer* (Cambridge: Cambridge UP, 2008); Rita Copeland, *Pedagogy, Intellectuals, and Dissent in the Later Middle Ages: Lollardy and Ideas of Learning* (Cambridge: Cambridge UP, 2001); Kantik Ghosh, *The Wycliffite Heresy: Authority and the Interpretation of Texts* (Cambridge: Cambridge UP, 2002); Anne Hudson, *The Premature Reformation: Wycliffite Texts and Lollard History* (Oxford: Clarendon Press, 1988); Fiona Somerset, Jill C. Havens, and Derrick G. Pitard, eds., *Lollards and Their Influence in Late Medieval England* (Woodbridge: Boydell, 2003). For an important recent evaluation of the field, see Mishtooni Bose and J. Patrick Hornbeck II, eds., *Wycliffite Controversies* (Turnhout, BE: Brepols, 2011).

7. Some notable exceptions are David Aers, *Sanctifying Signs: Making Christian Tradition in Late Medieval England* (Notre Dame, IN: Notre Dame UP, 2004); David Aers and Sarah Beckwith, "The Eucharist," in *Cultural Reformations: Medieval and Renaissance in Literary History*, ed. Brian Cummings and James Simpson (Oxford: Oxford UP, 2010), 153–65; Ann W. Astell, *Eating Beauty: The Eucharist and the Spiritual Arts of the Middle Ages* (Ithaca, NY, and London: Cornell UP, 2006); Sarah Beckwith, *Signifying God: Social Relation and Symbolic Act in the York Corpus Christi Plays* (Chicago: University of Chicago Press, 2001). Important historical treatments of the Eucharist include the following: Caroline Walker Bynum, *Holy Feast and Holy Fast: The Religious Significance of Food to Medieval Women* (Berkeley: University of California Press, 1987); Eamon Duffy, *The Stripping of the Altars: Traditional Religion in England c. 1400–c. 1580* (New Haven, CT: Yale UP, 1992); Rubin, *Corpus Christi*.

8. Mervyn James, "Ritual, Drama and Social Body in the Late Medieval English Town," *Past and Present* 98 (1983): 3–29; Rubin, *Corpus Christi*, 213–87.

between people."⁹ Though such theater shares many of the concerns of the texts I consider here, as Beckwith argues, the plays' particular reinterpretation of the Eucharist is distinct to the dramatic form, made possible by physical performance. My approach in this book is similar to Beckwith's insofar as the texts I consider also reflect on the Eucharist as a symbol of the Christian community. However, Beckwith's work is explicitly invested in celebrating versions of sacramentality that privilege the Eucharist as a sacramental action rather than a physical object; she goes so far as to argue that the York plays' vision of sacramentality is more legitimate than the medieval liturgy's version, which she calls "bastardized" because of its lack of focus on the community.¹⁰ In contrast, I am not interested in establishing which versions of the Eucharist are truer or theologically superior. And indeed, for the Middle English texts that I examine, the Eucharist's status as an object is part of its power and appeal.¹¹ They foreground their own status as textual objects in order to reflect on and celebrate the transubstantiated altar bread as itself a divinely inscribed textual object.

Medieval discussions of the Eucharist center on the very nature of materiality, and Christ's material presence was one that had profound political and social implications. Unlike the dramatic tradition that Beckwith describes, eucharistic poetics is a literary system of expression that considers the extent to which readers can access transcendent meaning through textual objects; this literary tradition thus extends beyond the genre of poetry, and its implications extend beyond texts that explicitly discuss the sacrament of the Eucharist. By emphasizing the physical form of the Eucharist alongside the literary forms of Middle English texts themselves, these texts trouble and explore the relationship between materiality and spirituality. My study builds upon recent medieval literary scholarship on form's complex entanglements with history. Scholars such as Christopher Cannon, Maura Nolan, Shannon Gayk, and Kathleen Tonry, to name but a few, emphasize the ways in which Middle English texts are often intensely interested in what literary form is and means within its historical and political context.¹² As Tonry points out, Middle Eng-

---

9. Beckwith, *Signifying God*, 235, n. 24.

10. Ibid., 115.

11. In this way, my project shares some of the same concerns as those of Shannon Gayk and Robyn Malo in their recent special issue of the *Journal of Medieval and Early Modern Studies*, "The Sacred Object," which explores "how sacred objects are understood as instruments of divine power." Shannon Gayk and Robyn Malo, "The Sacred Object," *Journal of Medieval and Early Modern Studies* 44.3 (2014): 460.

12. On this recent return to "form" as a category of analysis, see especially the following: Christopher Cannon, *The Grounds of English Literature* (Oxford: Oxford UP, 2004); Shannon Gayk and Kathleen Tonry, eds. *Form and Reform: Reading across the Fifteenth Century* (Colum-

lish literature is "a powerfully innovative corpus that offers up to the attentive reader often surprising configurations of the 'literary' and the 'thynges' of history."[13] If form, as Cannon argues, is the intersection between materiality and thought, the Eucharist is an example of form par excellence.[14] By using poetic techniques to block and invite readerly participation, eucharistic poetics encourage readers to consider the ways in which the political and ecclesiastical power structures mediate the believer's access to the divine body. The Christian understanding of language and the Eucharist both derive from the central mystery of the Incarnation; the Word became flesh and redeemed human language, and it is through the words of the priest that the Word again becomes flesh on the altar during the Mass.[15] Eucharistic poetics brings together the period's interest in literary form with its central cultural symbol.

Through their engagement in eucharistic poetics, Middle English writers depict the reading of literary language, particularly figurative language, as a spiritual, intellectual, and emotional process. By presenting the Eucharist as a text in need of both devotional and poetic interpretation, vernacular writers trouble our modern critical categories of affective piety and vernacular theology.[16] Recent scholarship on late medieval religious literature has sought to break down previous scholarly distinctions between intellectually serious theological texts and more emotional works of devotional literature. Previously, scholars had tended to assume that intellectual engagement with eucharistic theology in the vernacular was almost, by its very nature, always threatening to become heretical; by extension, affective explorations of the

---

bus: The Ohio State UP, 2011); Maura Nolan, *John Lydgate and the Making of Public Culture* (Cambridge: Cambride UP, 2005); D. Vance Smith, "Medieval *Forma*: The Logic of the Work," in *Reading for Form*, ed. Susan Wolfson and Marshall Brown (Seattle and London: University of Washington Press, 2006), 66–79.

13. Kathleen Tonry, "Introduction: The 'Sotil Fourmes' of the Fifteenth Century" in *Form and Reform*, 4.

14. Christopher Cannon argues that "form is that which thought and things have in common." Cannon, *Grounds of English Literature*, 5.

15. As Miri Rubin points out, the Eucharist was often directly associated with the Incarnation. Rubin, *Corpus Christi*, 142–47.

16. Over the past fifteen years, following the lead of Nicholas Watson, many literary scholars have begun to rethink the nature of Middle English religious writings by reclassifying many texts as "vernacular theology" rather than "devotional literature" in order to highlight the intellectual seriousness of such vernacular texts: Watson, "Censorship and Cultural Change." *English Language Notes* recently published a special issue in which many notable scholars of Middle English literature, including Elizabeth Robertson, Daniel Donoghue, Linda Georgiannna, Kate Crassons, C. David Benson, Katherine C. Little, Lynn Staley, James Simpson, and Nicholas Watson, examine the effect of this term on the field. See Bruce Holsinger, ed., *English Language Notes* 44.1 (2006): 77–137.

Eucharist would therefore be intellectually simple and uninteresting.[17] The erosion of these two categories as distinct within modern scholarship offers us an important opportunity to reconsider the Eucharist's importance to religious literature.[18]

My discussion of eucharistic poetics should further challenge any absolute boundary between vernacular theology and devotional literature by showing how literary treatments of the Eucharist demand both intellectual and emotional engagement.[19] This process often centers on moments of thwarted identification with the divine presence in the host. In contrast to Cristina Cervone's recent study in which she argues for a highly intellectual relationship between theology and poetic form in Middle English texts, I contend that eucharistic poetics does not make a sharp distinction between the theological and the devotional, or the intellectual and the affective.[20] Throughout this book, I use the term "identification" to include both the recognition of the self in the other and the self's attempts to become the other. Although I have drawn the term from psychoanalytic discourse, I do not use it in an exclusively psychoanalytic sense. Attempts to identify with Christ can range

---

17. Previous literary scholarship on the Eucharist has too often drawn exclusively on Caroline Walker Bynum's descriptions of female mystics' ecstatic eucharistic devotion to depict lay eucharistic piety as a wholly affective experience centered on the believer's identification with Christ's crucified body. For Bynum, the scholastic doctrine of transubstantiation is central to female mystics' devotion primarily because it enables an affective identification with Christ that transcends argument; these mystics respond to eucharistic doctrine primarily emotionally rather than intellectually: "The sense of *imitatio* as *becoming* or *being* (not merely feeling or understanding) lay in the background of eucharistic devotion. The eucharist was an especially appropriate vehicle for the effort to become Christ because the eucharist *is* Christ. The doctrine of transubstantiation was crucial. One *became* Christ in *eating* Christ's crucified body." Bynum, *Holy Feast and Holy Fast*, 256–57.

18. Some important examples of this trend are Jessica Barr, *Willing to Know God: Dreamers and Visionaries in the Later Middle Ages* (Columbus: Ohio State UP, 2010); Jennifer Bryan, *Looking Inward: Devotional Reading and the Private Self in Late Medieval England* (Philadelphia: University of Pennsylvania Press, 2007); Gillespie and Ghosh, eds. *After Arundel*; Sarah McNamer, *Affective Meditation and the Invention of Medieval Compassion* (Philadelphia: University of Pennsylvania Press, 2010); Nicole R. Rice, *Lay Piety and Religious Discipline in Middle English Literature* (Cambridge: Cambridge UP, 2008); Fiona Somerset, *Feeling Like Saints: Lollard Writings after Wyclif* (Ithaca, NY: Cornell UP, 2014).

19. As John Arnold notes, scholars have tended wrongly to assume a uniformity of lay belief in the Eucharist. Belief necessarily will depend upon a variety of social, economic, and personal factors, including a level of individual choice. John H. Arnold, "The Materiality of Unbelief in Late Medieval England," in *The Unorthodox Imagination in Late Medieval England*, ed. Sophie Page (Manchester: Manchester UP, 2010), 65–95.

20. Cristina Cervone has recently argued for a connection between theology and poetic form. Her focus is decidedly intellectual, rather than devotional or affective, and focuses on the poetics of the incarnation. Cristina Maria Cervone, *Poetics of the Incarnation: Middle English Writing and the Leap of Love* (Philadelphia: University of Pennsylvania Press, 2012).

from Margery Kempe's emotional attempts to become one with Christ to William Langland's intellectual assessments of the similarities between Christ and the human community. However, in all the texts I examine, these attempts at identification are similar in that they all end with the recognition of human lack. The writers use this lack in order to show the necessity of the Church and its sacraments to Christians' struggle for union with God even as they recognize that full union is not possible during earthly life. This process of simultaneous identification and resistance to identification is a function of literary language. In one of the most influential modern discussions of allegory, Paul de Man argues that, because allegory makes visible the distance between the literal sign and the allegorical abstraction it represents, allegory prevents the reader's emotional identification with the text. As he argues, "allegory designates primarily a distance in relation to its own origin. . . . [In] so doing, it prevents the self from an illusory identification with the non-self, which is now fully though painfully, recognized as a non-self."[21] Though De Man's particular focus is allegory, his statement holds true for eucharistic poetics more broadly. Instead of offering a moment of identification with the divine, eucharistic poetics invite the reader to participate in the creation of the text's meaning even as it highlights the fact that representation and transcendent reality fail to perfectly coincide. De Man's description gestures toward one of the most startling aspects of eucharistic poetics: Figurative language works in concert with affective piety in Middle English religious writing not by inviting communion but by resisting affective identification between the reader and the divine. In doing so, these texts offer their readers the opportunity to redefine the Eucharist and reimagine the nature of Christian identity and Christian community.

POETIC THEOLOGIES

Middle English texts often examine the nature of both individual and community identities by exploring an uncertainty that lies at the heart of most eucharistic theology: ideas of Christ's material presence in the consecrated host trouble and resist ideas about the host's allegorical representation of the Christian community as the mystical body of Christ. In this section, I will show how Latin theology itself highlighted disjunctions between the literal and allegorical in its definitions of Christ's eucharistic presence.

---

21. Paul de Man, "The Rhetoric of Temporality," in *Blindness and Insight: Essays in the Rhetoric of Contemporary Criticism*, 2nd ed. rev. (Minneapolis: University of Minnesota Press, 1983), 207.

Broadly speaking, there were two basic medieval approaches to the theology of the Eucharist based on the writings of two church fathers: what modern scholars often identify as the Augustinian approach and the Ambrosian approach.[22] Augustine and Ambrose themselves did not suggest that their viewpoints were contradictory in any way, and medieval theologians likewise did not argue that the works of Ambrose and Augustine were anything other than complementary. However, those medieval theologians who tended to argue for a more figurative and spiritual understanding of Christ's presence in the Eucharist drew predominately from Augustine, and those who argued for a more literal physical understanding drew mostly from the work of Ambrose. In the end, the views that won out and became seen as orthodox by the beginning of the fourteenth century were those views most heavily influenced by Ambrose. Though the Ambrosian approach became dominant in Latin theology, both approaches were available to vernacular writers.

Augustine viewed Christ as present in the Eucharist figuratively through the presence of the Christian community. The faith community becomes the mystical body of Christ through its faith and charity; the reality of the sacrament is Christ's mystical body, the faithful. He argues that "the faithful know the body of Christ if they should not neglect to be the body of Christ."[23] In fact, Augustine warns against understanding the Eucharist in any way that could be construed as cannibalism. In his explication of Psalm 98, Augustine argues that Christ's meaning in the institution of the Eucharist was fundamentally spiritual: "Understand spiritually what I have said. You are not to eat this body which you see, nor to drink that blood which they who will crucify me will pour forth. I have commended to you a certain sacrament; spiritually understood, it will give life. Although it is necessary that it be visibly celebrated, it must be spiritually understood."[24] Augustine never wrote a tract solely on the Eucharist, but his discussions of the Eucharist in various other

---

22. Ian Christopher Levy, *John Wyclif: Scriptural Logic, Real Presence, and the Parameters of Orthodoxy* (Milwaukee, WI: Marquette UP, 2003), 123–26; Gary Macy, *The Theologies of the Eucharist in the Early Scholastic Period: A Study of the Salvific Function of the Sacrament According to the Theologians c. 1080–c. 1220* (Oxford: Clarendon Press, 1984), 18–43; James F. McCue, "The Doctrine of Transubstantiation from Berengar through Trent: The Point at Issue," *Harvard Theological Review* 61 (1968): 385–430.

23. "Norunt fideles corpus Christi, si corpus Christi esse non negligant." Augustine, *In Iohannis Evangelium Tractatus CXXIV,* Corpus Christianorum Series Latina, vol. 36 (Turnhout, BE: Brepols, 1954), 266. Tractate 26.13. Translation is from Augustine, *Tractates on the Gospel of John,* trans. John W. Rettig, The Fathers of the Church, A New Translation, vol. 79, (Washington, DC: Catholic University of America Press, 1988), 271.

24. "Spiritaliter intellegite quod locutus sum; non hoc corpus quod uidetis, manducaturi estis, et bibituri illum sanguinem, quem fusuri sunt qui me crucifigent. Sacramentum aliquod uobis commendaui; spiritaliter intellectum uiuificabit uos. Etsi necesse est illud uisibiliter celebrari, oportet tamen inuisibiliter intellegi." Augustine, *Enarrationes in Psalmos, LI-C,* Corpus

works enabled later theologians to argue authoritatively that the Eucharist should be understood primarily in a spiritual, communal, and, ultimately, a figurative sense.

In contrast, Ambrose saw the Eucharist as Christ's literal, physical body and the appearance of the altar bread as a thin veil rendering the presence of Christ invisible. In *On the Sacraments* and *On the Mysteries,* Ambrose addresses a group of newly initiated Christians and explains the sacrament in strikingly literal terms. For Ambrose, the same body that was born of Mary and crucified is physically present in the consecrated host; his presence is just beyond the realm of human sensation. He argues that Christ is physically present in the host and the only reason believers cannot sense the presence of flesh and blood is that God knows it would horrify them.[25] As we saw in the exemplum that began this introduction, this argument—that God shields his followers from sensing the true nature of the act of cannibalism in which they engage—became enormously influential in the Middle Ages. Although Augustine saw the presence of Christ realized through the actions of the faithful, Ambrose saw Christ's Real Presence as something from which the faithful needed to be shielded.

The eleventh-century Berengarian controversy, the first major victory for the Ambrosian approach to the eucharistic presence, vividly illustrates the extent to which a literal understanding of Christ's presence in the consecrated host began to dominate orthodox medieval theology. Berengar of Tours was a theologian trained in Chartres who strongly believed in the use of reason in theology. By 1047, he began to publish his eucharistic doctrine, a doctrine that started to be condemned as early as 1049.[26] Berengar argued that, since Christ is not deceptive, bread must be present in the host after the consecration.[27] Making an appeal to metaphor with reference to Augustine's *On Christian Doctrine,* Berengar argued that the host is a visible sign (*sacramentum*) of Christ's presence (*res sacramenti*) and not the presence itself. The Eucharist establishes a real but spiritual communion between the believer and the body of Christ. Berengar's opponents, most notably Lanfranc of Bec,

---

Christianorum Series Latina, vol. 39, (Turnhout, BE: Brepols, 1956), 1386. Psalm 98.9. Translation is my own.

25. Ambrose, "De Sacramentis" in *Sancti Ambrosii Opera,* Pars Septima, Corpus Scriptorum Ecclesiasticorum Latinorum, vol. 73 (Vienna, AT: Höelder-Pichler-Tempsky, 1955), 13–85.

26. Levy, *John Wyclif,* 137–38.

27. On Berengar's eucharistic doctrine, see Rachel Fulton, *From Judgment to Passion: Devotion to Christ and the Virgin Mary, 800–1200* (New York: Columbia UP, 2002), 118–40; Levy, *John Wyclif,* 137–54; Macy, *Theologies of the Eucharist,* 44–72; Nathan Mitchell, *Cult and Controversy: The Worship of the Eucharist Outside Mass* (New York: Pueblo, 1982), 129–98; Rubin, *Corpus Christi,* 16–20.

drew on Ambrose's writings and were unwilling to accept such a radical split between *sacramentum* and *res sacramenti*. In 1059, at the Easter Council of Rome, Berengar's writings were burnt, and he was forced to sign a confession that affirmed that "the bread and wine which are placed on the altar are, after consecration, not only a sacrament, but are the true body and blood of our Lord Jesus Christ. And they are sensibly, not only in a sacrament, but in truth, handled and broken in the hands of the priest, and crushed by the teeth of the faithful."[28] The result of the controversy and the horrifyingly literal nature of Berengar's oath was that no orthodox theologian of the Middle Ages would seriously challenge Christ's Real Presence in the Eucharist.[29]

Two centuries later, Thomas Aquinas defined "transubstantiation" in a distinctly Ambrosian sense and established what was to become the orthodox understanding of the Eucharist for centuries. His definition firmly established the transformation of the consecrated bread as literal, physical transformation and further enforced the idea of the Eucharist as a sacred object rather than a communal event. At the time Aquinas was writing, "transubstantiation" had been in use for about a century, but there was little agreement on the precise meaning of the term; it could encompass a whole range of explanations for the nature of eucharistic transformation.[30] Drawing on Aristotle, Aquinas defines transubstantiation as a process during which the accidents (sensible qualities) of the sacramental bread remain unchanged, but the substance (essence) of the bread is transformed into the body and blood of Christ and none of the substance of the bread remains. However literal his definition of transubstantiation is, Aquinas does not conceive of the Eucharist in a graphic, physical sense. Instead, his use of Aristotle's definition of "substance" allows him to conceive of Christ's presence as both a physical reality and something that is completely beyond the senses. Christ is really, physically, substantially present in the Eucharist, but one can only sense that presence through the intellect and through faith.

Although later medieval eucharistic theology took a decidedly more Ambrosian approach, the more figurative and literary Augustinian approach still persisted, even among the most apparently orthodox versions of eucha-

---

28. "panem et uinum, que in altari ponuntur, post consecrationem non solum sacramentum, sed etiam uerum corpus et sanguinem Domini nostri Iesu Christi esse, et sensualiter, non solum sacramento, sed in ueritate, manibus sacerdotum tractari, frangi, et fidelium dentibus atteri." Original and translation are taken from: Levy, *John Wyclif,* 139.

29. Macy, *Theologies of the Eucharist,* 69.

30. Joseph Goering, "The Invention of Transubstantiation," *Traditio* 46 (1991): 147–70; Gary Macy, "The 'Dogma of Transubstantiation' in the Middle Ages" in *Treasures from the Storeroom: Medieval Religion and the Eucharist* (Collegeville, MN: Liturgical Press, 1999), 81–120. Originally published in *Journal of Ecclesiastical History* 45 (1994): 11–41.

ristic theology. Many theological texts insist on understanding the Eucharist in terms of the complex relationship between truth and figure that it enacts. Throughout the Middle Ages, most orthodox theologians understood the nature of Christ's eucharistic presence through reference to figurative language. Almost every theologian, whether orthodox or heretical, recognized that the physical host was an allegorical sign in the sense that it represented something other than or beyond itself; they typically used the terms *figura* (figure) and *veritas* (truth) to distinguish between the sign and signified in the sacrament. Transubstantiation became an essential component of mainstream theological thought in the fourteenth century, but discussions of the Eucharist's allegorical nature continued both in the vernacular and in Latin.

One important way in which figurative readings of the Eucharist shifted over the course of the Middle Ages was that later medieval theologians placed far less emphasis on Augustine's understanding of the host as a sign of the Christian community, the corporate body of Christ. The increased emphasis on transubstantiation meant that any such Augustinian communal interpretations of the host had to become explicitly allegorical. As Henri de Lubac has shown, there were three basic categories of Christ's body in the Middle Ages: (1) the historical body of Christ, (2) Christ as present in the sacrament of the Eucharist, and (3) the corporate body of Christ as manifest in the community of the faithful.[31] In the earlier Middle Ages, theologians used the term *corpus mysticum* to signify the body of Christ as it was mysteriously present in the Eucharist. However, once theologians became increasingly focused on defining the precise physical nature of Christ's presence in the host they began referring to the sacramental body as the *corpus verum*.[32] Starting around 1050, the corporate body of Christ, which had been referred to as simply *corpus Christi*, began to be referred to as *corpus mysticum* and *corpus Christi* referred only to the sacramental and historical bodies of Christ.[33] The Berengarian controversy effectively fused the historical and sacramental bodies of Christ, and the idea of the corporate body gradually became more separate from the Eucharist because the ecclesial body could not be physically present in the host in the same way that Christ's historical body could. Since the community of the faithful could only be figuratively present in the consecrated host, the

---

31. Henri de Lubac, *Corpus Mysticum: L'eucharistie et L'église au Moyen Age*, 2nd ed., rev. (Paris: Aubier, 1949). I cite from the recent English translation: *Corpus Mysticum: The Eucharist and the Church in the Middle Ages* trans. Gemma Simmonds with Richard Price and Christopher Stephens, ed. Laurence Paul Hemming and Susan Frank Parsons (London: SCM Press, 2006).

32. de Lubac, *Corpus Mysticum*, 221.

33. P. J. Fitzpatrick, *In Breaking of Bread: The Eucharist and Ritual* (Cambridge: Cambridge UP, 1993), 176; de Lubac, *Corpus Mysticum*.

corporate body did not easily fit into definitions of the Eucharist that insisted on Christ's body as physically present. At the same time as the definition of *corpus mysticum* as the community of the faithful arose, scholastic theology began to refer less and less to the host as an ecclesiological symbol.

Although they were not a central feature of all eucharistic theology in the late Middle Ages, discussions of the Eucharist as a sign of community were far from radical; such discussions appear in many medieval texts, both orthodox and heretical. In order to discuss the Eucharist while remaining within the boundaries of orthodoxy, many writers clearly differentiated between the literal presence of Christ's physical body and the way in which the host signifies but does not contain the corporate body of Christ. Even Thomas Aquinas regarded the Christian community as essential to the meaning of the Eucharist. He distinguishes between *corpus Christi* and *corpus mysticum* by arguing: "Now the reality of this sacrament is twofold, as we have explained, one which is signified and contained, namely Christ himself, the other which is signified yet not contained, namely Christ's mystical body which is the fellowship of the saints. Whoever, then, receives the sacrament by that very fact signifies that he is joined with Christ and incorporated in his members."[34] For many writers, both *corpus Christi* and *corpus mysticum* were signified in the host: the difference between the two methods of signification was that *corpus Christi* was literally present in the host while *corpus mysticum* was not. In this sense, communal readings of the Eucharist became more purely allegorical because they suggested a meaning for the host that was outside and other than the host itself. The distinction between Ambrosian and Augustinian approaches to the Eucharist was therefore by no means absolute. Indeed, theologians often celebrated the paradoxically highly literal and highly allegorical presence of Christ's body.

MIDDLE ENGLISH EUCHARISTS

It is precisely by reshaping the relationship between *corpus mysticum* and *corpus Christi* that Middle English writers challenge the belief in simplistic eucharistic promises of complete fulfillment. Middle English texts exploit the

---

34. "Duplex autem est res hujus sacramenti, sicut supra dictum est: una quidem quae est significata et contenta, scilicet ipse Christus; alia autem est significata et non contenta, scilicet corpus mysticum, quod est societas sanctorum. Quicumque ergo hoc sacramentum sumit, ex hoc ipso significate se esse Christo unitum, et membris ejus incorporatum." Original and translation from Thomas Aquinas, *Summa Theologiae,* Blackfriars edition (New York and London: McGraw-Hill, 1964), 3a.80, 4.

differences between Augustinian and Ambrosian approaches to the Eucharist and explore the ways in which both ecclesiastical and linguistic mediation of Christ's body simultaneously restrict and provide access to the divine. In doing so, they aim to transform Christian identity and Christian community.

The structure of this book is both thematic and roughly chronological, beginning with the surge of pastoralia produced at the end of the thirteenth century and extending into the fifteenth century. The first two chapters examine how two Middle English texts—*Handlyng Synne* and *Pearl*—use the specific literary tropes of exemplarity and metaphor respectively in order to challenge the ideal of perfect identity between individual believer and the divine. The next two chapters demonstrate how *Piers Plowman* and Julian of Norwich's *A Revelation of Love* use allegory to explore the Augustinian belief in the Eucharist as a sign of the corporate body of Christ. Finally, I turn to texts that examine the ways in which eucharistic poetics can provide a path to divine knowledge in ways that are either individualistic, as Nicholas Love and Margery Kempe suggest, or communal, as John Lydgate argues.

The eucharistic poetic tradition that I identify over the course of this book is widespread, and so I have aimed to demonstrate the tradition's pervasiveness by selecting texts from a wide range of genres, from lyric to penitential manual. To a certain extent, each of the texts and authors that I have chosen is representative of its genre and time period. However, each of my primary texts also makes an intellectually, poetically, and theologically complex and unique contribution to the eucharistic poetic tradition. Each uses intricate literary or poetic strategies in order to offer readers a practical and idealistic version of the Eucharist that aims at creating genuine spiritual community on earth.

My first chapter, "Resisting the Fantasy of Identification," takes as its focus Robert Mannyng's early-fourteenth-century penitential manual, *Handlyng Synne*. Through his use of exempla, Mannyng pokes holes in the eucharistic fantasy of perfect identity between human believer and the divine. Drawing on both scholastic theology's emphasis on mediation and popular late medieval modes of lay eucharistic piety that celebrated bloody sacrificial imagery and the idea of direct contact with Christ's body, Mannyng suggests to his lay audience that, although the Eucharist offers believers a fleeting union with Christ's body, it simultaneously demands they seek a deeper devotion through recognition of their own distance from the divine. Mannyng uses the intrinsic resources of the exemplum genre—a genre that persuades readers by asking them to identify themselves with its characters—in order to highlight the impossibility of total identification with Christ.

From Mannyng's exempla aimed at a broad lay audience, I turn my attention to highly sophisticated metaphors meant for aristocrats. My second chapter, "Devotional Submission and the *Pearl*-Poet," investigates the poetic engagements with eucharistic theology in the most formally intricate extant poem in Middle English: *Pearl*. Focusing on the four works of the *Pearl*-poet—*Pearl, Cleanness, Patience,* and *Sir Gawain and the Green Knight*—I argue that the poet presents the Mass as a ritual way for the aristocratic subject to secure a stable Christian identity through practicing emotional control. In *Pearl*, through his elaborate use of the pearl metaphor, the poet depicts the dreamer's attempts to possess both his lost pearl and the eucharistic host as futile. The Eucharist, which appears as a piece of bread that looks nothing like the physical body of Christ, teaches the aristocratic subject to be satisfied with simultaneous absence and presence, and to recognize what it is that he truly lacks: Christ.

In the next chapter, "Christ's Allegorical Bodies and the Failure of Community," my focus shifts to allegory, the literary trope that theologians most frequently associate with eucharistic theology. My discussion centers on the relationship between allegory and eucharistic theology in William Langland's *Piers Plowman*. The poem takes on simplistic assertions that the Christian community is one body in Christ—seemingly effortless in its communal solidarity and unity—and replaces them with an invitation to readers to engage in the frustrating and ongoing work of reforming a fractured community. I focus on the poem's penultimate passus, which begins with Will falling asleep during the Mass immediately before he would have received the Eucharist and ends with the Christian community in Unity refusing Conscience's call to eucharistic reception. Framed by these two eucharistic moments, the middle of the passus is an investigation of the way in which signs, particularly Christ's name and the church as a sign of Christ's presence on earth, challenge and enable the human community's access to Christ.

Julian of Norwich's *A Revelation of Love,* the subject of my fourth chapter, also focuses on the allegorical corporate body and actively resists the ideal of personal identification with Christ. Instead, Julian argues that believers ought to long for a communal unification with the body of Christ, a unification that is not realized in earthly life but is instead suspended across both time and individual identity. Throughout her text, Julian uses eucharistic language—images of blood, feeding, and union—to reflect on the power of signs to bring about union between Christ and his earthly church. Julian depicts the Eucharist as essential to human devotion precisely because it is a sign of a union with God that is not yet realized but for which the human community ought to long continually. The institutional church is thus a necessary part of Julian's model of human devotion because it provides the sacraments and therefore invites the Christian community as a whole to thirst for fulfillment in Christ. Although mystical experiences, because they offer direct contact with the divine outside of an institutional context, pose a potential threat to the ecclesiastical hierarchy's monopoly on access to Christ's body, Julian uses eucharistic poetics in order to argue for the importance of church mediation to salvation.

In the penultimate chapter, "The Willful Surrender of Eucharistic Reading," I examine two texts not often associated with poetics: Nicholas Love's *Mirror of the Blessed Life of Jesus Christ* and *The Book of Margery Kempe*. I argue that both texts dwell on eucharistic fulfillment in order to underscore the ways personal expectations of perfect understanding must be set aside and replaced with willed, disciplined acceptance of lack of knowledge and certainty. With his series of meditations on Christ's life, Love provides a tool for lay people to engage in a pleasurable surrender of the will to the ecclesiastical hierarchy, a surrender dependent on the intangible nature of Christ's presence in the Eucharist. *The Book of Margery Kempe* not only enacts Love's model of devotion but also asks readers to consider the eucharistic nature of their own reading practices. The *Book* frequently depicts both Margery and her ecstatic eucharistic piety as alienating to the community around her and thus challenges readers to accept the alienation and distance that is so often at the heart of even the most fervent literary depictions of eucharistic devotion.

John Lydgate, the central English poet of the fifteenth century, recognizes and deliberately draws upon the tradition of Middle English eucharistic poetics in order to explore the spiritual power of poetic form. In my final chapter, "John Lydgate and the Eucharistic Poetic Tradition: The Making of Community," I argue that, according to Lydgate, the Eucharist and the poetic have a reciprocal relationship: not only is poetic language a powerful tool for understanding the Eucharist, but the Eucharist is also fundamental to an understanding of the nature of poetry. The Eucharist is the highest form of figurative language, containing and bringing into conflict the multiple meanings of *figure,* including human body, representation, symbol, written character, metaphor, and prophecy. Poetry and the Eucharist share the social function of illuminating the Christian church by drawing the believer into an interpretive relationship mediated by the authority of both the poet and the ecclesiastical hierarchy; this relationship leads the reader from figurative language to divine truth. Drawing particularly on *A Procession of Corpus Christi* and *Pilgrimage of the Life of Man,* I show how Lydgate self-consciously describes the medieval Christian community as only legible through a Christian figural poetics made possible through Christ's body in the Eucharist. Lydgate resists simplistic beliefs in the divine presence and replaces them with a eucharistic poetics that demands intellectual and affective exertion in order to make Christian community possible.

For Middle English writers, the Eucharist and the poetic provide vital access to transcendence and that access comes because of, rather than in spite of, the limitations placed on the reader's experience of the divine. As I will show in the chapters that follow, these writers refute easy promises of eucharistic fulfillment in order to offer instead the joy and satisfaction that comes as a result of readers' affective, spiritual, and intellectual work of poetic and textual interpretation.

CHAPTER 1

~

Resisting the Fantasy of Identification in Robert Mannyng's *Handlyng Synne*

Robert Mannyng's well-known but seldom-studied early fourteenth-century penitential manual, *Handlyng Synne,* capitalizes on mainstream believers' taste for the sensational and the miraculous. Amidst his seemingly straightforward doctrinal statements, Mannyng weaves in some of the most vivid and entertaining exempla in Middle English literature, including, as I will discuss below, a crucifix coming to life in order to kiss a knight and the Eucharist transforming into the mutilated body of the baby Jesus on the altar. Given its often sensational content, it may be surprising that *Handlyng Synne* is, as I will argue, one of the earliest texts in Middle English to challenge the simplistic eucharistic ideal of perfect identification between Christ and believer.

Mannyng uses a quintessentially pastoral literary form—the penitential exemplum—in order to discuss the importance of the Eucharist to lay salvation.[1] As many scholars have noted, a surge in vernacular literary production

---

1. In this way, my argument is similar to Joyce Coleman's reading of the manual insofar as she argues, on the basis of its interest in the Eucharist, that Mannyng used the text to garner donations for his own Gilbertine order. Joyce Coleman, "Handling Pilgrims: Robert Mannyng and the Gilbertine Cult," *Philological Quarterly* 81 (2002): 311–26.

Although *Handlyng Synne* is well known, the poem has attracted very little scholarship, and most of that is descriptive rather than analytic and interpretive. Fritz Kemmler, *'Exempla' in Context: A Historical and Critical Study of Robert Mannyng of Brunne's 'Handlyng Synne'* (Tübingen, DE: Narr, 1984); Derek Pearsall, *Old English and Middle English Poetry* (London: Routledge, 1977), 108; D. W. Robertson Jr., "The Cultural Tradition of Handlyng Synne," *Specu-*

in England arose following the Fourth Lateran Council of 1215; in response to the most well-known conciliar decree, *omnis utriusque sexus,* requiring yearly confession, many writers began to produce works of pastoralia designed to help lay readers prepare for confession by encouraging self-examination and teaching the basics of the Christian faith.[2] And so, beginning in the late thirteenth century, Middle English texts begin to appear that discuss the Eucharist in ways ranging from sensational to thoughtful.[3] Mannyng's text is a particularly sophisticated example of such early English pastoralia.

---

lum 22 (1947): 162–85; R. A. Shoaf, "'Mutatio Amoris': 'Penitentia' and the Form of the Book of the Duchess," *Genre* 14 (1981): 163–89. A notable exception is Mark Miller, "Displaced Souls, Idle Talk, Spectacular Scenes: Handlyng Synne and the Perspective of Agency," *Speculum* 71 (1996): 606–32.

Some scholars have implicitly acknowledged *Handlyng Synne*'s textual complexity but have limited their discussions to Mannyng's seven "original" exempla, the exempla that do not appear in Mannyng's source, the thirteenth-century Anglo-Norman *Manuel des Pechiez*. Scholarship that focuses on the original exempla includes John M. Ganim, "The Devil's Writing Lesson," in *Oral Poetics in Middle English Poetry,* ed. Mark C. Amodio with Sarah Gray Miller (New York: Garland, 1994), 109–23; Carl Lindahl, "The Re-Oralized Legends of Robert Mannyng's *Handlyng Synne*," *Contemporary Legend* 2 (1999): 34–62; Anne M. Scott, "'For lewed men y vndyr toke on englyssh tonge to make this boke': *Handlyng Synne* and English Didactic Writing for the Laity" in *What Nature Does Not Teach: Didactic Literature in the Medieval and Early Modern Periods,* ed. Juanita Feros Ruys (Turnhout, BE: Brepols, 2008), 377–400.

2. Leonard E. Boyle, "The Fourth Lateran Council and Manuals of Popular Theology," *The Popular Literature of Medieval England,* ed. Thomas J. Heffernan (Knoxville: University of Tennessee Press, 1985), 30–43; Alastair Minnis, "1215–1349: Culture and History" in *The Cambridge Companion to Medieval English Mysticism,* ed. Vincent Gillespie and Samuel Fanous (Cambridge: Cambridge UP, 2011), 69–89. Thomas N. Tentler, *Sin and Confession on the Eve of the Reformation* (Princeton, NJ: Princeton UP, 1977).

3. Many medievalists incorrectly date the serious discussion of eucharistic theology in the vernacular to the last third of the fourteenth century with the rise of Wyclif and the Lollard movement. For example, Margaret Aston even goes so far as to state that, prior to the end of the fourteenth century, the discussion of the doctrine of the Eucharist in the vernacular was "as impossible as it had seemed undesirable." However, some of the texts that we know definitively to have been produced before the emergence of the Lollards include: *The Southern Passion* (c. 1275–1285), the *Lay Folks Mass Book* (late thirteenth century), William of Shoreham's "De Septem Sacramentis" (early fourteenth century), and *Meditations on the Supper of our Lord* (c. 1315–1330). Margaret Aston, "Wyclif and the Vernacular" in *From Ockham to Wyclif,* ed. Anne Hudson and Michael Wilks, Studies in Church History, Subsidia 5 (Oxford: Blackwell, 1987), 303. Guides to the mass include F. J. Furnivall, ed., "How to Hear Mass," in *The Minor Poems of the Vernon Manuscript, Part 2.* EETS o.s. 117 (London: Kegan Paul, 1901), 493–511; *The Lay Folks Mass Book,* ed. Thomas Frederick Simmons, EETS o.s. 71 (London: Oxford UP, 1968). For lyrics, see Rossell Hope Robbins, "Levation Prayers in Middle English Verse," *Modern Philology* 39 (1942): 131–46. Passion meditations include *Meditations on the Supper of our Lord, and the Hours of the Passion,* ed. J. Meadows Cowper, EETS o.s. 60 (London: N. Trübner & Co., 1875); *The Southern Passion,* ed. Beatrice Daw Brown, EETS o.s. 169 (London: Oxford UP, 1927);

Throughout *Handlyng Synne*'s doctrine and exempla, Mannyng presents the eucharistic sacrifice as the solution to all sorts of predicaments—from mining accidents to purgatory—and argues that this sacrifice is essential to lay devotion and salvation.[4] By engaging with both scholastic and vernacular discourses on the nature of Christ's presence in the host, Mannyng reveals that the exemplum genre itself reflects and informs his understanding of the Eucharist. Rather than simply illustrate moral principles, exemplary narratives persuade by demanding audience identification. However, such identification can only ever be partial and Mannyng exploits this aspect of the exemplum in order to argue that both the Eucharist and the exemplum center on failed identification, particularly the failure of the the lay reader to identify with the divine. Although popular belief and vernacular narratives often imply that the Eucharist offers an opportunity for individual union with Christ, for Mannyng, the fleeting union with Christ that the Eucharist offers believers simultaneously demands they seek a deeper devotion through recognition of their own distance from the divine.

I offer my argument in four stages. First, I show how Mannyng's decision to write about the Eucharist in vernacular narrative reflects his particular interest in exploring the fraught nature of the laity's access to the divine. Next, I place Mannyng's text in the context of pre-fourteenth-century scholastic debates about the Real Presence, debates that I argue reveal an internal contradiction: although medieval theologians insisted that Christ's presence in the consecrated host was physical and immediate, at the same time they also suggested that that very presence had to be perceived through some form of mediation, whether that mediation was the appearance of the host or doctrines that told believers what they ought to think when they saw the host elevated at Mass. I then contrast this scholastic tradition with later medieval vernacular texts and lay devotional practices that encouraged lay believers to imagine the Eucharist as providing direct contact with Christ's suffering, sacrificial body. Finally, drawing primarily on four of Mannyng's exempla, I show that *Handlyng Synne* uses the exemplum genre to bridge the scholastic and vernacular discourses on the Eucharist and invites its lay readers to reflect on the roles of both mediation and physical presence in their worship of the divine.

William of Shoreham, "De Septem Sacramentis," in *The Poems of William of Shoreham*, ed. M. Konrath, EETS e.s. 86 (London: Kegan Paul, 1902), 1–78.

4. It is worth noting that, although the predicaments may vary drastically, the solution is often the same mundane one. Family members and friends must pay for masses in order to have their loved one released, whether from purgatory or a collapsed mine.

VERNACULAR NARRATIVE AND LAY SALVATION

Mannyng writes *Handlyng Synne* in English because he regards lay salvation as important and the laity's theological education as vital to that salvation; one of the primary ways in which he explores this issue of lay access to the divine is through an insistent focus on the Eucharist—a sacrament that he believes both invites and refuses direct contact with Christ. *Handlyng Synne* aims to engage its primarily lay audience in theological thought through its use of both narrative and the vernacular, two aspects of the text that Mannyng views as interdependent. By choosing to translate the thirteenth-century Anglo-Norman *Manuel des Pechiez* into the vernacular, Mannyng imagines an uneducated lay English audience that is distinctive by virtue of its thirst for narrative entertainment. For Mannyng, English is not only the language of the people but also the language of narrative.[5] He begins *Handlyng Synne* by presenting lay piety as inadequate, a problem in which vernacular narrative plays an important role. His prologue laments that the laity are unknowingly falling into sin for two distinct reasons: doctrinal texts are not widely available in the vernacular and lay people prefer entertaining tales to sermons. He therefore ambitiously sets out to remedy the situation:

> For lewed men y vndyr toke
> On englyssh tonge to make þis boke,
> For many beyn of swyche manere
> Þat talys & rymys wyle bleþly here
> Yn gamys, yn festys, & at þe ale.
> (43–47)[6]

By interspersing penitential doctrine with entertaining exempla, he hopes that his text will compete with popular forms of entertainment. Instead of insisting that his lay readers must entirely renounce their old habits, such

---

5. As Anne Scott notes, *Handlyng Synne* is a "self-consciously English text." Scott, "For lewed men," 383. As recent scholarship on vernacular theory has shown, a medieval English author's decision to write in the vernacular is not just an indicator of that author's desire to communicate across the range of professions and social classes; many medieval writers argued that English had a particular symbolic value and unique method of creating meaning. Jocelyn Wogan-Browne, Nicholas Watson, Andrew Taylor, and Ruth Evans, eds., *The Idea of the Vernacular: An Anthology of Middle English Literary Theory, 1280–1520* (University Park: Pennsylvania State UP, 1999). On the relationship between Middle English and Anglo-Norman, see Nicholas Watson and Jocelyn Wogan-Browne, "The French of England: The *Compileison, Ancrene Wisse,* and the idea of Anglo-Norman," *Journal of Romance Studies* 4 (2004): 35–58.

6. All quotations of *Handlyng Synne* are taken from: Robert Mannyng of Brunne, *Handlyng Synne,* ed. Idelle Sullens (Binghamton, NY: Medieval & Renaissance Texts & Studies, 1983).

as storytelling, *Handlyng Synne* asks them to integrate greater piety into the practices in which they already engage. Although Mannyng aims to entertain, he does not use the literary form of the exemplum in order to simplify his doctrine. On the contrary: the exemplum demands that readers recognize themselves in the narratives' characters. Mannyng uses this generic feature in order to make his complex discussions of theology personally relevant to his lay readers. Through this complex and strategic use of exempla, *Handlyng Synne* participates in what Ralph Hanna has recently identified as an early fourteenth-century tradition of vernacular texts that conceive of their audience as "responsible religious agents."[7]

Mannyng consciously writes in the vernacular specifically for the laity. Recognizing that there are not enough religious texts available to lay readers, he writes *Handlyng Synne* in order to enrich lay piety and make lay salvation possible. To the best of our knowledge, the Gilbertine canon Robert Mannyng of Brunne only produced two written works, both of which are highly ambitious vernacular projects: the 12,638-line *Handlyng Synne* begun in 1303 and *The Chronicle*, a 24,304-line history of England completed in 1338. Mannyng composes both his texts "not for þe lerid bot for þe lewed."[8] Many scholars have suggested various immediate audiences for *Handlyng Synne*: the Gilbertine novices, the lay brothers, pilgrims, preachers, wealthy patrons, the lower classes, or parish congregations.[9] Although we will probably never know for certain, it is clear that he imagines a broad readership, a readership that only understands English and that engages in secular distractions, such as going to taverns and attending jousts. He directs particular exempla to people who would likely not have been in holy orders, such as parents and wives. Given the lack of exempla aimed solely at exhorting proper behavior for priests and canons, it is highly unlikely that Mannyng's primary audience was would-be Gilbertine canons unless his goal was to provide them with material for preaching to the laity. It is therefore clear from Mannyng's discussions of secular affairs and lay modes of worship that the 'lewed' readership he imagines was primarily the laity.

One of the primary ways in which *Handlyng Synne* grapples with the problem of lay access to the divine is through its focus on the Eucharist. The

---

7. Ralph Hanna, *London Literature, 1300–1380* (Cambridge: Cambridge UP, 2005), 212.

8. Robert Mannyng of Brunne, *The Chronicle*, ed. Idelle Sullens (Binghamton, NY: Medieval & Renaissance Texts & Studies, 1996), 91.

9. Coleman, "Handling Pilgrims"; Ruth Crosby, "Robert Mannyng of Brunne: A New Biography," *PMLA* 57 (1942): 15–28; Kate Greenspan, "Lessons for the Priest, Lessons for the People: Robert Mannyng of Brunne's Audiences for Handlyng Synne," *Essays in Medieval Studies* 21 (2005): 109–21; Lindahl, "Re-Oralized Legends"; Idelle Sullens, "Introduction," in *The Chronicle* (Binghamton, NY: Medieval & Renaissance Texts & Studies, 1996), 17.

Eucharist is central to *Handlyng Synne;* the section devoted to the Eucharist is roughly one thousand lines of the twelve-thousand-line poem. One of the most significant changes Mannyng made when translating the *Manuel des Pechiez* was to double the length of the section on the sacraments, with the majority of the additions occurring in the section on the Eucharist.[10] Mannyng's text has discrete sections—the Ten Commandments, the Seven Deadly Sins, sacrilege, the Seven Sacraments, and confession—but Mannyng's discussion of the Mass's power permeates the other sections of the poem, as well. In one exemplum, included under the section on sacrilege, a deacon sees the Holy Spirit descend onto the altar in the form of a dove during the consecration (8820). In the section on covetousness, an exemplum condemns executors whose chief fault is neglecting to have Masses said for the dead man's soul (1179–80). Many exempla encourage the laity to purchase and participate in Masses for their loved ones because the Eucharist has the power to free slaves, rescue buried miners, send souls to heaven, and release prisoners. Mannyng examines how the transformation of the host into the body and blood of Christ particularly benefits the laity through its assurance of the immediate presence of the divine.

Though Mannyng participates in an already vigorous vernacular discourse on the Eucharist, his treatment of the sacrament is distinctive because of his emphasis on a paradoxical relationship between the Eucharist and the laity: the Eucharist promises direct contact with the body of Christ, but the laity must be cautious to approach it precisely because of the immediate contact it provides. In his prologue, Mannyng presents sin as something tangible, something that each believer literally handles "wyþ honde" (83). According to Mannyng, regardless of one's best intentions, one sins every day. The good Christian must not deny his sinful nature but instead learn to handle his sins properly through penance. For the laity, the Eucharist, in contrast to penance, was a sacrament that was completely untouchable. Since lay people typically only received the host once a year at Easter, the Eucharist was often an entirely visual experience. By the Carolingian period, the church began anointing priests' hands at ordinations and only the priest's specially anointed hands

---

10. Mannyng increases the length of this section from roughly 869 lines to 1,809 lines. He increases the length of the subsection on the Eucharist from roughly 415 lines to 919 lines. These observations are based on my own examination of the two manuscripts of the *Manuel* that are generally thought to most closely resemble the texts from which Mannyng translated: London, British Library, MS Harley 273 and London, British Library, MS Harley 4657. E. J. Arnould also notes Mannyng's expansion of the section on the sacraments. See E. J. Arnould, *Le Manuel des Péchés: Étude de Littérature Religieuse Anglo-Normande* (Paris: Libraire E. Droz, 1940), 298.

ever touched the host.[11] When a lay person did receive the host, he had to receive it directly in his mouth because his hands were not worthy. Mannyng highlights this intangibility in his introduction to his section on the Eucharist. Mannyng prays, "Forȝyue me to day, lord, my synne, / Þat y þys wrþy sacrament mowe begynne, / And wrshypfully þer of to speke / Þat we neure þe beleue breke" (9903–6). This trepidation does not appear in the introductions to any of the other sections of *Handlyng Synne*. Mannyng suggests that it is dangerous to approach the Eucharist, even if only through speech. Although the Eucharist ostensibly brings Christ's body into close contact with the faithful by bringing it down to earth in the form of bread, the Eucharist does not ultimately make Christ's presence into something that the laity could ever approach without fear, let alone dare to handle. By asking his readers to contemplate the Eucharist, Mannyng also asks them to contemplate this paradoxical intangibility of Christ.

MEDIATION AND EUCHARISTIC THEOLOGY

In order to examine how Mannyng negotiates this disjunction between Christ's immediate physical presence in the Eucharist and his divine intangibility, it is essential to explore at some length the specific historical and theological framework from which his thinking about the Eucharist arose and in which he directly engages: theological definitions of the Real Presence of Christ in the Eucharist.[12] From the early Middle Ages on, even Latin theological treatments of the Eucharist struggled to explain this apparent conflict. By the fourteenth century, theologians often attempted to overcome the paradox by relying on the idea that the human experience of Christ's presence in the Eucharist must always be mediated: both in the sense that Christ's physical presence can only be perceived indirectly through the physical appearance of bread and in the sense that individual believers ought to submit to the church hierarchy's definition of transubstantiation rather than rely on their own intellects. This strategy only masked the paradoxical nature of Christ's presence.

The Eucharist was a highly volatile subject throughout the Middle Ages, but virtually every theologian who engaged in debates about the Eucha-

---

11. Mitchell, *Cult and Controversy,* 66–128. See also Ronald Knox, "Finding the Law: Developments in Canon Law during the Gregorian Reform," *Studi Gregoriani* 9 (1972): 419–66.
12. Since records of Gilbertine libraries and education are few, it is difficult to define precisely the nature of Mannyng's theological training and knowledge. However, the theologians whom I discuss in this overview were highly influential figures, and it is almost a certainty that Mannyng would have been familiar with their versions of eucharistic theology.

rist acknowledged the centrality of the sacrament to Christian worship and Christian life. From the eleventh to the early fourteenth century, the belief that Christ was truly present in the Eucharist was required for orthodoxy; the recognition of Christ's "Real Presence" in the host was not up for debate. However, what became a focus of debate was what exactly constitutes a "real" presence: What did it mean to say that Christ was present in a piece of bread when it was impossible to taste, touch, smell, or see him? The precise definition of Christ's Real Presence in the Eucharist was highly important because the very definition of the relationship between humanity and the divine was at stake. If Christ was physically present in the host, then there was the distinct possibility that humans had the power to harm Christ's body by eating it. If Christ was only spiritually present in the host, then it was possible that Christ lied when he said, "This is my body," during the Last Supper. Many theologians struggled to find ways to describe Christ's presence that made him accessible without being vulnerable, and omnipotent without being unapproachable.

As theologians became more Ambrosian in their understandings of the Eucharist by focusing on the literal physical presence of Christ's historical body in the host, they found it increasingly challenging to explain how Christ's body could remain impassible in the consecrated host.[13] As I discussed in my introduction, the first major victory for the Ambrosian understanding of the eucharistic presence came during the Berengarian controversy in the eleventh century; however, this victory also resulted in theological models that threatened to undermine Christ's impassibility. This threat arose from the oath that Berengar was forced to sign, which affirmed that "the bread and wine which are placed on the altar are, after consecration, not only a sacrament, but are the true body and blood of our Lord Jesus Christ. And they are sensibly, not only in a sacrament, but in truth, handled and broken in the hands of the priest, and crushed by the teeth of the faithful."[14] Berengar's oath was widely accepted as a statement of orthodoxy, but the literal and cannibalistic nature of it suggested the disturbing possibility that believers have the power to literally tear Christ apart during the Mass.[15] The oath implies that Christ

---

13. On the distinction between Ambrosian and Augustinian approaches, see my introduction.

14. "panem et uinum, que in altari ponuntur, post consecrationem non solum sacramentum, sed etiam uerum corpus et sanguinem Domini nostri Iesu Christi esse, et sensualiter, non solum sacramento, sed in ueritate, manibus sacerdotum tractari, frangi, et fidelium dentibus atteri." Original and translation from: Levy, *John Wyclif,* 139.

15. Indeed, the oath was so widely accepted as orthodox that it was included in the twelfth-century collection of canon law, the *Decretum Gratiani*. On the legacy of the oath, see Gary Macy, "The Theological Fate of Berengar's Oath of 1059: Interpreting a Blunder Become Tradition," in *Treasures from the Storeroom: Medieval Religion and the Eucharist* (Collegeville, MN:

is a vulnerable, weak God, powerless against the actions of his subjects, and undermines the long-accepted argument that Christ is impassible—unchanging and indestructible—in the host. Unwilling to accept this description of Christ's body as completely accessible and vulnerable to every believer, many major theologians, ranging from Alger of Liège to Peter Lombard, scrambled to find ways both to affirm the orthodoxy of Berengar's oath and to confirm the impassibility of Christ's body in the Eucharist.[16] As a result of the controversy, theologians often struggled with the challenge of understanding how Christ could be really present in the host and still not be subject to the control of the faithful.[17]

At the Fourth Lateran Council in 1215, the church began narrowing the definition of Christ's eucharistic presence and affirmed the necessity of priestly mediation to an experience of that presence. The Council's first canon, *Firmiter*, used the term *transubstantiatio* to describe the change that the bread undergoes during the consecration, a change that it argued could only be effected by a duly ordained priest. At the time, "transubstantiation" had been in use for about seventy years, but there was no agreement on the precise meaning of the term; it could encompass a whole range of explanations for the nature of eucharistic transformation.[18] Indeed Pope Innocent III, in his own writings on the Eucharist, never posited the precise nature of eucharistic transformation as a matter of faith.[19] Instead, he had called the Council partly in response to the Cathar and Waldensian heresies, heresies that contested the power structure of the church and the efficacy of the sacraments. As such, the Council never set out to define the precise nature of the eucharistic presence but only to affirm that there was some sort of eucharistic presence in the first place. What was important to the Council was asserting that believers could not experience that presence without the mediation of church authority.

In contrast to Lateran IV, Thomas Aquinas had a much more rigid understanding of transubstantiation, and his definition helped to shape the Eucharist into a sacrament that could only be understood through submission to church authority. When he wrote the *Summa Theologiae* in the later thirteenth century, Aquinas defined the transformation of the host into the body of Christ in a way that was to become the orthodox understanding of the

---

Liturgical Press, 1999), 36–58. Originally published in *Interpreting Tradition: The Art of Theological Reflection*, ed. Jane Kopas (Chico, CA: Scholars Press, 1984), 27–38.

16. Ibid.

17. Macy, *Theologies of the Eucharist*, 69.

18. Goering, "Invention of Transubstantiation," 147–70; Macy, "'Dogma of Transubstantiation,'" 81–120.

19. Levy, *John Wyclif*, 172–75.

Eucharist for centuries. He used the term *transubstantiatio* in a very specific way to describe the transmutation of the host into Christ, and he proclaimed that all other definitions of the eucharistic transformation were heterodox. Aquinas based his definition of transubstantiation on Aristotelian metaphysics. According to Aquinas, the process of eucharistic conversion is properly called "transubstantiation," and he used the documents of Lateran IV as evidence for the support of his particular definition.[20] During this process, the accidents of the bread and wine stay the same, but their substance is transformed into the body and blood of Christ, and none of the substance of the bread and wine remains. He argues that "there is no other way in which the body of Christ can begin to be in this sacrament except through the substance of the bread being changed into it."[21] Only transubstantiation can account for Christ's presence, and therefore the process of substantial conversion is essential to a belief in Christ's real presence. At the time that Aquinas proposed the model of conversion, there were two rival models to explain the real presence: annihilation and consubstantiation. The annihilation model suggested that the substance of the bread was destroyed and then replaced by the substance of Christ. Consubstantiation was the belief that the substance of Christ coexisted with the substance of the bread. Prior to the work of Aquinas, all three models could be classified as transubstantiation. Aquinas considered consubstantiation and annihilation both heretical and impossible.

After Aquinas, the parameters of orthodox eucharistic belief began to get much narrower and more rigid. Aquinas's understanding of Christ's presence in the Eucharist is distinctly Ambrosian in the sense that it focuses on the Eucharist as an object that is consecrated rather than a communal event to be celebrated. However, Aquinas does not conceive of the Eucharist in a graphic, physical sense. Instead, his use of Aristotle's definition of "substance" allows him to conceive of Christ's presence as both a physical reality and something that is completely beyond the senses. Drawing on both Augustine and a reinterpretation of Berengar's oath, Aquinas argues that the faithful do not physically chew Christ's body; they chew only the accidents underneath which Christ is really present.[22] Therefore, Christ remains impassible. Aquinas argues that, when believers claim to see a child or a piece of bloody flesh in place of the host, such visions are not reality but merely representations of the truth.

---

20. Levy, *John Wyclif,* 182–90.

21. "relinquitur quod non possit aliter corpus Christi incipere esse de novo in hoc sacramento nisi per conversionem substantiae panis in ipsum." Latin text and English translation are taken from Aquinas, *Summa Theologiae,* v. 58, 62–63 (3a.75, 2). All citations of the *ST* are from volumes 58 and 59.

22. *ST* 3a.77, 7

As Steven Justice explains, "Beholders may feel they now see Christ's body unmediated, but in fact, a new layer of mediation has been added: the appearance of bread still conceals the substance of Christ's body but now is itself concealed under the miraculous apparition."[23] Aquinas claims that one can only see Christ's natural form in heaven and, therefore, God forms such visions in the eye of the beholder, and they do not take place in the sacrament itself.[24] God does not intend for humans to have an unmediated view of the body of Christ; such a connection with God can only take place in the afterlife. Aquinas contends that sacraments correspond to faith and faith, by nature, has to do with unseen realities.[25] Christ is really, physically, substantially present in the Eucharist but one can only sense that presence through the intellect and through faith, both of which ought to be dependent upon official church doctrine.

After Aquinas, several theologians—notably including Duns Scotus and later William of Ockham and Thomas of Strasbourg—began to argue that the only correct way to understand the eucharistic presence was through the mediation of church authority.[26] At the turn of the fourteenth century, the Franciscan theologian Duns Scotus presented a view on the Eucharist that challenged the role of human reason in theology by suggesting that, although transubstantiation was illogical, it must be the true explanation of the eucharistic transformation because the church had decreed it to be so. Scotus contradicted Aquinas and argued that transubstantiation was not the only possible explanation for the eucharistic presence. In fact, transubstantiation was not even particularly logical. According to Scotus, consubstantiation was the simplest and most scripturally sound explanation. Failing that, even annihilation was less complicated and therefore more logical. But Scotus ultimately decided that transubstantiation was the only orthodox belief with regard to the eucharistic presence because he interpreted the *Firmiter* canon of the Fourth Lateran Council as endorsing Aquinas's definition of transubstantiation as the only possible explanation of the Real Presence.[27] To explain why the church would accept transubstantiation as dogma when the words of scripture could be satisfied in a simpler and apparently truer way, Scotus argues: "I reply that Scripture is expounded by the same Spirit by which it was created; and so we

---

23. Steven Justice, "Eucharistic Miracle and Eucharistic Doubt," *Journal of Medieval and Early Modern Studies* 42 (2012): 316.
24. *ST* 3a.76, 8.
25. *ST* 3a.75, 1.
26. McCue, "Doctrine of Transubstantiation," 403–7.
27. David Burr, *Eucharistic Presence and Conversion in Late Thirteenth-Century Franciscan Thought* (Philadelphia: American Philosophical Society, 1984), 76–98; Levy, *John Wyclif*, 191–98; McCue, "Doctrine of Transubstantiation," 403–7.

must suppose that the Catholic Church has expounded these matters by the same Spirit by which the faith is handed on to us, taught, that is, by the Spirit of truth, and has chosen *this* understanding of things because this is the true understanding."[28] For Scotus, the doctrine of transubstantiation became more a question of the authority of the postapostolic church than of an understanding of the Eucharist. Essentially, he conceded that the dogma had no purpose and no support other than the authority of the church. Aquinas's theology emphasized that all human knowledge begins with sense perception, but Scotus found that he could only agree with Aquinas's explanation of the eucharistic presence by suspending his own knowledge in favor of church authority. After Scotus, it became common for theologians to appeal to Lateran IV as the ultimate authority on the mode of eucharistic change.[29]

At the beginning of the fourteenth century, the mode of Christ's presence in the Eucharist became a touchstone for orthodoxy not because alternate beliefs indicated a misunderstanding of the nature of God but because they indicated an unwillingness to submit to the will of the church. Even for the scholastics, mediation became an intrinsic part of the experience of the Eucharist because nothing an individual possessed—from physical sense to the intellect—could help one understand Christ's presence. For Scotus and those that followed him, an understanding of the Eucharist necessitated a recognition that the Eucharist was actually beyond any individual's understanding; the only true understanding came from the authority of the church.

VERNACULAR NARRATIVE AND CHRIST'S SACRIFICIAL BODY

In contrast to late medieval scholasticism, which defined eucharistic reception as a mediated experience of Christ's presence, the vernacular narratives about the Eucharist increasingly centered on physical contact and identification with Christ's sacrificial, suffering body. As the theologians' definitions of the Eucharist became more Ambrosian, the structure of the Mass itself shifted away from Augustine's understanding of the Eucharist as a celebration of the entire Christian community to an Ambrosian understanding of the Eucha-

---

28. "dico, quod eo spiritu expositae sunt Scripturae, quo conditae. Et ita supponendum est, quo Ecclesia Catholica eo Spiritu exposuit, quo tradita est nobis fides, Spiritu scilicet veritatis docta, et idea hunc intellectum eligit, quia verus est." Latin text and translation are from McCue, "Doctrine of Transubstantiation," 406–7.

29. Macy, "'Dogma of Transubstantiation'"; McCue, "Doctrine of Transubstantiation," 411–12.

rist as sacred object. Over the course of the Middle Ages, the laity became estranged from the action of the Mass.[30] During the liturgy, they prayed silently and had no spoken responses to make. Greater attention to the Real Presence ultimately led to the withdrawal of the cup from the laity, largely out of fears of spillage.[31] In addition, lay reception of the host typically occurred only once a year at Easter, because, from a clerical perspective, limiting the number of times that lay people received the Eucharist both shielded the laity from further sin and protected the host from any contamination.[32] The canon of the Mass was often inaudible to the laity and in a language they did not understand; it was sometimes not even a particularly clear visual experience since screens obscured the high altar.[33] For the laity, the Mass was typically an experience of various barriers between Christ's body and oneself, not the least of which was a doctrine of transubstantiation that told believers that their physical senses were not to be believed.

The barriers that clerics erected between the laity and the consecrated host seem to have heightened the lay desire to see Christ in the host and increased the importance of Christ's physical presence to lay devotion. Alongside the theologians' development of complex theologies of the Real Presence, the laity developed an increasingly fervent cult of the Eucharist that reached its height in the thirteenth and fourteenth centuries.[34] In the first decade of the thirteenth century, in order to prevent the laity from engaging in idolatry by adoring an unconsecrated host, church officials decreed that the host ought to be hidden until just after the consecration, when it should be elevated to be seen and worshipped by the congregation.[35] Since they received the host so infrequently, the elevation quickly became the height of the Mass for many lay people. By the thirteenth century, we find stories of people attending Mass only to see the moment of elevation.[36] Seeing the host was understood as a form of reception, a form that did not involve the risk of mortal sin.

---

30. John Harper, *The Forms and Orders of the Western Liturgy: From the Tenth to the Eighteenth Century* (Oxford: Clarendon Press, 1991), 40–41; Joseph A. Jungmann, *The Mass of the Roman Rite: Its Origins and Development*, trans. Francis A. Brunner, vol. 1 (Dublin: Four Courts Press, 1951), 117.

31. Mitchell, *Cult and Controversy*; Rubin, *Corpus Christi*, 72.

32. Rubin, *Corpus Christi*, 73.

33. John Bossy, "The Mass as a Social Institution, 1200–1700," *Past and Present* 100 (1983): 29–61; Harper, *Forms and Orders*, 119.

34. J. I. Catto, "John Wyclif and the Cult of the Eucharist," in *The Bible in the Medieval World: Essays in Memory of Beryl Smalley*, ed. Katherine Walsh and Diana Wood, Studies in Church History, Subsidia 4 (Oxford: Blackwell, 1985), 269–86.

35. V. L. Kennedy, "The Moment of Consecration and the Elevation of the Host," *Medieval Studies* 6 (1944): 121–50.

36. Caroline Walker Bynum, *Holy Feast*, 55.

Narratives that insisted on the literal presence came to substitute for hands-on participation in the liturgy. In sermon collections and legendaries, miracle tales abounded that assured believers that Christ's body was literally physically present in the consecrated host and that they were therefore in direct contact with Christ when they saw it.[37] Vernacular descriptions of the Eucharist in late medieval sermons and manuals of religious instruction typically favored direct modes of devotion, preferring to promise believers a direct visual encounter with Christ.[38] For example, the thirteenth-century *Lay Folks Mass Book* tells its readers to imagine Christ's crucifixion during the consecration and instructs them to behold the moment of elevation "for þat is he þat iudas salde, / and sithen was scourged & don on rode, / and for mankynde þere shad his blode."[39] Likewise, in an early fourteenth-century poem, William of Shoreham urges his readers to believe that, in the host, "Þat hys swete ihesu cryst / Ine flesche and eke ine bloude, / Þat þolede pyne and passyoun, / And diaþ opone þe roude."[40] Such texts invite worshippers to imagine the sight of the Eucharist as a personal vision of Calvary. Though these texts, like *Handlyng Synne*, often highlight alienation from the divine alongside identification with it, they do suggest that worshippers should strive to identify with Christ on an intense emotional level.

From the thirteenth century until the end of the Middle Ages, many vernacular texts—especially guides to the Mass, prayers in books of hours, and sermon collections—highlighted Christ's immediacy by describing the Eucharist itself in the language of blood sacrifice.[41] However, such direct access to

---

37. For a comprehensive study of the various types of eucharistic miracles and the texts in which they appear, see Peter Browe, *Die Eucharistichen Wunder des Mittelalters* (Breslau: Verlag Müller & Seiffert, 1938).

38. As is well known, the late Middle Ages witnessed a new focus on Christ's Passion. The Franciscans in particular encouraged lay affective devotion through writings and teachings that suggested that people could bypass complex theology and Latin learning through personal identification with the wounded, suffering Christ. For the Franciscans, the pain and suffering of Christ was a devotional tool perfectly suited to the laity's desire to understand and personally engage in the Christian faith. Late medieval Passion devotion and eucharistic devotion were virtually indistinguishable because both focused so intently on imagining Christ's suffering body. R. N. Swanson, "Passion and Practice: the Social and Ecclesiastical Implications of Passion Devotion in the Late Middle Ages," in *The Broken Body: Passion Devotion in Late-Medieval Culture*, ed. A. A. MacDonald et al. (Groningen: Egbert Forsten, 1998), 1–30.

39. *Lay Folks Mass Book*, B.407-9.

40. William of Shoreham, "De Septem Sacramentis," 25.

41. Even one of the most popular verses for vernacular doctrinal instruction on the Eucharist, which begins with the line "Hyt semes quite and is red," implies a bloody sacrifice by imagining Christ's true body as red and bloody rather than whole and impassible. Rossell Hope Robbins, "Popular Prayers in Middle English Verse," *Modern Philology* 36 (1939): 344. A few illustrative examples of the sacrificial language in vernacular treatments of the Eucharist include the

Christ's body is necessarily mediated by the text itself. Such devotional literature often invited its readers to imagine the host as a particularly gory, bleeding Christ in order that they might more fully understand the Eucharist. Across Europe, miracle tales and sermon exempla abounded in which hosts bled or turned into fingers, and such tales frequently encouraged worshippers to pity Christ by portraying him as a suffering, helpless infant, rather than a willing adult victim.[42] Since such devotional literature was almost always written by clerics and—especially in the case of sermon collections—written for priests as a resource for preaching to the laity, these texts do not provide definitive proof that the laity themselves were primarily interested in descriptions of sacrifice. However, the dominance of sacrificial imagery in these texts certainly indicates that clerical authors perceived that such imagery was or should be one of the laity's preferred ways of thinking about the Eucharist.

The interest in sacrifice is typically much more pronounced and literal-minded in texts intended for the laity than it is in the works of most medieval theologians. Most theologians tended to view Christ's sacrifice on the cross as unique and the Eucharist as a sacrifice in a commemorative and representative sense. Along with Aquinas, most theologians claimed that the "Eucharist is at once a sacrifice and a sacrament."[43] However, they rarely elaborated on its sacrificial nature.[44] In contrast, many sermon exempla implied that the Eucharist was an actual repetition of Christ's sacrifice. For example, in a late-fourteenth/early-fifteenth-century sermon on the Eucharist, John Mirk relates two bloody exempla: one in which the host begins to bleed profusely and one in which it turns into a chunk of flesh.[45] Although he never says that Christ is mutilated on the altar, his narratives persuade his audience by suggesting exactly that. Such tales imply that priests reperform Christ's slaughter at every

---

following: Carl Horstmann, ed., "De Festo Corporis Cristi," in *Minor Poems*, 168–97; Robbins, "Levation Prayers," 138–39; Siegfried Wenzel, ed., *Verses in Sermons: Fasciculus morum and its Middle English poems* (Cambridge, MA: Medieval Academy, 1978), 162. For a more comprehensive treatment of the sacrificial language associated with the Mass, see Rubin, *Corpus Christi*, 302–10.

42. Examples of such widely circulated tales and exempla can be found in such texts as Arnulf of Liège's fourteenth-century *Alphabetum Narrationum* and Caesarius of Heisterbach's thirteenth-century *Dialogus Miraculorum*. Miri Rubin provides a comprehensive examination of collections of eucharistic miracle tales and exempla. See Rubin, *Corpus Christi*, 108–29.

43. "hoc sacramentum simul est sacrificium et sacramentum." *ST* 3a.79, 5.

44. Francis Clark, *Eucharistic Sacrifice and the Reformation* (Westminster, MD: Newman Press, 1960), 225; P. J. Fitzpatrick, "On Eucharistic Sacrifice in the Middle Ages," in *Sacrifice and Redemption: Durham Essays in Theology*, ed. S. W. Sykes (Cambridge: Cambridge UP, 1990), 129–56; Jungmann, *Mass of the Roman Rite*, 181–82.

45. John Mirk, "De Solempnitate Corporis Cristi," in *Mirk's Festial: A Collection of Homilies*, ed. Theodor Erbe, EETS e.s. 96 (London: Kegan Paul, 1905), 168–75.

Mass and sacrifice Christ in much the same way that Old Testament priests sacrificed animals. Most medieval theologians—from Thomas Aquinas to Nicholas of Cusa—did not accept that bloody visions at the consecration were visions of reality,[46] but it was tales of such bloody visions and the promise of direct contact with Christ's sacrificial body that seem to have fueled much of the popular desire for the Eucharist.

Although there was no official doctrine that explicitly claimed that the Mass was a literal blood sacrifice, the church tacitly encouraged the laity to hold such a view by urging them to buy Masses. It depicted the offering of Masses as a good work that worked like a repeatable blood sacrifice in the sense that its repetition automatically exerted an influence on God. The practice of paying priests to offer Masses as sacrifices in satisfaction for sins was one of the most significant ways in which the laity could participate in the Mass. Indeed, the lay desire to offer the Mass as a sacrifice is fundamental to the way in which we understand religious practices of the Middle Ages. As John Bossy argues, "The devotion, theology, liturgy, architecture, finances, social structure and institutions of late medieval Christianity are inconceivable without the assumption that the friends and relations of the souls in purgatory had an absolute obligation to procure their release, above all by having masses said for them."[47] The Mass as sacrifice was integral to lay medieval piety, and vernacular texts often depict that sacrifice in terms of a visual and affective identification with the mutilated body of Christ.

MANNYNG'S EUCHARISTIC EXEMPLA

In *Handlyng Synne*, Mannyng recognizes the disjunctions between and within the scholastic understanding of the Eucharist as mediated and the apparent lay desire for Christ's immediate presence. He engages with both these discourses in his effort to show how Christ's intangibility in the host ought to lead the lay believer to personal reform. Although Mannyng does conceive of the host as an object that ought to be worshipped, he argues that Christ's mediated presence in the host should encourage believers to live more virtuous Christian lives within their own immediate communities.

---

46. One notable exception is Duns Scotus, but even the majority of Franciscans tended to agree with Aquinas. Caroline Walker Bynum, "Seeing and Seeing Beyond: The Mass of St. Gregory in the Fifteenth Century," in *The Mind's Eye: Art and Theological Argument in the Middle Ages*, ed. Jeffrey F. Hamburger and Anne-Marie Bouché (Princeton, NJ: Department of Art and Archaeology, 2006), 208–40.

47. Bossy, "Mass as a Social Institution."

Handlyng Synne embraces many conventional aspects of lay eucharistic devotion, including the popular conception of the Mass as sacrificial. Mannyng explains that, during the Mass, "Þe sone ys offred to fader in heuene / For þo soules þat þe prest wyl neuene" (10505–6). To emphasize its sacrificial nature, he begins his section on the Eucharist with a description of the Last Supper. Assuming his readers know the story, Mannyng glosses over the narrative to highlight what he considers essential: the institution of the Eucharist at the Last Supper is indistinguishable from the pain Christ suffers on the cross. He begins by explaining "For whan hys passyoun neyher nye, / To hys dyscyplys þat were hym bye / He 3af hys body hem to fede" (9913–15). Instead of explaining that Christ gave his body to his disciples in the form of bread, Mannyng marks the event as cannibalistic by describing how Christ simply gave them his body to eat. When Mannyng later uses the phrase "ful vyle deþ & pynyng wo," he describes both Christ's experience on the cross and how Christ feels when he gives his disciples his flesh to eat (9920). It is the Eucharist's status as a bloody and painful sacrifice that assures its continual efficacy. Mannyng explains that every single Mass aids the salvation of souls in purgatory "for no þyng may hem so moche auayle / Of here peyne and here trauayle / As þe sacrament of þe autere / Ne makþ hem of peyne so clere" (10321–24). The second half of the section on the Eucharist focuses on the Mass's sacrificial efficacy, supported by four successive exempla, all illustrating the same teaching: saying Masses for a person, whether living or dead, has a tangible effect on that person's well-being and salvation.[48] As in many vernacular discussions of the Eucharist, *Handlyng Synne* unites the Eucharist with the Passion in order to show the sacrament's inherently sacrificial nature.

However, Mannyng carefully places this sacrificial and physical understanding within a Thomistic framework that insists on the necessity of both sensory and intellectual mediation. In his introduction to the section on the Eucharist, Mannyng explains the eucharistic transformation in the newly orthodox terms of transubstantiation: to consecrate is to "chaunge þe lyknes / Yn to a nouþer þyng þat es: / Þe lyknes of brede & wyne, / Yn flesshe & blod to turne hyt ynne" (9977–80). Demonstrating his understanding of the distinction between substantial and accidental change, Mannyng carefully points out that "hyt semeþ brede as by syght, / And as brede sauer haþ ryght. / Noþer þy

---

48. In the first exemplum (10327–86), a dead man appears to a priest and asks him to say six Masses so that the man's sins may be forgiven and he may finally enter heaven. In the second (10405–95), a man in purgatory appears to his wife and convinces her to purchase private Masses so he can enter heaven. In the third (10527–718), a knight is captured and enslaved, but because his brother the abbot says a Mass for him every day, no one is able to bind the knight in fetters, and he is therefore freed. In the fourth (10733–806), a buried miner survives for a year in a collapsed mine because his wife has a Mass said for him every day.

syghte no þy felyng / Hast þou on no certeyn þyng" (9995–98). Mannyng stays within the bounds of scholastic orthodoxy by affirming the imperceptibility of Christ's presence in the host.

However, Mannyng also emphasizes that reception of the Eucharist is a tangible experience when he describes the physical properties of the host itself (10089–164).[49] He suggests that, since a person who receives the host ought to be free from sin, believers ought to imitate the physical properties of the host rather than directly imitating Christ's sacrifice. Readers ought to become like the altar bread; he names seven properties of the host that signify the ways in which Christians should stand against the Seven Deadly Sins. For example, Christians ought not to be prideful because "Þou wost weyl þat þe vbble / Ys but a lytyl þyng to se. / So shul we be lytyl yn wyl, / Lytyl & meke wyþ outen yl" (10091–94). Likewise, since the host is white, Christians should not fall into the blackness of lechery (10143–46). Mannyng's explanation urges Christians to imitate the physical properties of the bread itself, rather than the person whom the bread signifies. At first glance, this explanation of the significance of the properties of the host might seem to confuse substance and accidents by aligning the physical accidents of the bread with Christian virtues.

On the contrary, Mannyng expands transubstantiation to include not only the transformation of bread but also the transformation of believers themselves into the body of Christ. Mannyng explains that Christ is not present in hosts made of sour dough because sourness signifies envy and "Þarfore makþ he noun herbergerye / Þere he fyndes byfore enuye" (10113–14). Christ will not dwell in bread that represents envy through its sourness, just as he will not be present in an envious person. Recipients of the host must commit to being like the host so that they too might experience substantial conversion. Through reception of the Eucharist, Christ transforms the believer's substance into his own while leaving the believer's accidents intact. Mannyng's exposition of the host's physical nature broadens his focus from the Real Presence in the host to include the mystical body of Christ, the whole community of believers.

By focusing on the physical attributes of the host—while recognizing that they are not indications of Christ's presence—Mannyng endorses host devotion as a vital albeit indirect method of worshipping Christ. Mannyng foregrounds host devotion as a mediated experience. He does not claim that seeing the host is identical to seeing Christ face to face. However, Mannyng

---

49. An analogous passage also occurs in the *Manuel*, with slightly different descriptions and ordering. Although the content of Mannyng's explication of the properties of the host is not markedly different from that which appears in the *Manuel*, the historical context—particularly the new emphasis on the orthodoxy of transubstantiation—significantly alters the implications of the passage.

still regards the Eucharist as essential to salvation. The mediation that the bread's accidents and the rituals of the church provide helps to increase the believer's faith and commitment to a life free from the seven deadly sins. Even though the ostensible purpose of the Eucharist is the conversion of the soul and communion with Christ, Mannyng insists that that purpose must be achieved through mediation. The intangibility of Christ's presence in the bread is not a detriment to the faith, but is actually an essential part of it.

According to Mannyng, the sacrifice of the Mass has many benefits, but it does not provide the individual believer with direct contact with the divine. It is in his four exempla that portray encounters with the suffering body of Christ—two that depict him as an adult and two that depict him as a mutilated infant—that Mannyng most clearly contests the possibility of personal union with the sacrificial body of Christ. These exempla will be the focus of the remainder of this chapter. Only one of these exempla directly supports a doctrine on the Eucharist, but all four are eucharistic. All four narratives and their surrounding commentary develop arguments about identification with Christ, the desire to incorporate Christ's identity into one's own; all four directly deal with the individual believer's relationship to Christ's body, a relationship most frequently associated with the Eucharist. Only one of these four exempla is original to Mannyng.[50] Nevertheless, he makes all of them distinctly his own through a particular focus on the process of identification, accomplished mainly by marked increases in both the amount of direct discourse and narrative detail.

Through this insistent focus on identification, he draws on the exemplum's intrinsic generic resources. As recent scholarship has recognized, exempla are rarely if ever passive vehicles of church doctrine. On the contrary, as the scholarship of Elizabeth Allen, Mark Miller, Susan Phillips, Catherine Sanok, and Larry Scanlon shows, exemplary narratives often exceed the general rule they purport to exemplify and highlight the psychologically contingent nature of moral choices. That makes individual subjectivity central to the exemplum's narrative function,[51] a function upon which Mannyng extensively draws. In

---

50. The "Bloody Child" exemplum does not appear in the *Manuel*, but does have a few analogues. See Frederic C. Tubach, *Index Exemplorum: A Handbook of Medieval Religious Tales* (Helsinki: Suomalainene Tiedeakatemia, 1969), 386, no. 5103 (misnumbered as no. 5013).

51. Although their approaches and arguments often differ considerably, all of the following scholars emphasize the role of the audience and individual psychology in making meaning: Elizabeth Allen, *False Fables and Exemplary Truth in Later Middle English Literature* (New York: Palgrave Macmillan, 2005); Miller, "Displaced Souls"; Susan E. Phillips, *Transforming Talk: The Problem with Gossip in Late Medieval England* (University Park: Pennsylvania State UP, 2007), 13–63; Catherine Sanok, *Her Life Historical: Exemplarity and Female Saints' Lives in Late Medieval England* (Philadelphia: University of Pennsylvania Press, 2007); Larry Scanlon,

these four exempla, he presents encounters with the presence of Christ as fundamentally alienating because the individual believer can never fully identify with Christ.

Mannyng's theological point is straightforward: sin keeps believers from recognizing themselves in the image of God. The exemplum is an ideal form for discussing the limits of identification because, rather than simply illustrate moral principles, exemplary narratives persuade by demanding audience identification. As Larry Scanlon argues, "The exemplum expects the members of its audience to be convinced by its *sententia* precisely because it expects them to put themselves in the position of its protagonist's moral success, or avoid his or her moral failure."[52] In Mannyng's four exempla, there are two levels of identification at work. Firstly, the narrative invites readers to recognize themselves in the main characters' sinful behavior and to empathize with their difficulties. Perhaps more importantly, however, these exempla depict Christians who attempt to make that same identificatory connection with Christ. They want to label Christ as a part of themselves, just as they would incorporate him into their bodies through eating the consecrated host. In these four exempla, such attempts at identification are never complete in and of themselves. Encounters with Christ remind the sinner and the reader of their own sins and their own need for reform, rather than lead them to an ecstatic union with Christ. These four exempla challenge sacrificial models of eucharistic piety by contesting the idea that direct visual encounters with the crucified Christ can provide affective union with him.

In the exemplum of the forgiving knight, Mannyng argues that direct, visual encounters with Christ are central to an understanding of popular devotion, but such encounters ought not to be ends in themselves. In this narrative, included in the section on wrath, two knights are at war because the older one has killed the younger one's father. On Good Friday, after having been trapped in his castle for a year, the older knight decides to go to church to ask for God's mercy. When the younger knight sees the older knight leave his castle, he intends to kill the older knight, but the older knight begs for mercy in the name of him that "suffrede deþ on þe rode tre / Þys day to saue boþe me and þe / and forȝaf hem þat hys blode spylte" (3845–47). Their shared recognition of Christ's Passion provides them both with reason enough to demonstrate Christian forgiveness. The younger knight kisses the older knight, and they go to church together. When the younger knight kneels down to kiss the crucifix, the image of the crucified Christ leans down and kisses the knight instead. The

---

Narrative, Authority, and Power: The Medieval Exemplum and the Chaucerian Tradition (Cambridge: Cambridge UP, 1994).

52. Scanlon, *Narrative, Authority, and Power*, 35.

miracle leads to widespread changes in both lay and clerical behavior: "Eury man þer of gan telle, / Prestes yn prechyng þer of gun spelle, / So þat eury man yn þe cuntre / Leuede weyl þe more yn charyte" (3897–900). The visual encounter with Christ is what spurs the bystanders into greater belief and to lead more Christian lives.

For Mannyng, unlike the wondering churchgoers, the miraculous element of the story is secondary to the personal transformation that the younger knight undergoes as a result of reading Christ's actions figurally. Mannyng introduces the narrative by describing the relationship between Christ and the individual believer as one of fundamental similarity; the most significant difference between the two is sin. He explains that "God louyþ eury creature / Þat he furmede to hys fygure. / But þe synne þat ys wroght, / Þat louede he neure noght" (3779–82). In the context of the exemplum, his use of the word "fygure" is provocative. In addition to conveying that man is formed in the physical likeness of God, the term "fygure" suggests that God endows each creature with figural significance, and that sin thwarts a person's ability to signify God. This claim thus offers an important variation on the mode of exegesis made famous by Erich Auerbach, wherein a believer hears about a particular event in Christ's life and then considers how to act in a given situation based on Christ's actions.[53] Reading Christ as a figure for one's own life was simultaneously a fulfilment of Christ's teaching in the present day and a reference back to the historical life of Christ. As Mannyng suggests, when one sins, one's actions no longer have this same sort of figural significance because sin has severed the love relationship between God and the self. Once the older knight invokes Christ's crucifixion, the younger knight reflects on Christ's forgiving actions and decides to directly imitate that loving forgiveness by kissing the older knight. The younger knight encounters Christ in the crucifix because he read his own actions figurally.

The exemplum's central moral action is the younger knight's decision to imitate and identify with Christ rather than his earthly father. In the beginning of the tale, the knights' wrath makes them indistinguishable. In other exempla, Mannyng sometimes names his characters, but he deliberately confuses these knights' identities by leaving them unnamed. His frequent use of the pronouns "he" and "hys" forces his readers to work hard at distinguishing one knight's actions from the other. When the younger knight kisses the older one, he imitates Christ's forgiveness and refuses to engage in his father's feud; he thus shifts his identification and imitation to Christ and away

---

53. Erich Auerbach, "Figura," in *Scenes from the Drama of European Literature* (Minneapolis: University of Minnesota Press, 1984), 11–76.

from a human knightly community based on wrath. From this point on, the exemplum ceases to confuse the two knights, but instead blurs the distinction between the younger knight and Christ. The knight's merciful actions—actions he performs explicitly, "For Ihu loue þat dere vs boghte" (3856)—are an imitation of Christ's love and sacrifice on the cross. However, when the crucifix kisses the knight, it imitates the knight's own action even as it signifies Christ on the cross. After the crucifix kisses the knight, Mannyng remarks, "Y trowe yn hys herte were moche blys" (3892), but he never makes it clear whether Christ or the knight is the antecedent of "hys." Over the course of the exemplum, Christ and the knight become figures who signify each other. The forgiving knight makes a radical shift from pursuing vengeance in the name of his earthly father to imitating Christ's forgiveness. In doing so, he recovers the "fygure" of Christ within himself.

In this exemplum, the ordinary churchgoers miss this complex model of identity transformation because they overemphasize the importance of the miraculous encounter with the image of Christ. For them, the miraculous takes precedence over the knight's conversion of heart and the knowledge of Christ's sacrifice. Although they had all been reflecting on Christ's Passion and all witnessed two warring parties achieve peace on account of Christ's sacrifice, these things do not affect their actions. Witnessing the suffering body of Christ in action, however, affects the way they talk and changes the way they interact with their broader social world; everyone there repeats the story and "alle men þe sunner forʒaue / Here wraþþe þat þey to ouþre dede houe" (3901–2). The faith community is only able to fully understand the significance of the crucifixion when they see the crucifix in motion and then "þey saye hyt alle & weyl hyt wyste" (3886). The image of the bleeding Christ had to be very immediate in order to be effective in inspiring their charity and forgiveness.

Mannyng certainly hails the churchgoers' immediate visual contact with Christ's body as a powerful sign, but he also asks his readers to question the necessity of such encounters. The animation of the crucifix is a confirmation of Christ's infinite mercy and power, and Mannyng encourages the reader to consider this animated crucifix as an instance of a real, physical encounter with the body of Christ by referring to it as the "creatour" (3874). In contrast to the churchgoers, Mannyng's readers do not encounter an affective image. The idea of Christ's suffering is present throughout this exemplum, and the characters witness Christ on the cross, but Christ's pain goes unmentioned. The churchgoers in the narrative are reflecting on Christ's Passion, but the narrative itself focuses on their process of reflection, rather than encouraging readers to make their experience of reading parallel the churchgoers' act of worship. Although the members of the parish only believe that they must live more mercifully once they have seen the physical presence of Christ on the cross, Mannyng encourages his readers to see proof of Christ's sacrifice in the merciful works of others. One of this exemplum's most pointed critiques is of the predominantly lay modes of worship that value miraculous visions over learned Christian truths and the good works of other Christians.

Mannyng launches a similar critique in his story of Fr. Carpus. In this exemplum on the sin of sloth, he argues that visual encounters with Christ can be profoundly alienating. This narrative examines to what extent a devotional focus on the image of Christ's wounded body can bridge the distance between Christ and the believer. At the start of the tale, a priest named Carpus converts a Saracen to Christianity, but this Saracen soon turns away from his newfound faith. Carpus dreams he sees the Saracen crossing an unstable bridge over hell and prays that the Saracen will fall into the pit with the devils. Carpus looks up to heaven in prayer and sees Christ on the cross with "hys woundes al blody" (5287). Christ speaks directly to him:

"Carpus," he seyde, "se wyþ þyn yne
What y suffrede for mannes pyne.
Man to saue y lete me slo
Why wst þou dampne hym to wo?
Why hast þou hym so moche wyþ yll
And for mankynde y lete me spyll?
Wyþ pyne and hard passyoun,
My blode y ȝaf for hys raunsoun.
Why wst þou he hadde helle fere,
Syn y haue boght hym so dere?
(5289–98)

Christ offers his own bleeding body as proof of the Saracen's worth. Since Christ was willing to suffer such torture for every individual's chance at salvation, the Saracen's soul is of great importance to God. According to Christ, in condemning the Saracen's soul, Carpus is also devaluing Christ's body.

Christ makes this argument primarily through the immediacy of vision, telling Carpus to look "wyþ þyn yne" on his suffering body. Carpus's faith can no longer be a purely intellectual or theological reflection; his eyes must encounter the real physical presence of Christ's pain. Through vision, Christ blurs the distinction between the individual and the community by suggesting that damning this one Saracen would be equivalent to damning all humankind and therefore render Christ's sacrifice worthless. Christ's wounds and blood are therefore a reflection of every person's worth. In the image of Christ's Passion, the identity of the human and divine intermingle. The wounds belong to Christ's body and to all of humanity. To have a vision of Christ's body is also to envision one's own salvation.

However, sin keeps the identities of Christ and believer from folding into each other. The exemplum makes this point by shifting the reader's identification at key moments. It first asks readers to identify with Carpus, then with Christ, and finally with both Carpus and the Saracen on the basis of their shared sin. This narrative is the final one in the section on sloth, a section that primarily condemns believers who neglect to live out their faith because of apathy and laziness. When the tale begins, readers are ready to identify with Carpus. After all, Carpus has done his Christian duty very diligently and has put a great deal of effort into educating and converting this Saracen; when the Saracen falls back into his former faith, it is easy to label his sin as sloth and condemn him, just as Carpus does. However, the tale does not make this easy judgement. It moves quickly to a detailed description of the Saracen's perilous journey over the bridge on which Carpus sees him:

> Yn ful gret perel and kare,
> And eure yn point to mys fare.
> Yn poynt he was to falle adown
> Of hys heued formest þe crown.
> Þe fendes þat were yn þe pytte
> Smote vpward ȝyf þey myghte hym hytte,
> And addres bete hym by þe fete.
> (5269–75)

This description evokes sympathy for the Saracen's position and makes Carpus's prayer that the Saracen suffer "dampnacyoun wyþ outen ende" seem particularly cruel (5250). When Christ appears, he demands that readers identify with him, and recognize him as the true victim. After Carpus thanks God for this revelation, Mannyng exhorts his readers to resist sloth, "For þat he loueþ vs alle so dere," creating a distinction between "he" and "us" based on humanity's sinful disinclination to love one's enemy (5317). Mannyng places all his readers in the position of Carpus and the Saracen, both of whom need divine forgiveness because both gave up on believing in and actively imitating Christ.

Although affective reflections on the suffering of Christ open up the possibility to emotionally identify with him, this exemplum suggests that such reflections also reveal the sharp divide between Christ and the self, forcing the believer to recognize the ways in which he cannot fully identify with Christ. The ultimate result of Carpus's vision is that he realizes he is not as Christ-like as he had once thought. In Christ's initial speech to Carpus, he uses highly accusatory language, asking three questions beginning with "why" (5292–94; 5297–98). The questions demand no response, suggesting there is no justification possible for Carpus's actions. Christ repeatedly uses the words "y" and "þou" in order to create a sharp contrast between their two positions. Christ's wounds prove that he is superior to Carpus because Christ allows himself to be open to betrayal and pain while Carpus does not. When Christ describes his crucifixion, he describes it as an act of will rather than suggesting that he was passively acted upon. He exclaims, "Man to saue y lete me slo" and "for mankynde y lete me spyll" (5291; 5295). Christ allows himself to be continually open to bear the sins of others in a way that Carpus simply does not tolerate. However Christ-like Carpus had thought himself to be before his vision, Christ's ever-bleeding body forces him to recognize the vast gulf his sin has created between Christ and himself.

The exemplum's concentration on Carpus's experience as a primarily visual one encourages readers to gain a critical distance on the affective encounter with Christ's sacrificial body. Christ tells Carpus, "But y haue shewed hym so moche yn ded / Wyþ my woundes þat þou seest blede, / Þat y þarfore ne wlde noght / Lese þat y so dere haue boght" (5301–4). Christ expresses his investment in humanity in particularly visual terms; his own crucifixion is a "shewing." Although Carpus has presumably spent much time contemplating the meaning of Christ's suffering during his duties as a priest, Christ suggests that Carpus can only truly understand the Passion and its meaning by viewing Christ's actively bleeding wounds. Mannyng uses the visual as a way to show the self-evident nature of Christian truth and the immediacy of Christ, but his readers do not access the same immediacy of this visual register. Instead, the narrative form mediates the image of Christ's bleeding wounds for the reader. This mediation invites the reader to think critically about the purpose of the vision, rather than regard the vision as an end in itself. Ultimately, Carpus experiences a call to inner conversion not through an intense emotional connection with Christ but through reflection on the impossibility of a total connection. Focusing on the visual register, a register that readers can only imagine and not directly experience, encourages readers to recognize their own distance from the bleeding body of Christ so that they too can see their own need to reform.

Both the exemplum of Fr. Carpus and the exemplum of the forgiving knight encourage reflection on the necessity of the immediacy of Christ's body to devotion. Both affirm the value of a visual encounter with Christ's body, but ask readers to place that encounter within a broader context. Seeing Christ's crucified body is not an end in itself. The forgiving knight must imitate the model of Christ's suffering, and Carpus must recognize his own sin. These two exempla ask their audience to think critically about the ways in which the sacrificial body of Christ demands that believers enlarge their devotional focus.

Mannyng becomes most critical of the devotional focus on the sacrificial body when his discussion of it is most eucharistic. In his discussion of the second commandment—"swere nat goddes name in ydylnes" (607)—Mannyng tells a tale that evokes horror at sacrificial imagery. The exemplum of the bloody child focuses on a rich man who swears excessive oaths. One night, after falling ill, the rich man hears a woman moaning:

> Þat yche womman com hym before
> Wyþ a chyld yn here armys bore.
> Of þe chyld þat she bare yn here armys
> Al to drawe were þe þarmys.
> Of handys, of fete, Þe flesh of drawyn,
> Mouþ, eȝynn, & nose were al tognawyn,
> Bak and sydys were al blody.
> (699–705)

Although it becomes clear later in the tale that the child is Christ and the woman is Mary, Mannyng never names the child. Mannyng intends for his audience to initially imagine this child as just that: a child. Many medieval Christians were accustomed to eucharistic images of the mutilated Christ child on the altar, but this tale deliberately unsettles its readers by asking them to imagine a nameless, innocent infant whose body has been torn apart in almost every way imaginable.[54] Mannyng keeps the idea of pain in the forefront of readers' minds by using the word "sor" repeatedly throughout the tale and his introduction to it. Christ's wounds are not a demonstration of his mercy and generosity as they are in the story of Fr. Carpus. Mary angrily explains to the rich man, "Al hys flessh þan þou teryst / Whan þou falsly by hym sweryst" (725–26). In this narrative, the appearance of a familiar eucharistic image—the mutilated Christ child—is not evidence of Christ's loving and benevolent sacrifice but is instead only proof of sin.

The tale's insistence on the visual brings the reader's attention to the nature of sin and not union with Christ. Mary presents proof of the rich man's sins in particularly visual terms when she says, "Hys manhede þat he toke for þe, / Þou pynyst hyt, as þou mayst se" (716–17). Since Christ is an infant and muti-

---

54. Rubin, *Corpus Christi*, 135–39.

lated beyond all recognition, he cannot and does not speak for himself; the only way to understand his pain is through vision. Mary asks the rich man to undertake an impossible task: to understand the immediate physical pain of a body quite distinct from his own through entirely visual means. Neither the rich man nor the reader can fully identify with the bloody child; they must instead primarily understand Christ's pain and sacrifice through watching Mary watch Christ. When the rich man first sees Mary and the child's mutilated body, but before Mary speaks and identifies herself, "Þys womman soruful and sory, / Þys man for here wax sor agreysyn" (706–7). The narrator twice describes the rich man's response to Mary's emotional pain and outrage as "sor," blurring the distinction between physical and emotional pain (707; 734). Although he cannot understand Christ's pain through vision alone, he can understand Mary's because he can identify with her act of viewing.

For the sinner, expressions and experiences of suffering are indirect; one experiences pain through watching another experience it or, in this case, watching one person witness another's pain. This section on the second commandment raises the breakdown of identity boundaries as a goal of personal reform, suggesting that readers should learn that "euery man vnto oþer, / Þe pore to þe ryche ys broþer" (771–72). For holy people, like Mary and Christ, identity categories need not be rigid. Mary interprets sins against her son as offences against her, and Christ feels the same way about sins against Mary. For example, Mary does not suggest that the rich man will be damned or that Christ will condemn him. Instead, Mary threatens the rich man that, if he does not give up swearing false oaths, she will cease to pray for him because, since the man is so cruel to her son, "How shulde y þan be meke to ȝow?" (732). A large part of the rich man's anguish in this exemplum is his recognition that his sin created boundaries between himself and Christ. The text constructs distinct divisions between the rich man and Christ so that it is possible for him to see Christ's pain but not to claim any of it as his own.

The horror and Mary's response to it alienate both the reader and the rich man from Christ's physical experience. For an exemplum that centers on Christ's mutilated body, the narrative is surprisingly unconcerned with the eventual fate of the Christ child. In fact, despite all the generous descriptions of the blood and gore, the narrator never describes the child crying or the child's pain; as far as the reader is concerned, the child may as well already be dead, but the narrative does not even provide that important detail. Although Mannyng prefaces this tale by saying that those who swear false oaths dismember Christ (668), he does not suggest that repentance will heal Christ's body. Mary herself even seems to forget about the bloody infant she is holding and gives a speech on the conditions of her own intercession.[55] She then walks away "wyþ her chylde" (757), but the narrator does not describe the state of the child himself.

This exemplum encourages readers to recognize their own sins in the wounds of Christ. According to Mannyng, the second commandment forbids both swearing false oaths and misinterpreting theology because both are defamations of Christ's true nature. For example, he explains, "3yf þou trowst þat god was nat before / Ar he was of þe maydyn bore / . . . / Hyt ys a3ens þys comaundement" (647–52).[56] Since many Christians, particularly the ill-informed readers that Mannyng imagines, could easily be ignorant of complex theological concepts like Christology, many readers could see their own sins in the representation of Christ's wounds. Instead of recognizing their shared dignity in Christ's divinity, Mannyng encourages readers to recognize their faults in his mutilation. Mannyng hopes that his readers will recognize their need to remove the sin that keeps the identity categories of self and God so distinct.[57] The identification that the rich man experiences is his recognition of his own sins in Christ's wounds.

The sight of the child's mutilated body is both horrifying and implicitly eucharistic. Mannyng's use of the word "tognawyn" to describe Christ's disfigurement not only suggests that Christ's body is torn apart but also that it has been literally gnawed upon. Mary accuses the rich man of cruelly forcing Christ to repeatedly undergo the suffering of the crucifixion: "Þyn oþys doun hym more greuusnesse / Þan al þe Iewys wykkydnesse. / Þey pynyde hym onys

---

55. "3yf þou wylt of oþys blynne, / þan wyle y preye for þy synne / þat þey may be þe for3eue / And do þy penaunce whan þou art shreue. / For alle men þat hauntyn grete oþys, / To helpe hem at need, certys me loþys" (747–52).

56. Mannyng details various blasphemous beliefs in this passage:

> Or 3yf þou trowyst þat he was noght
> Before or þe world was wroght
> Hyt ys a3ens þys comaundement.
> God was euer wyþ outen bygynnyng
> Ar the worlde, or man, or ouþer þyng.
> 3yf þou trowyst þat hys manhede
> Haþ no powere with þe godhead,
> Repente þe, þou art yn synne,
> For ydylnes hast þou hys name ynne.
> (649–58)

57. Literary scholars have often remarked on the relationship between the construction of the self and confessional literature. Katherine C. Little, *Confession and Resistance: Defining the Self in Late Medieval England* (Notre Dame, IN: University of Notre Dame Press, 2006); Karma Lochrie, *Covert Operations: The Medieval Uses of Secrecy* (Philadelphia: University of Pennsylvania Press, 1999); Lee Patterson, *Chaucer and the Subject of History* (Madison: University of Wisconsin Press, 1991).

& passyd away, / But þou pynyst hym euery day" (719–22). The tale describes the rich man tearing Christ's flesh with his mouth daily, an act uncannily similar to reception of the Eucharist. Like the conventional conflation of Passion and Eucharist, Mannyng equates the sacrifice of the crucifixion with the rending of Christ's flesh through blasphemy. When we swear false oaths, Mannyng explains, we both "dysmembre Ihu" (668) and "vpbreyd hys pyne" that he suffered on the cross (672). He takes the crucifixion out of its historical context by accusing his readers of causing Christ's wounds. However, he also claims that his readers mock the historical wounds of Christ by explaining how "we eft pyne hym so sore" (680). Contemporary sinners both mock and cause Christ's wounds. This confusion of causation is evocative of the Eucharist because, in many sacrificial explanations of the Mass, the sacrament is both a remembrance of Christ's suffering and a reenactment of it.[58] There is no doubt that Mannyng regards the eucharistic sacrifice as spiritually beneficial, but the eucharistic elements of this exemplum are also cruel and repulsive.

In the first exemplum of the Eucharist section, Mannyng directly confronts this conflict between the horror of the sacrificial and its spiritual benefits in the Eucharist. This exemplum, whose ultimate source is a sixth-century story from the *Vitas Patrum*, is one of the oldest and most frequently repeated Eucharist exempla of the Middle Ages. In the story, an old man doubts that the Eucharist is truly the body of Christ. With the encouragement and prayer of two concerned abbots, he prays that God will reveal to him the truth, and after a week of prayer, he attends Mass. As the priest begins to consecrate the host, an angel appears with a small child, and as the priest breaks the host, the angel proceeds to cut the infant into pieces and collect its blood in a chalice. When the priest approaches the old man with chunks of the child's flesh on the paten, the old man shouts out in horror that he now believes in the Eucharist, and the chunks of flesh appear to be bread once again.

This tale deliberately represents the eucharistic sacrifice as horrific. In the sixth-century Latin version of the tale, the narrator gives the conventional Ambrosian explanation for why humans do not ordinarily see the infant Christ, who is always present in the host: "God understands human nature—that it cannot enjoy bloody flesh—and therefore transforms his body into bread and his blood into wine."[59] The Latin text thus attempts to make the story slightly more palatable by suggesting that God fully understands that

---

58. Caroline Walker Bynum, *Wonderful Blood: Theology and Practice in Late Medieval Northern Germany and Beyond* (Philadelphia: University of Pennsylvania Press, 2007), 210–48; Fitzpatrick, "On Eucharistic Sacrifice."

59. "Deus scit humanam naturam; quia non potest vesci carnibus crudis, et propterea transformat corpus suum in panem, et sanguinem suum in vinum." J. P. Migne, ed. *Patrologia Latina*, cursus completus, 1844–55, 73:979. Translation is my own.

the natural reaction to the ingestion of raw human flesh is revulsion. However, Mannyng's version does not try to explain away any of the horror. For readers who have already heard the earlier exemplum of the bloody child, this image of Christ would look very similar except that the butchering of the child takes place within a liturgical setting. It is not sufficient to dismiss this tale by saying that, by the fourteenth century, such images of infanticide had become acceptable within the context of the Eucharist. Nor is it sufficient to suggest that such imagery merely emphasizes the cruelty of Christ's initial sacrifice on the cross. This tale purposefully highlights the horrific and repellent nature of ideas of eucharistic blood sacrifice even as it supports those selfsame ideas. The old man's reaction to seeing the flesh behind the appearance of bread—"on þe pateyn / Morselles of þe child al newe sleyn" (10065–66)—is understandably more a reaction of disgust than of wonder. When the priest is about to give him a chunk of the child's bloody flesh, he does not thank God for allowing him to see this miracle. Instead, he shouts "Mercy, goddes sone of heuene!" (10070). This man achieves a vision of the true nature of the Eucharist, but that vision ultimately portrays the central celebration of Christianity as bloodthirsty and cruel. Mannyng introduces this tale by saying of the Eucharist that "some haue seye hyt bodyly / To whom he shewed hys mercy" (10003–4), but the tale ultimately suggests that it is God's mercy that allows the old man to see the Eucharist as bread; lack of vision is the mercy that humans should desire.

In this narrative, Mannyng positions sight as a powerful conversion tool, but encourages believers not to require visions of Christ's sacrificial body. The tale clearly depicts the old man as a doubting Thomas figure. Like Thomas, who would not believe in the resurrection until he had seen and touched Christ's wounds, this old man is a faithful Christian who fails only in his unwillingness to believe in the miraculous transformation of Christ's body. He imitates Thomas's statement of doubt when "he seyde þat hyt was lye / But ȝyf he say hyt wyþ hys ye" (10025–26). In contrast to the biblical story of Thomas, this old man only needs to see Christ's body in the Eucharist, but does not desire to touch it. In the oldest known Latin version of this tale, when the old man goes to receive the Eucharist, the host only transforms from flesh into bread once it is in his hand.[60] However, partly because believ-

---

60. "Cum autem accessisset senex, ut acciperet sanctum communionem, data est ipsi soli caro sanguine cruentata. Quod cum vidisset, pertimuit, et clamavit, dicens: 'Credo, Domine, quia panis qui in Atari ponitur, corpus tuum est, et calyx tuus et sanguis.' Et statim facta est pars ill in manu ejus panis." PL 73:979. (When the old man approached to receive Holy Communion, he alone was given flesh stained with blood. When he had seen this, he became afraid, and shouted, saying, "I believe, Lord, that the bread placed on the altar is your body and the chalice is your blood." And at once the piece in his hand became bread.) Translation is my own.

ers did not receive the host in their hands in the late Middle Ages, the Middle English version only requires the sight of the flesh. The old man only needs to see the priest offer him "a morsel of þe flesshe / Wyþ al þe blod þer on al fresshe" in order to be horrified into believing in the Eucharist (10067–68). As in the story of doubting Thomas—which concludes with Christ's statement that "blessed are those who have not seen and yet have come to believe" (John 20:28)—this tale urges readers to be more faithful than the doubting man. Hearing the story should be enough to convince them of the Real Presence in the Eucharist. Mannyng concludes that, although this tale emphasizes vision as the vehicle for conversion, "alle ouþre beþ þe bettre / Þat heren þys tale or reden þys lettre" (10081–82). The vision of Christ's flesh is important for conversion, but belief without vision can be even better.

Mannyng argues that a faith that focuses primarily on visualizing Christ's sacrifice is one that risks undermining its own belief in the impassibility of God. In order to prove that the Eucharist is a literal blood sacrifice, this tale contests the idea that Christ's body can survive the consecration. Mannyng describes how all three men perceive "byfore þe prest þat a chyld lay quyk / Yn feyr form of flesshe & blode" (10054–55), emphasizing that the child is alive prior to the consecration. The process of the consecration, in which an angel cuts Christ into pieces, looks very much like murder; the bread is no longer the living Christ but pieces of a dead corpse. This tale implies that, during the sacrifice of the Mass, the priest commits infanticide, and the congregation engages in ritual cannibalism. Rather than suggest that Christ's sacrifice of himself was perfect and for all time, the tale argues that Christians must reenact this sacrifice again and again in order to achieve salvation. This vision of Christ's body in the Eucharist threatens to undermine the belief that Mannyng suggests it proves: the presence of an all-powerful God in the host.

Mannyng never rejects sacrificial images of Christ's body. On the contrary, he uses such images throughout *Handlyng Synne* to encourage deeper devotion in his readers. He affirms that belief in the efficacy of blood sacrifice is orthodox, but insists that it is only a starting point of faith. It is noteworthy that, in a text filled with fantastic tales, Mannyng only uses one miracle tale that involves the literal transformation of the host into flesh. Immediately after this exemplum, Mannyng shifts his audience's attention to his explication of the physical properties of the host. As his readers become more familiar with doctrines of the Eucharist, he invites them to concentrate on devotional practices that demand a more indirect approach to Christ's sacrifice. Like Ambrose, Mannyng believes that Christ's flesh is physically present in the host, but it is better for believers not to see it. The horror of the sacrifice is disgusting to humans and ultimately beyond human comprehension. For

Mannyng, the appearance of bread, the barrier between the believer and the body of Christ, is the ideal way to see the Eucharist.

In these four exempla, Mannyng argues that aiming for a full communion with the crucified body of Christ can be distorting and keep one from personal conversion. For Mannyng, one of the best aspects of eucharistic devotion is that it reveals to the believer his own state of sin. In all four exempla that feature encounters with the mutilated body of Christ, there is a positive spiritual outcome. The crucifix in the exemplum of the forgiving knight inspires greater charity, Fr. Carpus repents his sloth, the rich man gives up swearing false oaths, and the old man publicly declares his belief in the Eucharist. However, none of these outcomes arises from an ecstatic identification with Christ or an entirely positive vision of him. In *Handlyng Synne*, the best faith in the Eucharist occurs when the faithful cannot fully identify with Christ, when their experience of Christ is imperfect and therefore spurs them on to their own spiritual perfection through penance and personal reform.

Throughout *Handlyng Synne*, Mannyng uses eucharistic theology in order to examine lay religious practices. He concludes that the role the laity have been given—either through their own choice or through restrictions that the church has placed upon them—often limits their access to the divine. The very structure of the Mass constantly reminds the laity that they do not have direct access to God; they rarely receive the host, never receive the cup, and the Mass is almost incomprehensible. Perhaps most importantly, despite some believers' claims to see flesh in the consecrated host, most Christians had to settle for gazing upon a white circle of bread. By interweaving scholastic theology and popular devotional practices, Mannyng argues that the barriers between God and the self that the individual believer experiences in the Eucharist provide an indispensable spiritual experience precisely because the Eucharist fails to fulfill the promise of complete connection with the suffering of Christ. The Eucharist helps the laity to achieve salvation by encouraging them to handle the sin that keeps them from experiencing union with God.

For Mannyng, the material appearance of the Eucharist and the process of reading pastoral texts are both important for lay salvation; the transformation of individual identity takes place through a process of rumination and interpretation of both host and text. In the next chapter, I will consider a text that likewise productively explores the individual's inability to identify with Christ in the Eucharist. In *Pearl*, the most formally intricate poem in Middle English, the *Pearl*-poet extends eucharistic poetics beyond the pastoral genre in order to explore the function of the literary and the poetic in shaping the Eucharist and the Christian self.

CHAPTER 2

Devotional Submission and the *Pearl*-Poet

Transubstantiation is an invisible process. In this way, as writers of Middle English such as Robert Mannyng are fond of pointing out, the host's transformation is analogous to an individual believer's spiritual reform: it is internal and intangible but with very real consequences for the individual soul. Within Middle English writings, both transformative processes lend themselves especially well to metaphorical representation because a metaphor, by its very nature, highlights the dissimilarity between tenor and vehicle, even as it explicitly declares their equivalence. For the reader of Middle English texts, discerning Christ's presence in the host, recognizing the spiritual in one's own earthly life, and understanding a metaphor all demand the intellectual work of interpreting a material object in order to access another level of meaning. In many Middle English writings, metaphor and the Eucharist simultaneously invite and refuse interpretation, a feature that allows writers to explore the alienating nature of spiritual devotion to a God that is materially present but invisible. This mutually defining relationship between metaphor and the Eucharist is most fully developed in the most formally intricate poem in the Middle English canon: *Pearl*.

Pearl explicitly brings together its interest in both the Eucharist and metaphor in relation to individual spiritual transformation in its final stanza, a stanza that modern scholars too often ignore or dismiss. After 1,200 lines that explore the dreamer's resistance to Christian consolation in the wake of personal grief, the poem exhorts its audience:

> To pay the Prince other sete saghte,
> Hit is ful ethe to the god Krystyin.
> For I haf founden Hym, bothe day and naghte,
> A God, a Lorde, a frende ful fyin.
> Over this hyul this lote I laghte
> For pyty of my perle enclyin;
> And sythen to God I hit bytaghte
> In Krystes dere blessing and myn,
> That in the forme of bred and wyn
> The preste uus schewes uch a daye.
> He gef uus to be His homly hyne
> And precious perles unto His pay.
> (1201–12)[1]

Following his failed attempt to join the pearl maiden in the New Jerusalem, the awakened dreamer claims that he has learned to turn away from his lost beloved, his pearl, and toward God alone. In this closing stanza, he argues that liturgical devotion to Christ in the Eucharist is the solution to his problems of grief and longing. For many scholars, this claim seems disingenuous; they argue it provides an overly simplistic solution to a problem the poem has otherwise portrayed as spiritually and psychologically complex.[2] I disagree. In this chapter, I take *Pearl*'s closing stanza seriously and argue that the poem's

---

1. All citations of *Pearl* are from: *Pearl*, ed. Sarah Stanbury (Kalamazoo, MI: Medieval Institute Publications, 2001).

2. For example, David Aers calls the ending "theologically superficial and psychologically superficial," while John Bowers labels it a "gratuitous assertion of the Real Presence." David Aers, "The Self Mourning: Reflections on Pearl," *Speculum* 68 (1993): 70; John M. Bowers, *The Politics of* Pearl: *Court Poetry in the Age of Richard II* (Cambridge: D. S. Brewer, 2001), 53. Other critics who read this final stanza as either unsatisfying or unconvincing include: J. J. Anderson, *Language and Imagination in the* Gawain-*poems* (Manchester and New York: Manchester UP, 2005), 77; Denise Louise Despres, *Ghostly Sights: Visual Meditation in Late-Medieval Literature* (Norman, OK: Pilgrim Books, 1989); Sarah Stanbury, *Seeing the* Gawain-*Poet: Description and the Act of Perception* (Philadelphia: University of Pennsylvania Press, 1991), 32. Even the few scholars who have shown that eucharistic allusions occur throughout the poem are reluctant to take this ending at face value. The few modern critics who have written on the Eucharist in *Pearl* are decidedly apologetic in tone, seemingly unconvinced by the importance of the connections between the Mass and *Pearl*. See John Gatta Jr., "Transformation Symbolism and the Liturgy of the Mass in *Pearl*," *Modern Philology* 71 (1974): 243–56; Heather Phillips, "The Eucharistic Allusions of Pearl," *Mediaeval Studies* 47 (1985): 474–86. No doubt part of this reticence stems from a desire to distance themselves from Robert Max Garrett's early and largely unsupported claim that the Eucharist provides the poem's entire meaning: *The Pearl: An Interpretation* (Seattle: University of Washington, 1918). Arthur Bahr has recently addressed the difficulty of the final stanza from the perspective of manuscript studies and the singularity of *Pearl*'s manuscript. Arthur Bahr, "The Manifold Singularity of *Pearl*," *ELH* 82 (2015): 729–58.

poetic complexity enables an equally intricate understanding of the Eucharist. In all four of the *Pearl*-poet's works, the poet draws on figurative language in order to argue that the Eucharist can effect personal spiritual reform. Particularly in *Pearl*, he argues Mass is a ritual that demands that the worshipper accept God's simultaneous presence and absence, a moment in which the divine is almost tangible but impossible to grasp. This focus on representing the intangible brings together the poem's interests in figurative representation and individual spiritual reform. Instead of constantly longing for that which is outside and beyond his grasp, *Pearl* insists that the dreamer must learn to recognize what it is he truly lacks: Christ. The Eucharist becomes a ritual method for the aristocratic subject to reform himself in light of this recognition.

THE *PEARL*-POET AND ARISTOCRATIC DEVOTION

Pearl's depiction of the individual subject's need for interior spiritual and emotional reform is dependent upon late medieval aristocratic understandings of the Mass.[3] Fourteenth-century aristocratic liturgical practices particularly lend themselves to figurative representations precisely because of their internal and private nature. Drawing on these practices, the *Pearl*-poet consistently argues in all four of his poems that internal states have moral relevance and that liturgical devotion is essential to constructing a stable Christian identity for the aristocratic subject.

Fourteenth-century aristocratic liturgical practices were often individual—both in the sense that the aristocracy's experiences of the Mass were typically internal and in the sense that they used their wealth in order to mark out their individual social status within their churches.[4] As I discussed in the previous

---

3. *Pearl* treats the Eucharist in the context of fourteenth-century aristocratic liturgical practice, a historical context that scholars too often dismiss or ignore. In recent years, *Pearl* scholarship has increasingly turned toward sociohistoricism. Several scholars have explicitly resisted discussing the poem's theology because they regard such a focus as a move away from its immediate historical moment and cultural context. However, when such scholarship ignores the Eucharist in favor of history, it denies the fact that the Eucharist itself has a cultural history. Historicist readings that explicitly resist theology include the following: Helen Barr, "*Pearl*—or 'The Jeweller's Tale,'" *Medium Ævum* 69 (2000): 59–79; Lynn Staley, "*Pearl* and the Contingencies of Love and Piety," in *Medieval Literature and Historical Inquiry: Essays in Honor of Derek Pearsall*, ed. David Aers (Cambridge: D. S. Brewer, 2000), 83–114; John Watkins, "'Sengeley in synglere': *Pearl* and Late Medieval Individualism," *Chaucer Yearbook* 2 (1995): 117–36.

4. I use the terms "internal" and "interiority" to denote the aspects of a person that exist consciously within the self, but do not necessarily bear a direct relationship to physical behavior and experience. This interiority includes the elements that Caroline Walker Bynum has identified as composing medieval ideas of the self, such as thoughts, inner motivation, emotions, and

chapter, the late medieval form of the Mass encouraged lay people to engage in increasingly personal, inward-looking modes of devotion because their participation in the Mass was usually limited to silent reflection.[5] Some members of the aristocracy would have been literate enough to understand the parts of the Mass spoken aloud in Latin, but the canon—the most sacred part of the Mass in which the consecration of the bread and wine takes place—was inaudible, said silently by the priest in order to avoid revealing the secrets of God.[6] Late medieval guides to the Mass, such as the thirteenth-century *Lay Folks Mass Book,* encouraged their lay readers to devote themselves to prayers that often had little connection to the priest's prayers and actions.[7] The late fourteenth-century poem, "How to Hear Mass" suggests that, during the Mass, its lay readers ought to "priueliche ȝor preyers preye / To him þat may vn-bynde, / In saluyng of ȝor synnes seuene / To þe mihtful kyng of heuene."[8] Like Mannyng's *Handlyng Synne,* Middle English devotional literature frequently depicts the Mass, in general, and the elevation of the host, in particular, as a highly personalized encounter between Christ and believer in which believers reflect upon their own sins and individual need for redemption.[9] Although Mass was ostensibly a social occasion, the fourteenth-century laity were encouraged to see the liturgy as an opportunity for inward reflection on the state of their own souls.[10]

This tendency toward personal devotion during the Mass is particularly characteristic of the aristocracy. Fourteenth-century aristocrats often used their wealth to set themselves apart physically from the wider parish community, thereby publicly performing their distinctly individual modes of worship. Beginning in the fourteenth century, members of the aristocracy and wealthy

---

psychological development. Caroline Walker Bynum, "Did the Twelfth Century Discover the Individual?" in *Jesus as Mother: Studies in the Spirituality of the High Middle Ages* (Berkeley: University of California Press, 1982), 82–109.

5. Harper, *Forms and Orders,* 40–41; Jungmann, *Mass of the Roman Rite,* 1.117.

6. Harper, *Forms and Orders,* 119.

7. For example, the *Lay Folks Mass Book* directs its readers, during the consecration, to pray for such things as good weather or to simply repeat the pater noster until the elevation occurs. However, the *Book* does name several of the parts of Mass and gives its readers a general sense of the significance of the priest's actions.

8. Furnivall, "How to Hear Mass," in *Minor Poems of the Vernon MS,* ed. F.J. Furnivall, EETS o.s. 117 (London: Kegan Paul, 1901, 493–511, lines 24–27.

9. See, for example, John Audelay, *The Poems of John Audelay,* ed. Ella Keats Whiting, EETS o.s. 184 (London: Oxford University Press, 1931), 62–81; "A Prayer to the Sacrament of the Altar," in *Medieval English Lyrics: A Critical Anthology,* ed. R. T. Davies (London: Northwestern UP, 1963), 115; Robbins, "Levation Prayers," 131–46.

10. Discussing a slightly later period, Eamon Duffy notes that, with the increased use of prayer books, "devotion at Mass ... became a matter of inner meditation on the Passion, using the stages of the liturgy as triggers or points of departure." Duffy, *Stripping of the Altars,* 119.

members of the upper gentry often carried highly ornate and expensive books of hours with them to guide their prayers during the Mass.[11] By the end of the fourteenth century, the public use of the book of hours during Mass became so prevalent that many historians regard it as "the characteristic instrument of noble piety."[12] Such books typically encourage their readers to have an instrumental view of prayer that focuses on gaining personal benefits for oneself and one's family.[13] When prayers in books of hours describe the Eucharist, they typically concentrate on the consecrated host as offering a personal encounter between Christ and the individual worshipper, and the accompanying illuminations usually depict the host in a monstrance or otherwise divorced from its liturgical, social context.[14] Thus, the book of hours became an object that both marked aristocratic worshippers as socially distinct and encouraged them to turn increasingly to their own personal concerns and private devotions.[15] Also in the fourteenth century, the aristocracy began to build private pews and private chapels for themselves within their parish churches.[16] Even the pax—a sacred object passed from person to person at the end of Mass as a substitute for the reception of the Eucharist—was no longer a symbol of community and equality. Not only was the pax often passed according to rank but many members of the upper classes actually had private paxes.[17] From the thirteenth to the fifteenth century, wealthy individuals frequently donated decorations to cathedrals and parish churches—such as stained-glass windows depicting the donor in a devotional scene—a practice that individuated a communal space by simultaneously demonstrating the donor's wealth and the donor's

---

11. It was not until the early fifteenth century that books of hours became more affordable and available to a wider audience. See Eamon Duffy, *Marking the Hours: English People and Their Prayers 1240–1570* (New Haven, CT: Yale UP, 2006), 4.

12. Jeremy Catto, "Religion and the English Nobility in the Later Fourteenth Century," in *History and Imagination: Essays in Honour of H. R. Trevor-Roper*, ed. Hugh Lloyd-Jones, Valerie Pearl, and Blair Worden (London: Duckworth, 1981), 49. See also John Bossy, "Christian Life in the Later Middle Ages: Prayers," *Transactions of the Royal Historical Society* 6th series, 1 (1991): 137–48; Duffy, *Marking the Hours*.

13. Bossy, "Prayers"; Duffy, *Marking the Hours*, 64.

14. Rubin, *Corpus Christi*, 156–59, 293, 297, 302.

15. On the connection between texts and the religious devotion of the upper classes, see Lawrence Besserman, *Chaucer's Biblical Poetics* (Norman: University of Oklahoma Press, 1998), 8–26; Diana Webb, *Privacy and Solitude in the Middle Ages* (London: Hambledon Continuum, 2007), 119–33.

16. Pamela C. Graves, "Social Space in the English Medieval Parish Church," *Economy and Society* 18 (1989): 297–322; Colin Richmond, "Religion and the Fifteenth-Century English Gentleman," in *The Church, Politics and Patronage in the Fifteenth Century*, ed. Barrie Dobson (Gloucester: Alan Sutton, 1984), 193–203.

17. Duffy, *Stripping of the Altars*, 116. On the pax as social ritual, see Bossy, "Mass as a Social Institution."

personal relationship with the divine. Fourteenth-century windows suggest a particularly intimate relationship between donor and the divine because they typically depict the donor praying alone at the feet of the saints or Christ himself.[18] As the Middle Ages progressed, more members of the aristocracy and even the gentry were building private chapels in their own homes and receiving papal approval to allow Masses to be performed there.[19] Between the years of 1342 and 1352 alone, Pope Clement VI granted licences for the possession of portable altars to some hundred and fifty individuals in England.[20] More chantries were established for personal intentions and more Masses were celebrated outside of the parish setting.[21] Although it is impossible to know what any given individual was thinking of or praying for during Mass, it is clear that the aristocracy was beginning to conceive of the Mass as an act of devotion that could be directed primarily toward personal growth and personal benefit. In contrast to histories of medieval selfhood that argue that medieval individual self-consciousness arose primarily out of a desire to identify oneself with a group,[22] aristocratic liturgical practices suggest a different picture: being a member of the aristocracy actually enabled an increased focus on the individual as a self distinct from other selves.

The fourteenth-century aristocracy used public displays of their wealth and devotion as ways of constructing their own individual spiritual lives. In general, fourteenth-century vernacular religious texts increasingly focused on the internal and subjective elements of Christian devotion, a shift in focus that many scholars attribute to the influence of confessional discourse.[23] In a sense, the aristocratic focus on personal devotion during Mass is therefore typical of a larger trend in lay religious experience. What makes aristocratic liturgical practices unique, however, is both aristocrats' intent focus on interior states

---

18. Sarah Stanbury, *The Visual Object of Desire in Late Medieval England* (Philadelphia: University of Pennsylvania Press, 2008), 191–218.

19. As Diana Webb has shown, during the fourteenth century, there was a marked increase in private domestic piety, an increase largely limited to the upper classes because wealth provided unique opportunities for a more diversified living space and a larger number of material possessions, including books. Webb, *Privacy and Solitude,* 120–33.

20. Diana Webb, "Domestic Space and Devotion in the Middle Ages," in *Defining the Holy: Sacred Space in Medieval and Early Modern Europe,* ed. Andrew Spicer and Sarah Hamilton (Aldershot: Ashgate, 2005), 37.

21. Catto, "Religion and the English Nobility."

22. This argument is most famously made in Bynum, "Did the Twelfth Century Discover the Individual?"

23. For an overview of the increased interiorization of fourteenth-century devotional literature, see Nicholas Watson, "The *Gawain*-Poet as a Vernacular Theologian," in *A Companion to the* Gawain-*Poet,* ed. Derek Brewer and Jonathan Gibson (Cambridge: D. S. Brewer, 1997), 293–313.

and the way in which they publicly performed their interiorization and individualization of religious practice. In her study of secular court rituals, Susan Crane argues that the late medieval aristocracy typically understood identity to be constituted through external performance: "What people manifest and articulate is what counts about them, not what is hidden and unexpressed. Performance is a reliable measure of who one actually is."[24] Although Crane does not discuss religious practices at length—practices that I would argue tend to assume a sense of self that to some extent precedes social interaction—her work highlights the important role of performance in the formation of aristocratic selfhood. For the aristocracy, one's interior life, including one's emotions, thoughts, and motivation, was complex and absolutely central to the understanding of the Mass. Aristocrats seem to have felt that staging the distinctiveness of their religious devotion was an essential aspect of the practice of their Christian faith, an aspect that enabled and authorized devotion centered on individual self-examination.

Though, as we will see in the next chapter on *Piers Plowman*, some Middle English texts depict the Mass as both social and egalitarian, the *Pearl*-poet presents a version of eucharistic piety that is decidedly individualist and entirely focused on members of the aristocracy. For this reason, several scholars have suggested that the poet's theology cannot be taken seriously precisely because it is not community oriented.[25] For example, Nicholas Watson argues that the poet demonstrates a watered-down "aristocratized theology," and David Aers laments that, in the poet's four poems, "The eucharist is assimilated to a discourse which has nothing to say about its role in cultivating union between fellow creatures in Christian communities."[26] While it is

---

24. Susan Crane, *The Performance of Self: Ritual, Clothing, and Identity During the Hundred Years War* (Philadelphia: University of Pennsylvania Press, 2002), 176. Also useful on the relationship between identity and bodily performance in medieval texts are J. A. Burrow, *Gestures and Looks in Medieval Narrative* (Cambridge: Cambridge UP, 2002); Clifford Davidson, ed., *Gesture in Medieval Drama and Art* (Kalamazoo, MI: Medieval Institute Publications, 2001).

25. Colin Richmond makes such an explicit judgment of late medieval religious practices when he criticizes the fifteenth-century gentry's religious practices by arguing, "Such folk, in becoming isolated from their neighbours, were also insulating themselves against communal religion, possibly even religion *per se*, for how can you be religious on your own?" Richmond, "Religion and the Fifteenth-Century," 199. See also Colin Richmond, "Margins and Marginality: English Devotion in the Later Middle Ages," in *England in the Fifteenth Century: Proceedings of the 1992 Harlaxton Symposium*, ed. Nicholas Rogers (Stamford, CA: Paul Watkins, 1994), 242–52.

26. David Aers, "Christianity for Courtly Subjects: Reflections on the *Gawain*-Poet," in *A Companion to the Gawain-Poet*, ed. Derek Brewer and Jonathan Gibson (Cambridge: D. S. Brewer, 1997), 100. Nicholas Watson also criticizes the *Pearl*-poet for making his theology too suited to aristocratic tastes. However, Watson does not make this point through reference to the poet's lack of social concern. Watson, "*Gawain*-Poet," 312.

true that many fourteenth-century aristocratic practices were profoundly self-centered—in the sense of being primarily interested in the individual soul's relationship to God—that does not make the theological thinking associated with them merely a shallow celebration of individual wealth. On the contrary, as the works of the *Pearl*-poet show, the aristocracy's inward-looking religious practices enable complex theological thinking about the nature of the individual soul's relationship with the divine.

In all four poems of Cotton Nero A.x, the *Pearl*-poet draws on the Christian liturgy in order to argue that emotional control and the maintenance of a stable identity are Christian virtues. With his almost obsessive use of jewels, rank, courtly manners, and rich clothing as ways of expressing the nature of the divine, the poet is intently interested in examining how material objects correspond to divine reality; he thus presents his theological thinking in a way that is particularly suited to aristocratic tastes.[27] He appeals directly to the aristocracy by seriously exploring the aristocracy's interest in liturgical devotion as a largely inward-looking experience. In all four poems, the poet's primary interest with regard to Christian devotion is the individual Christian's inner life, particularly the believer's emotional control. For the poet, good external actions are important, but properly controlled thoughts and emotions are the cornerstone of being a good Christian subject; external acts are often significant primarily because of the way in which they reflect or affect internal states. He frequently expresses his fascination with interiority in reference to liturgy. In the three most explicitly didactic texts, *Pearl, Cleanness,* and *Patience,* the poet refers to moral lessons heard at Mass in order to point out methods of individual reform.[28] *Patience,* a text intensely focused on the prophet Jonah's inner response to God's commands, begins by referring to a Gospel reading that "I herde on a holyday, at a hyȝe masse" (9). The poet goes on to retell Matthew's Beatitudes in a way that, far from emphasizing good works or issues of social justice, focuses on self-control. Most radically, he replaces "blessed are those who suffer persecution" with those "þat con her hert stere" (27). He thus

---

27. Class distinctions were very apparent to clerical authors, and it was not uncommon for pastoral texts to give class-specific guidance. For one example, see Michael Haren's work on the mid-fourteenth-century *Memoriale presbitorum*: "Confession, Social Ethics and Social Discipline in the *Memoriale presbitorum*," in *Handling Sin: Confession in the Middle Ages,* ed. Peter Biller and A. J. Minnis (York: University of York Press, 1998), 109–22.

28. See *Pearl* 497, *Cleanness* 51, and *Patience* 9. I recognize that the poet cites the Mass partly because the Mass would have been most lay people's only direct source of scripture passages. However, his citation of the Mass also invokes a liturgical context within the poems. All citations from Malcolm Andrew and Ronald Waldron, ed., *Cleanness, Patience,* and *Sir Gawain and the Green Knight* are from: *The Poems of the Pearl Manuscript: Pearl, Cleanness, Patience, Sir Gawain and the Green Knight,* 4th ed. (Exeter: University of Exeter Press, 2002).

invokes a liturgical setting in order to place his Old Testament subject in the context of controlled Christian interiority. *Cleanness* is much more explicit in its exploration of liturgy; it directly links internal virtue to the Mass by beginning with an explanation of priests' need for internal purity at the consecration. Even in *Sir Gawain and the Green Knight,* the least devotional of the four poems, Gawain intersperses his struggles to maintain self-control with regular attendance at Mass. At the center of all four poems is the individual's struggles to perfect and control his interior state—the dreamer's quest to overcome grief in *Pearl, Cleanness*'s exhortations that readers must strive to remove the spots on their souls, Jonah's failures to acquire patience and understanding in *Patience,* and Gawain's continual dissatisfaction with what he perceives as his own moral failure at the end of *Sir Gawain*—and the poet views this struggle through the interpretive framework of Christian liturgy and ritual. Before discussing *Pearl,* I want to turn briefly to *Cleanness* in order to show the poet's abiding interest in exploring the importance of inward-looking liturgical piety by troubling the boundaries between literal and figurative meaning.

In *Cleanness,* the poet explicitly takes up the relationship between internal piety and external courtly behavior. *Cleanness* presents Christian interiority and courtly life as not only reconcilable but inherently complementary. The poet often makes this argument for the coincidence of internal Christian devotion and external courtly behavior through particular reference to the Mass.[29] *Cleanness* opens with the assertion that spiritual purity is essential to Christian life, and to prove this point, the poet draws on one instance in which the need for such purity is self-evident: when a priest prepares to celebrate the Eucharist. The poet explains the necessity of priestly purity in detail:

> For wonder wroth is þe Wyȝ þat wroȝt alle þinges
> Wyth þe freke þat in fylþe folȝes Hym after—
> As renkez of relygioun þat redden and syngen,
> And aprochen to Hys presens, and prestez arn called;
> Thay teen vnto His temmple and temen to Hymseluen,
> Reken with reuerence þay richen His auter,
> Þay hondel þer His aune body and vsen hit boþe.
> If þay in clannes be clos þay cleche gret mede;
> Bot if þay conterfete crafte and cortaysye wont,

---

29. The amount of scholarship on *Cleanness* is small. However, Amity Reading also notes the importance of the Mass to the poem, arguing that the poem focuses on ritual sacrifice and feasting in order to explore "the hierarchical relationship between man and God." Amity Reading, "'The Ende of Alle Kynez Flesch': Ritual Sacrifice and Feasting in *Cleanness,*" *Exemplaria* 21 (2009): 275.

> As be honest vtwyth and inwith all fylþez,
> Þen are þay sinful himself, and sulpen altogeder
> Boþe God and His gere, and Hym to greme cachen.
> (5–16)

Although the Mass generally rewards those who participate in it, a priest who touches Christ's body in the host without first ensuring his own internal purity is guilty of sacrilege and incurs God's wrath. A priest's internal impurity transforms the effects of his external public act. The Mass, as an outward performance that demands inner belief, is the ultimate example of a moment in which outer behavior and inner virtue must operate together.

Using this discussion of the Mass as a starting point, the poet equates proper priestly and aristocratic behavior on the grounds that both require external courtly displays of internal purity. The poet compares the Mass to an aristocratic feast at which God is presiding as a king in his court. According to the poet, God is distinctly courtly in appearance:

> He is so clene in His courte, þe Kyng þat al weldez,
> And honeste in His housholde, and hagherlych serued
> With angelez enourled in alle þat is clene,
> Boþe withinne and withouten in wedez ful bry3t.
> (17–20)

The physical beauty and richness of God's court is clear evidence of its holiness. Throughout the poem, proper aristocratic manners and dress are indicators of internal purity. In one of Christ's most explicitly sacramental acts—the breaking of bread—his spiritual purity is most evident in the extreme delicacy and neatness with which he tears the loaf of bread. Christ is so clean, the poet tells us,

> Forþy brek He þe bred blades wythouten,
> For hit ferde freloker in fete in His fayre honde,
> Displayed more pryuyly when He hit part schulde,
> Þenne alle þe toles of Tolowse mo3t ty3t hit to kerue.
> (1105–8)

Christ displays his holiness by serving food like a proper aristocrat would. For the poet, priests and aristocrats are fundamentally similar in that, in order to please God, both must match their internal piety with "cortaysye," a model of virtuous behavior that ultimately finds its origin in proper court manners.

Unlike *Sir Gawain*, in which the poet alludes to his characters' complex inner lives, *Cleanness* does not focus on the believer's internal state other than to suggest that spiritual purity is fundamentally internal. In *Cleanness*, the clearest indicator of one's internal state is the courtliness of one's actions.

The distinction between external and internal purity, between courtly manners and Christian piety, collapses over the course of the poem; the poem ultimately regards the two as inseparable. This conflation is most marked in the poem's refusal to consistently distinguish between literal and figurative filth. Near the start of the poem, the poet tells his readers that, when they come to the heavenly feast, they must wear clean and beautiful clothing. To demonstrate that clothing is only a figure for works, he explains,

> Wich arn þenne þy wedez þou wrappez þe inne,
> Þat schal schewe hem so schene schrowde of þe best?
> Hit arn þy werkez, wyterly, þat þou wroȝt hauez,
> And lyued with þe lykyng þat lyȝe in þyn hert.
> (169–72)

After this point, however, the distinction between literal dirt and the figurative filth of sin begins to disappear. When the poet describes Christ's nativity, he dwells almost exclusively on the spotlessly clean nature of the manger. As he envisions it, "Þaȝ þay pouer were, / Watz neuer so blysful a bour as watz a bos þenne, / Ne no schroude-hous so schene as a schepon þare" (1074–76). In order to demonstrate the sanctity of Christ's birth, the poet has to imagine the stable as a different location; it becomes both aristocratic and priestly as the poet compares it to a bower and a sacristy, respectively. The poet prevents readers from understanding these comparisons as wholly figurative by insisting on such details as the stable's mysterious rose scent (1079). Although this description of the manger might seem to suggest that spiritual purity transcends physical filth, it also implies that it is almost unthinkable for the two to be found together. The poem thus makes a plea for its readers to engage in greater piety by aligning such piety with the aristocratic taste for physical opulence and cleanliness.

As the poet makes clear through the negative example of Belshazzar's feast, liturgical piety is essential to proper courtly behavior. At his feast, Belshazzar commits two interrelated sins. First, he defiles Jewish altar vessels and, second, he fails to make his feast courtly enough. The defilement of altar vessels is the first step away from proper court behavior. The poet finds it horrifying that the altar vessels would be used for anything other than religious purposes and, although the vessels are ostensibly Jewish, he implicitly invokes the sacred vessels of the Mass by reminding readers that "in His sacrafyce summe wer anointed" (1497). Belshazzar's feast becomes a sacrilegious parody of the Mass. However, this sacrilege is only the start of his sins. The poet explains that God is angry because "His jueles so gent with jaueles wer fouled" (1495), arguing that God believes his vessels to be of too high and noble a value to be used by those of low rank. The mixing of people of various classes and ranks is morally abhorrent; the poet explains with disgust how "þenne derfly arn dressed dukez and pryncez, / Concubines and kny3tes" (1518–19). Like the sinful priests whom the poet condemns at the start of the poem, Belshazzar sins by touching liturgical vessels when he is internally impure; his internal filth is particularly manifest in his failure to observe proper courtly protocols of behavior.

Although the Mass is not the poem's central focus, the poet continually invokes it to illustrate the urgent need for readers to maintain the cleanliness of their souls. In the middle of the poem, he warns readers that God is particularly angry at the impurity of his own followers because God considers Christian bodies to be holy vessels consecrated to him. Christians must therefore be wary because "His wrath is achaufed / For þat þat ones watz His schulde efte be vnclene, / Þa3 hit be bot a bassyn, a bolle oþer a scole, / A dysche oþer a dobler, þat Dry3tyn onez serued" (1143–46). This liturgical comparison is essential to the structure of the poem because, without it, there is no logical transition from Sodom and Gomorrah to Belshazzar's feast. Both Belshazzar and the Sodomites sin against purity because they have made improper use of holy vessels; the difference is that the holy vessels defiled in Sodom were made of human flesh. The poet uses the liturgy as the ultimate example of an instance in which the coincidence of external courtly behavior and internal Christian purity is absolutely essential. Thinking about the Mass enables the poem to blur the line between figurative and literal cleanness and, in so doing, construct a model of purity that unites aristocratic behavior and Christian interiority perfectly. For the *Pearl*-poet, the Mass provides the aristocratic subject with an opportunity for personal reform, and that reform is best understood through figurative language.

METAPHOR AND SUBMISSION

Pearl, like the three poems that share its manuscript, argues that internal states have moral relevance for the aristocratic subject. Throughout the poem, the dreamer becomes increasingly frustrated because he cannot identify with either his lost beloved or with Christ, primarily because he can only perceive them through textual mediation: the continually shifting pearl metaphor and the Lamb as an allegorical sign of Christ. The poem's emphasis on metaphor highlights the dreamer's own need to submit to external logic and to acknowledge his irreducible distance from the divine.

Of the four poems in Cotton Nero A.x, *Pearl* provides the fullest exploration of the relationship between liturgy and Christian interiority. Like *Sir Gawain* and *Cleanness*, it examines aristocratic Christian identity construction, but *Pearl* is unique in its explicit focus on interiority and emotional reform rather than social acts. The other three poems explore various ways in which external, social actions are results of internal states, but *Pearl* only examines external acts insofar as the dreamer allows them to affect his internal sense of identity and emotional control. The poet's choice of the dream vision genre is itself indicative of the poem's intensely inward focus. While *Sir Gawain* often refuses to discuss its protagonist's internal state, *Pearl* takes the dreamer's thoughts and emotions as its primary subject. Unlike Sir Gawain, who faces physical challenges in which he has some level of agency, the dreamer's struggles are entirely internal; he must learn to cope with the loss of his pearl, a loss over which he has absolutely no control. Rather than being concerned with how to integrate piety into courtly life, the poem explores how the aristocratic subject can transform his interior state through Christian doctrine and ritual. For the *Pearl*-poet, religious ritual is a necessary part of internal reform, and *Pearl*, unlike the other three poems, makes the nature of such reform an object of intense focus. In this sense, *Pearl* most closely resembles *Patience* because both focus on the individual's internal response to the intractable will of God. However, the two protagonists differ radically in that the dreamer has access to Christian liturgy and consolation while Jonah, as an Old Testament figure, does not. This access to Christian consolation through ritual is what allows *Pearl* to conclude on the hopeful note that the Mass is central to the reform of the interior self.

Pearl begins by describing the dreamer's moral failure to cope with his personal grief in a way that is consonant with Christian belief in the resurrection. His excessive and paralyzing sorrow is not a result of a lack of knowledge of Christian consolation; rather the source of this excess is his lack of emotional control. Before being overcome with sorrow and collapsing into sleep, the dreamer reflects on his pearl's burial place and tries to console himself with the thought that "for uch gresse mot grow of graynes dede, / No whete were ells to wones wonne" (31–32). In thus imagining his pearl as a seed in the ground from which grain will grow, the dreamer depicts his pearl's death as the beginning of new life. This attempt at consolation alludes to a passage from the Gospel of John in which Christ explains the necessity of his own death by comparing human life to a grain of wheat: "Unless a grain of wheat falls into the earth and dies, it remains just a single grain; but if it dies, it bears much fruit" (John 12:24). With this statement, the dreamer attempts to console himself not only with an image of rebirth derived from his physical location on the grave but also through reference to orthodox Christian belief. However, neither is effective. Even though he knows intellectually through scripture that life does not end at physical death, he continues to regard his pearl as utterly lost. He remains entrenched in grief, "Thagh kynde of Kryst me comfort kenned" (55). The narrator admits that knowledge of Christ's human nature, and therefore Christ's resurrection from the dead, ought to have consoled him, but it failed to do so.[30] Instead of relying on his knowledge of Christian truth, the dreamer initially depends on his emotions and regards his pearl as a lost physical object rather than a soul that transcends physical existence. He locates her presence precisely in the ground when he reflects that "ther wonys that worthily, I wot and wene, / My precious perle wythouten spot" and mourns "my perle that ther was penned" (47–48; 53). Despite his prior knowledge of Christian truth, he emotionally relies on physical knowledge, a knowledge that leads him to wrongly believe that his pearl is firmly located in the earth.

The dreamer fails to rule his emotional state with rationality, instead allowing emotion to dominate over reason. The narrator reflects that "a deuely dele in my hert denned / Thagh resoun sette myselven saght" (51–52). Although reason would have been a remedy for grief, the dreamer allows his sorrow to dominate. When the pearl maiden enters the poem, she immediately rebukes the dreamer for allowing his emotions to work in opposition to his reason. She calls his overwhelming grief madness and criticizes him for not fully believing Christ's promise of resurrection. According to her, the dreamer's sorrow is misguided because "thow demes noght bot doel dystresse" (337). The dreamer only uses his rational judgment in the service of perpetuating his grief. He fails to realize what he should logically know: that Christ raised his pearl from the dead. In order to demonstrate the dreamer's lack of rationality, the pearl maiden compares him to a wild animal whose moaning serves no purpose: "Fo thogh thou daunce as any do, / Braundysch and bray thy brathes breme, / When thou no fyrre may to ne fro / Thou moste abyde that He schal deme" (345–48). Regardless of how loudly and endlessly he mourns, the dreamer is powerless to change God's decisions about life and death. According to the pearl maiden, God never forgoes reason, and God ought to be a model for

---

30. I use the terms "narrator" and "dreamer" to distinguish between the retrospective voice of the first-person narrator and the character experiencing the dream, respectively. The poem often makes very little distinction between these two figures, and so I use the term "narrator" only when the tone is clearly retrospective.

the dreamer's own internal state. The poem's sixth section, in which the pearl maiden repeatedly chastises the dreamer for his grief, centers on the concatenated word "deme" because the dreamer's misconceptions about the maiden's heavenly state stem from his refusal to "deme" correctly, in the sense of both "to judge" and "to rule." The dreamer does not lack knowledge or reason; instead he refuses to use proper judgment in applying them to his own emotional state. He fails to rule himself properly.

Within the world of the poem, interior states are nearly tangible realities that the individual must control. As the dreamer wanders in the dream landscape, he allows the exterior world too much control over his internal state and becomes unable to maintain a firm distinction between what is inside and outside of himself. When he first perceives the place's beauty, "The dubbement dere of doun and dales, / Of wod and water and wlonke playnes, / Bylde in me blys, abated my bales, / Fordidden my stresse, dystryed my paynes" (121–24). He imagines that the beauty of the place has actively overcome his emotional state of sorrow in a way that he himself was wholly unable to do. He allows the landscape to have such an emotional effect on him that he begins to imagine his own interior life as if it too were a landscape. When he follows the river, "I bowed in blys, bredful my braynes" (126). Just as the river rises to the limits of its banks, his emotions nearly overflow from his mind. Even though he is actively walking along the river and trying to find a way across it, he conceives of himself as passive and responding involuntarily to the effects of the external world. He refuses to acknowledge his own emotional agency and prefers to let external stimuli overwhelm him. When he first catches sight of the pearl maiden, he claims that the sight "meved my mynde ay more and more," and when he begins to recognize her, the "baysment gef my hert a brunt" (156–74). His heart and his mind are not active or in control; instead they are acted upon, and he feels that he must endure whatever violence they are dealt from the external world. At this moment in the poem, he recognizes the nearly tangible reality of his mental and emotional life, but he fails to see that he has any control over its construction.

The poem argues that the dreamer sins by not containing his emotions within the boundaries of his body. In response to the pearl maiden's accusations, the dreamer excuses his dramatic expressions of mourning by explaining that "my herte was al with mysse remorde / As wallande water gos out of welle" (364–65). The dreamer compares the loss of his pearl to a gap at the opening of a well, suggesting that his emotional loss is similar to a physical loss having physical consequences. He claims that his grief was natural and uncontrollable; it was impossible to contain because the loss created a hole in his heart analogous to the opening of a well. The poem rejects the dreamer's excuse by implying that he has a moral obligation to maintain the boundaries of his emotional state. It contrasts the dreamer's image of his emotions as water exceeding its boundaries with another image of flowing water that occurs throughout the poem: the river that marks the separation between the dreamer and the pearl maiden. The river has its origin in the New Jerusalem and serves as a mark of separation rather than overflow. For the Lamb, the river is a way of separating what is his—the community of the saved in the New Jerusalem—from what is not. In this image of ever-flowing but highly regulated water, the poem makes a morally charged contrast with the dreamer's emotions, which always threaten to exceed their proper boundaries.

In contrast, the pearl maiden perfectly controls the boundaries of her identity and emotions. There are many important differences between the dreamer and the pearl maiden—the most obvious being gender, age, and the maiden's resurrected state—but one of the most dramatic is their radically different levels of emotional control. Unlike the dreamer, the pearl maiden has sharp boundaries to her identity. When the dreamer first recognizes the maiden, he launches into a long description of her royal dress and appearance, with a focus on the boundaries of her body. The poem pays particular attention to the hems and borders of her garments, explaining that she wore sleeves "dubbed with double perle and dyghte, / Her cortel of self sute schene / Wyth precios perles al umbepyghte" (202–4). He describes the points of her crown and the outer covering of her hair. The maiden is like a jewel whose beauty is marked by its sharply defined edges. In part, this attention to the external indicates that the dreamer has not yet engaged discursively with the maiden, and so at this point, all of his knowledge is external; it also suggests that, to some extent, she holds the status of an object for him. However, the poem achieves both effects by revealing that the body of the pearl maiden has rigid boundaries, boundaries that are not only physical but also emotional. The dreamer is overjoyed to see the maiden and moves between grief, joy, shame, and disappointment over the course of the poem, but the pearl maiden herself expresses a very small range of emotions. Indeed, the dreamer is continually frustrated because of her refusal to engage him on an emotional level; she does not even acknowledge the intimacy of their previous earthly relationship. The only positive emotional response he receives from her occurs when she expresses pleasure that he professes to hold Christ as more important than her (400). She argues against emotional expression when she tells the dreamer that the only ultimate solution to grief is to stop external expressions of mourning altogether (349–60). For her, emotional containment is a moral imperative. As readers, we never get a sense of the pearl maiden's interior life because she is always in perfect emotional control. Although such containment is not particularly sympathetic to modern readers, the poem suggests that such control is the Christian ideal because the pearl maiden is perfect in the eyes of God.

The dreamer's grief undermines his ability to maintain a stable, contained identity, an identity that the pearl maiden has shown is essential for the Christian subject to have. The dreamer therefore attempts to overcome his grief through identification—the process of building up his own identity by claiming the pearl maiden's identity as a component of his own.[31] When the dreamer first speaks to the pearl maiden, he attempts to overcome the differences between them. He bewails the differences in their emotional states:

> Pensyf, payred, I am forpayned,
> And thou in a lyf of lykyng lyghte
> In Paradys erde, of stryf unstrained.
> What wyrde has hyder my juel vayned
> And don me in thys del and gret daunger?
> Fro we in twynne wern towen and twayned
> I haf ben a joyles jueler.
> (246–52)

The dreamer is not just lamenting his own emotional suffering but also expressing astonishment that the pearl maiden's experience was so emotionally different from his own. In protesting this disparity, the dreamer claims that they had a prior emotional unity: they were forced apart but their natural state is together. He identifies himself as a "jueler" for the first time at this

---

31. My description of identification in *Pearl* bears some resemblance to psychoanalytic discussions of the relationship between loss and identification. For Freudian psychoanalysis, identification occurs when the ego incorporates aspects of a love-object into itself in order to redirect love inward onto the ego; the subject only establishes a stable identity through this process of identification, which requires the ego to constitute itself with the elements of lost objects. My reading of *Pearl* differs from psychoanalysis in that, rather than propose that the ego must cover over and replace loss in service of pleasure, the poem argues that the Christian subject must acknowledge and accept the state of lack within the human self. See Sigmund Freud, "Mourning and Melancholia" in *The Standard Edition of the Complete Psychological Works of Sigmund Freud*, trans. James Strachey, vol. 14 (London: Hogarth Press, 1957), 243–58; Diana Fuss, *Identification Papers* (New York: Routledge, 1995). For an excellent discussion of the tensions between medieval religious literature and psychoanalysis, see Louise O. Fradenburg, "'Be not far from me': Psychoanalysis, Medieval Studies and the Subject of Religion," *Exemplaria* 7 (1995): 41–54. For readings of *Pearl* that more directly deal with the similarities between psychoanalytic discussions of loss and *Pearl*, see Aers, "Self Mourning"; George Edmondson, "*Pearl*: The Shadow of the Object, the Shape of the Law," *Studies in the Age of Chaucer* 26 (2004): 29–63; Sarah Stanbury, "The Body and the City in *Pearl*," *Representations* 48 (1994): 30–47.

moment, defining his identity as totally dependent on his possession of her because it is impossible to be a jeweler without a jewel. He implies that she is an essential part of his identity rather than a person with an independent subjectivity. Although the pearl maiden tells him that he ought not to grieve for her because she is not lost, he refuses to acknowledge that she understands herself as independent of him. Instead, he insists that, since she is able to enter the heavenly Jerusalem, he also must be entitled to do so. He exclaims, "I trawed my perle don out of dawes. / Now haf I fonde hyt, I schal ma feste / And wony with hyt in schyr wod-schawes" (282–84). At the moment he stakes a claim for his own right to enter paradise, he calls her "my perle" and uses the impersonal pronoun "hyt" to refer to her, treating her as his possession rather than a person. The dreamer's grief makes him feel incomplete, and he attempts to overcome this feeling by constructing a stable, independent identity for himself. In order to do so, he imagines the pearl maiden as merely an extension of him.

In *Pearl,* mourning poses a threat to the dreamer's individual identity precisely because mourning involves his admission that he is essentially incomplete without his pearl. The dreamer experiences the loss of his pearl as a loss to his own identity; he is initially unable to overcome his grief because he believes that, having lost her, he is missing an important part of himself. However, the dreamer's attempts to identify with her are continually thwarted. As the pearl maiden repeatedly points out, he needs to gain control over his emotions, but he cannot do so by identifying with her. Instead the dreamer must acknowledge that his identity will always be lacking as long as he lacks Christ, and he can never truly have Christ until he reaches the afterlife. The poem suggests that, although the dreamer cannot overcome this lack, he can construct a more stable Christian identity for himself by recognizing his need for Christ.

As the poem progresses, it becomes clear that identification with the pearl maiden is impossible because there is a radical difference between the earthly and the heavenly, the living and the resurrected dead. When the pearl maiden describes the New Jerusalem and the Lamb, she explains that this difference is both emotional and rational: "Althagh oure corses in clottes clynge / And ye remen for rauthe wythouten reste, / We thurghoutly haven cnawying" (857–59). She argues that one of the most important distinctions between those living on earth and those living in heaven is that the saved have a complete understanding of their relationship with God. Such knowledge creates a distinct emotional difference between the two states. The living are always crying out for God's pity because they cannot have full assurance and faith in their own resurrection, but the resurrected are able to cast out such cares and live in a state of perpetual joy. In response to the pearl maiden's explanation of the joys of the afterlife, the dreamer temporarily rejects his attempts at complete identification with her. Instead of imagining the pearl buried in the dirt as an extension of himself, he identifies with the dirt itself, claiming that "I am bot mokke and mul among" (905). In this image, he affirms the difference between earthly and heavenly life by imagining himself as the very definition of earthliness. The poem depicts the living as existing in a state of lack: they are in a perpetual state of emotional uncertainty because of their distance from the divine.

The dreamer repeatedly attempts to overcome this lack through identification, but he fails because he is striving to remake himself for his own fulfillment, rather than for Christ. When he sees the maidens worshipping the Lamb in the New Jerusalem, he is overwhelmed with the desire to be one of them. He is fascinated by his vision of the Lamb, but he does not identify with it; it is his attempted identification with the pearl maiden that makes him want to wade across the river. Once he sees her, his attention abruptly turns away from the Lamb in the middle of the stanza:

> Then saw I ther my lyttel queen
> Than I wende had standen by me in sclade.
> Lorde, much of mirthe was that ho made
> Among her feres that was so quyt!
> That sight me gart to thenk to wade
> For luf longyng in gret delyt.
> (1147–52)

Although the precise referent of "that sight" is unclear—whether it refers to the entire vision of the New Jerusalem or his view of her happiness among the community of the saved—the order of the description suggests that seeing her provides the impetus for his attempt to cross the river. At this moment, the dreamer's "luf longyng" is more obviously sinful than the emotion that drove his grief at the start of the poem. At the beginning of the poem, the dreamer feels that the return of his pearl would rescue her from death, but by this point, the pearl maiden has already told him explicitly that she neither wants to return to him nor does she wish him to attempt to enter the New Jerusalem with her. If he were to succeed in crossing the river, he would betray the pearl maiden, violate God's laws, and contaminate the extreme purity of the New Jerusalem. Instead of recognizing these reasons for remaining on his own side of the river, the dreamer returns to imagining his emotions as the products of external forces and asserting ownership of the pearl maiden. He uses identification as a way of trying to reclaim pleasure for himself, regardless of the consequences.

Throughout the poem, the dreamer identifies with people and things that are radically unlike him instead of recognizing his own limitations and failures. When the dreamer sees the Lamb, he first imagines that he understands the Lamb's delight but is then puzzled by the wound in the Lamb's side:

> Bot a wounde ful wyde and weete con wyse
> Anende Hys hert thurgh hyde torente.
> Of His quyte side his blod outsprent.
> Alas, thoght I, who did that spyt?
> Ani breste for bale aght haf forbrent
> Er he therto hade had delyt.
> (1135–40)

The dreamer fails to recognize one of the Christian truths familiar to almost every medieval reader of devotional texts: Christ's wounds are the result of humanity's sins. The answer to the dreamer's question—"who did that spyt?"—is that the dreamer himself caused the wound. Because the dreamer is unwilling to see his own sinfulness and unworthiness, he imagines himself as one of the saved rather than seeing himself as he truly is: the source of the Lamb's disfigurement. When the dreamer exclaims that any person who caused such a wound ought to burn up in grief rather than experience delight, he unconsciously shows that his own response to the Lamb is completely inappropriate. He does not recognize that, although the Lamb experiences great delight despite his bloody, open wound, the dreamer himself ought to be in a state of grief and repentance. The dreamer's attempts at identification are sinful because he strives to claim others' identities as his own instead of acknowledging his own identity as an unworthy sinner.

Pearl contends that there are limits to individual identity and explores these limits through its use of metaphor. Metaphor is strikingly similar to identification because both are processes in which the identity of one thing is apparent only through its appropriation of the characteristics of another. Metaphor functions by likening two objects even as it assumes that the two are in most ways dissimilar. Through the metaphor of the pearl, the poem calls attention to the boundaries of identity even as it seems to collapse them. The pearl is the vehicle for several different tenors over the course of the poem, and it is often difficult to determine which tenor the poem is referring to at any given moment. At the start of the poem, the pearl is literally a lost gem, but as the poem progresses, the word "pearl" has an increasing number of referents, including a dead girl, purity, the immortal soul, the kingdom of heaven, the Eucharist, and Christ himself. The pearl's constant shifts in meaning might to some extent signify the dreamer's spiritual progression from personal grief to divine contemplation; yet any such progression, to the extent that it occurs at all, is far from tidy. Even at the end of the poem, it is not entirely clear which meaning we are to finally attach to the word "pearl." The dreamer believes it is important and valuable to strive to be "precious perles unto His pay" (1212), but what precisely that involves is still an open question. However, trying to determine the final meaning of the pearl is not only futile but also beside the point. In its indeterminacy, the pearl represents precisely the failure of metaphor itself to totally appropriate meaning. Like the dreamer's failure to identify with the pearl maiden, the poem is never able to fully assimilate the pearl to a clear system of signification. The pearl's meaning must always remain just outside of the dreamer's, and the reader's, grasp. When the dreamer asserts that the pearl maiden is the pearl he once owned, she completely alters the terms of their discussion and argues that he never owned a pearl in the first place. She contends, "For that thou lestes was bot a rose / That flowred and fayled as kynde hyt gef; / Now thurgh kynde of the kyste that hyt con close / To a perle of prys hit is put in pref" (269–73). The implication of her argument is not only that the pearl maiden herself was not a pearl while alive but also that all living things on earth cannot be pearls because they are subject to the changes of nature. True pearls cannot be grasped on earth, either physically or intellectually. In the poem's first section, the poet underlines the pearl's unearthly nature by concluding each stanza with the phrase "perle withouten spot." He puns on "spot," a word he uses to describe both physical location and impurity. To be a pearl "withouten spot" also means to be without any earthly location.[32] The poet suggests that, although all Christians ought to strive to be pearls, the meaning and identity of the pearl remains fundamentally inassimilable to human earthly life. Although metaphor appears to collapse the boundaries of identity, the pearl as metaphor emphasizes the limits of similarity, comparison, and identification.

As the poem progresses, the dreamer gradually heeds the pearl maiden's advice and shifts at least some of his devotion from her to Christ. However, identification with the divine is even more difficult than identification with the pearl maiden. *Pearl* depicts an irreducible distance between the human and divine through its use of figurative language to describe Christ. In *Pearl*, the only way for humans to understand the divine during their earthly lives is

---

32. Sylvia Tomasch has extensively explored the shifting meanings of the word "spot" throughout the poem. Sylvia Tomasch, "A *Pearl* Punnology," *Journal of English and Germanic Philology* 88 (1989): 1–20.

through figuration; the divine can only be represented through that which it is not. When the pearl maiden initially describes the Lamb to the dreamer, she suggests that "the Lamb" is just a figurative name for Christ, calling him "My Lombe, my Lorde, my dere juelle, / My joy, my blys, my lemman fre" (795–96). In her formulation, "Lamb" is just one of the possible names of Christ and is therefore not a literal description of him. She furthers her depiction of Christ as Lamb by paraphrasing the prophet Isaiah: "As a schep to the slaght ther lad was He, / And as lombe that clypper in lande hem, / So closed He hys mouth fro uch query" (801–3). The word "as" explicitly indicates that the description of Christ as a Lamb is a simile. Because the pearl maiden insists that "the Lamb" is a figurative way of talking about Christ, it is startling for the reader to discover that, when the dreamer sees the New Jerusalem for himself, he does not see a human Christ. Instead, the Lamb is quite literally a lamb. When the dreamer notices the wound in the Lamb's side, a wound that Christ received on the cross, the poet describes it as located "anende Hys hert thurgh hyde torente" (1136). The poem places alliterative emphasis on the word "hyde," highlighting that the Lamb is literally an animal. The description requires readers to focus on the literal description of the Lamb rather than disregard it in favor of its allegorical referent. Unlike the pearl, whose relationship to its various tenors is constantly shifting, the Lamb is an allegorical sign with a single stable referent. The very stability of the sign highlights the distance between signifier and signified; the reader knows that Christ is not literally a lamb even though the poem insists on that representation. At the moment the dreamer expects to see God, he encounters a sign that refuses direct perception.

Within the dream, figural truths appear as if they were literal, but the pearl maiden insists that the dreamer ought to regard them as figurative. When the pearl maiden tells the dreamer about her home in the heavenly Jerusalem, the dreamer becomes confused, "Thou telles me of Jerusalem, the ryche ryalle, / Ther David dere was dyght on trone— / Bot by thyse holtes hit con not hone, / Bot in Judee hit is, that noble note" (919–22). The dreamer fails to recognize that the historical Jerusalem is a figuration of the heavenly Jerusalem because he wrongly assumes that his own experience is unmediated by signs and language. He thinks that, because he is directly experiencing it, the word "Jerusalem" must refer to a literal geographic location. This misunderstanding prompts the pearl maiden to teach him a lesson in biblical figuration, a lesson that seems to serve a more immediate purpose for the poem's readers than for the dreamer himself (937–60). The pearl maiden addresses him as if he were reading rather than experiencing the dream in order to show him that he ought to approach the dream as if it were a written text in need of interpretation.

Earthly humans can only perceive the divine through textual mediation. When the dreamer finally sees the New Jerusalem, he describes it through constant reference to a written text: the Book of Revelation. In the seventeenth section, every stanza ends with the concatenated words "the apostle John." This constant citation of John's voice both legitimates the dreamer's vision as orthodox and suggests that his vision could not be authoritative without textual support. His vision makes no claims to being unmediated; he details that "as John thise stones in Writ con nemme, / I knew the name after his tale" (997–98). The dreamer recognizes what he sees in front of his eyes through text rather than through vision. In the middle of his description, the dreamer explains, "I knew hit by his devysement" (1019), the word "knew" suggesting that he recognized it through John's description and that John's description actually enabled him to perceive it at all. In this section, knowledge of the afterlife is not possible without textual authority. At the beginning of the eighteenth section, however, the narrator recounts, "As John hym wrytes yet more I syye," suggesting that his description is about to go beyond John's (1033). And, in fact, the poem does describe elements not present in the Book of Revelation, but it rarely strays far from them, continuing to reference elements of the New Jerusalem that "John the appostel in termes tyghte" (1053). It is no coincidence that, at the moments when the dreamer relies on John's textual support the least, his reason and self-control also begin to fade. He describes these extratextual elements as such great wonders that "no fleschly hert ne might endure," and he becomes like a "dased quayle" upon seeing them (1082; 1085). The heavenly Jerusalem thwarts direct human understanding; a human becomes like an animal in witnessing it. The poem implies that to perceive the heavenly and remain both human and rational is necessarily to perceive it through textual mediation.

In order to even partly understand the divine, the individual believer must both accept mediation and totally submit to the external logic of divine authority. Throughout the poem, the dreamer misunderstands divine authority because he assumes that it must operate in exactly the same way as earthly royal authority does. When he hears that the pearl maiden is a queen in heaven, he is astonished because he thinks she died too young to merit such a high rank. He argues, "Of countes, damysel, par ma fay, / Wer fayr in heven to halde asstate / Other ells a lady of lasse aray— / Bot a queen! Hit is to dere a date" (489–92). Not only does he fail to understand the logic of heavenly reward, he struggles to grasp the idea that heaven might have a separate logic of reward at all. For him, there is no other system than the English aristocratic one. Even though the pearl maiden explains heavenly logic in detail, the dreamer cannot break outside of his earthly aristocratic logic. He even worries about material concerns, asking about her castle, "Haf ye no wones in castel walle, / Ne maner ther ye may mete and won?" (917–18). For the dreamer, courtly rank manifests itself in material objects, and he is uncertain what it might mean to have a heavenly rank if it does not entail castles and manors. The hierarchical system of heaven within this poem closely mirrors that of an earthly court, but the dreamer cannot accept even small differences between the two because to do so would mean to submit to a power he does not understand.

Royal and divine power are similar insofar as they both demand that the good subject submit to laws whose logic exceeds the subject's own perception. *Pearl*'s use of the phrase "princes paye" in both the opening stanza and the closing section demonstrates that royal and divine power both require individuals to subject their own desires to external judgment. In the very first lines of the poem, the dreamer praises his pearl on the grounds that royalty values it: "Perle, plesaunte to prynces paye / To clanly clos in golde so clere" (1–2). The value of the pearl is most evident in the fact that it is pleasing to princes; the dreamer does not believe that his own judgment is nearly as important or convincing. By the end of the poem, the dreamer has reexamined the pearl's value and now regards it in relation to divine rather than royal power. Nevertheless, he still suggests that it is a princely figure, a figure of courtly authority, that ultimately determines value when he hopes that Christ "gef uus to be His homly hyne / And precious perles unto His pay" (1211–12). Whether the power is royal or divine, the good subject is one who submits to its external judgment.

LITURGY AND INTERNAL REFORM

Throughout the poem, this external authority is one that is divinely inscribed in a material object: either a text or the host itself. Acceptance of this authority involves acceptance of simultaneous absence and presence, an acceptance of heavenly logic that is crucial to both a belief in the Eucharist and to the workings of figurative signification. Although the poem's ending is its most explicit reference to the Eucharist, liturgical themes pervade the poem to demonstrate that this submission to divine logic is essential to Christian worship. Eucharistic imagery circulates throughout the poem in a number of ways, not the least of which is in the pearl's resemblance to the host: both are round white objects that inspire devotion.

It is in the maiden's retelling of the vineyard parable, however, that the poem begins its exploration of the significance of liturgical practice to the individual subject. In this moment, *Pearl* argues that the Mass is an instance when earthbound humans encounter heavenly logic and must submit to what they do not fully understand. The pearl maiden introduces the parable with the words, "As Mathew meles in your Messe," directly linking the narrative to a liturgical setting (497). When she describes each laborer receiving his penny at the end of the day, her description is very similar to a eucharistic reception line. The lord, like a priest at Mass, orders the reeve to "set hem alle upon a rawe" so that the people might each receive a single flat disc in exchange for their labor (545). It is likely that many readers would have recognized this part of the parable as referring to eucharistic reception since several late medieval devotional texts explicitly associate this parable with the Eucharist. The fourteenth-century *Book of Vices and Virtues,* for example, states that the Eucharist "is þe peny þat he ȝyueþ to his werke-men whan þey comen at euen, þat is þe ende of here lif."[33] In the Mass, much like in the distribution of a penny to every worker, there is a radical equality among lay people, an equality that stands in sharp contrast to courtly rank. Although there are many ways in which lay people may seek to assert their social and economic dominance during the Mass—through location in the church, ownership of particular windows, the order of kissing the pax—every believer only receives one host, and each host is of equal value. The dreamer protests the logic of the parable precisely on these grounds of equality; he does not want to accept the idea that God will treat each Christian equally, regardless of rank or the number of his good works. In this parable, the poem thwarts direct correspondence between wealth and holiness. While this passage is not a rejection of all aristocratic liturgical practices—since the poem valorizes self-examination and a personal relationship with Christ in the host—it does critique the notion that wealth provides special access to God. It suggests that, despite all the aristocracy's efforts to gain personal spiritual benefits through private Masses and private prayer, God's favor is always beyond any individual's understanding and control. In this sense, the poem's version of the vineyard parable is

---

33. *The Book of Vices and Virtues,* ed. W. Nelson Francis, EETS 217 (London: Oxford University Press, 1942), 111. Parallel passages appear in *Le Somme des Vices et des Vertues* and *Aȝenbite of Inwyt.* For further details on the connection between the penny and host in *Pearl,* see Robert W. Ackerman, "The Pearl-Maiden and the Penny," *Romance Philology* 17 (1964): 615–23.

less interested in providing a vision of the Christian community than it is in pointing out the individual's inability to control God's judgment. The liturgy of the Mass demands that believers submit to the rules of God even though such rules do not correspond to those of the socioeconomic hierarchies of medieval England.

In particular, earthly devotion to the divine involves acceptance of simultaneous absence and presence, an acceptance of heavenly logic that is crucial to a belief in the Eucharist.[34] Despite the pearl maiden's continual criticism of his overzealous behavior, the dreamer refuses to settle for mediation and actively strives for direct contact with the objects of his fascination and desire. When she tells him that the two of them cannot live together, the dreamer laments that he will return to his grief: "Now haf I fonte that I forlete, / Schal I efte forgo hit er ever I fine? / Why schal I hit bothe mysse and mete?" (327–29). He complains that he will experience even greater pain than his original grief because she will no longer be either fully lost or fully present to him. She occupies a space between absolute absence and absolute presence, and he finds this situation almost impossible to accept both conceptually and emotionally. Over the course of the poem, the dreamer struggles to accept the unbridgeable distance between himself and the object of his devotion, whether that object is the Lamb or the pearl maiden. He always desires more immediacy, and this desire culminates in his failed attempt to cross the river into the New Jerusalem. At the end of the poem, the dreamer recognizes that his inability to control his desire is sinful and he therefore turns toward the Eucharist. The Eucharist, with its promise of Christ's presence in a piece of bread that does not in any way resemble the earthly body of Christ, is a sacrament that directly challenges the worshipper's ability to believe in the reality of simultaneous absence and presence. The consecrated host is a figure for the presence of Christ, and so just as the pearl metaphor calls attention to the difference between tenor and vehicle, it highlights the worshipper's distance from the divine at the same time as it signifies the divine's immediate presence.[35]

---

34. The paradoxical relationship between presence and absence in the Eucharist is an issue that theologians have long seen as central to an understanding of the sacrament. See, for example, Aquinas, *Summa Theologiae*, 3a.75. Modern scholars have also recognized this paradox's centrality. See Beckwith, *Signifying God*, 88–89; Bynum, "Seeing and Seeing Beyond,"; Catherine Pickstock, "Thomas Aquinas and the Quest for the Eucharist," in *Catholicism and Catholicity: Eucharistic Communities in Historical and Contemporary Perspectives*, ed. Sarah Beckwith (Oxford: Blackwell, 1999), 47–68.

35. Although modern scholarship sometimes implies otherwise, many orthodox theologians affirmed the idea that the consecrated host was both a figure for Christ's presence and that presence itself. For one of the earliest and most influential discussions of this idea, see Hugh of St. Victor, *On the Sacraments of the Christian Faith (De Sacramentis)*, trans. Roy J. Deferrari (Cambridge, MA: Mediaeval Academy of America, 1951), 304–15.

The Eucharist thus demands that believers submit to external authority and acknowledge the limits of identification because the distance between figure and reality is so readily apparent. It offers the dreamer the chance to learn to be satisfied with his distance from the divine.

The description of the virgins' procession into the New Jerusalem presents the Mass as a method of worship that acknowledges divine absence even as it celebrates Christ's sacramental presence. The maidens' procession toward and worship of the Lamb is one of the poem's most explicit liturgical allusions. Solemn processions were one of the most recognizable liturgical activities in late medieval England because they were particularly frequent in the Use of Salisbury, the variant of the Roman Rite used throughout most of England.[36] In the Use of Salisbury, the priest and the other liturgical ministers would process around the church at the beginning of Mass, and since the altar itself typically lay behind a screen, this procession was one of the most visible parts of the liturgy. The poet's use of the word "prosessyoun" to describe the maidens' entrance into the heavenly Jerusalem could not help but invoke liturgical practice (1096). Although the procession looks liturgical, the poet explains that the maidens are not taking part in a Mass because the Mass serves a purpose for earthly spirituality that is unnecessary in heaven. He describes how, in the New Jerusalem, "Kyrk therinne was non yete— / Chapel ne temple that ever was set. / The Almyghty was her mynster mete, / The Lombe the sakerfyse ther to refet" (1061–64). The immediate presence of Christ obviates the need for Mass because the celebration of Mass assumes Christ's absence; if Christ is fully present, there is no need to celebrate his invisible presence in the Eucharist. Since the image of Christ as a lamb draws on sacrificial language and the poet argues that the presence of the Lamb replaces earthly sacrifice, the ever-bleeding Lamb on his throne is analogous to the consecrated host on the altar. The maidens' worship of the Lamb is not a Mass but a perfection of it because it is a completely direct way of worshipping Christ. By arguing that God himself is the Church and the Lamb himself is the sacrifice, the poem depicts the heavenly Jerusalem in the terms of the Mass even though it recognizes that those terms have been superseded.

Through its description of the differing responses of the maidens and the dreamer to the Lamb, *Pearl* argues that participation in the Mass ought to involve emotional and physical control. In their perfect worship of the Lamb, the maidens model ideal liturgical devotion, in both their physical posture and emotional response. As they approach the Lamb's throne, "thagh thay

---

36. Terence Bailey, *The Processions of Sarum and the Western Church* (Toronto: Pontifical Institute of Mediaeval Studies, 1971). The Use of Salisbury is often referred to as the "Use of Sarum."

werne fele, no pres in plyt, / Bot mylde as maydenes seme at mas / So drov they forth with gret delyt" (1114–16). The poem praises the maidens because, although they are experiencing the utmost joy, they are completely emotionally contained and physically orderly. The word "seme" is highly significant to this description. It suggests that a particular set of thoughts and emotions is not essential to proper liturgical devotion. What is most important is that the worshipper exercise control over her emotions so that she can "seme" mild from the outside. In contrast to the maidens, the dreamer has exactly the wrong response to Christ's presence within this liturgical setting. First, he misunderstands the sacramental meaning of the Lamb's wound and is horrified rather than engaged in worship or penitence. However, the dreamer's greatest failure in liturgical behavior is his inability to contain his emotional response. The dreamer is allowed to see this celebration only until he lets his emotions overtake his physical actions, until "delyt me drof in yye and ere" (1153). Once his emotions drive his devotion, he attempts to cross the river and is forced to awaken from his dream. The poem presents emotional containment as an ideal of liturgical behavior, an ideal that the dreamer utterly fails to achieve.

Although it is the site of the dreamer's greatest failure, the poem argues that repeated participation in the liturgy is the only way for him to reform; the poem enacts this call to inner change through ritual in its form. The repetition of the Mass—as a religious ritual that requires the worshipper to accept simultaneous presence and absence, and to accept the limits of one's own subjectivity—is a way of training the self into proper spiritual discipline. Repetition itself lies at the heart of *Pearl*'s formal artistry. Each stanza of the poem begins by repeating the concluding words of the previous stanza, and the poem's last line echoes its first line; within each section, every stanza ends with a variation on the same concatenated word or phrase. The poem thus uses repetition to create internal connections between each stanza and section and, as virtually every formal analysis of the poem remarks, the form itself strives to imitate the perfection and roundness of a pearl.[37] This form—with its rigid structure and symbolic use of repetition—also imitates the repetitive nature of religious ritual. By showing how each repetition alters the meaning of the repeated word, *Pearl* argues that repetition itself can be a catalyst for inner change. Repetition is both a marker and a cause of inner transformation during the seventh section, which concatenates the phrase "grounde of alle my blysse." Over the course of this section, the repetition of this phrase draws attention to the dreamer's shifting understanding of the true nature of bliss. At

---

37. For an overview of the highly complex formal structure of *Pearl*, see H. N. Duggan, "Meter, Stanza, Vocabulary, Dialect," in *A Companion to the* Gawain-*Poet*, ed. Derek Brewer and Jonathan Gibson (Cambridge: D. S. Brewer, 1997), 221–42.

the beginning of the section, the dreamer asserts that, in life, the pearl maiden was the source of his bliss. Over the course of a few stanzas, he reinterprets the concatenated phrase to refer only to Christ, whom he now considers the only true and lasting source of happiness. The repetition of key words forces the dreamer to continually reformulate those words' meanings and highlights the way that meaning changes over the course of the section. Through its formal focus on repetition, the poem enacts what the dreamer realizes when he turns to the Eucharist at the end of the poem: regular repetition is the key to meaningful internal change.

Pearl's final stanza argues that eucharistic devotion provides a way for the individual subject to practice emotional and spiritual control. Upon awaking from his dream, the dreamer recognizes that his lack of emotional control forced him out of his vision of the New Jerusalem. He allowed his desire to push him to the point of madness when he should have submitted wholly to God's will, "And yerned no more then was me gyven, / And halden me ther in trwe entent" (1190–91). The dreamer was unworthy of the vision because he failed to contain and control his desire. When the dreamer then proposes the worship of the Eucharist as a solution to his sinfulness, he suggests that the sacrament can help the individual believer to gain control of his inner self. Although this suggestion may initially seem simplistic, the poem argues that the process of emotional containment and accepting the state of lack within the self is ongoing and therefore always incomplete; like the Mass, it must happen "uch a daye" (1210). When the dreamer proclaims, "To pay the Prince other sete saghte, / Hit is ful ethe to the god Krystyin" (1201–2), he is not stating that it is easy for him to please God. On the contrary, he has gone into great detail to show that he himself is not a good Christian. Eucharistic worship is a process of identity reform, a process whose goal it is to create that "god Krystyin" within the self so that pleasing Christ can eventually become a task that is "ful ethe." The Mass is not the end point of spiritual perfection; it is a ritual in which the individual learns and practices self-control.

In her introduction to *Pearl*, Sarah Stanbury describes critics' interpretive dilemma with regard to its final stanza in the following way: "Does [the dreamer] become, as he asserts, a docile subject (taking the sacrament), or does he remain a single consciousness, separate from the vision of metaphoric accumulation that he witnesses?"[38] Although this formulation accurately describes current scholarly approaches to this stanza, it creates an inaccurate opposition between eucharistic devotion and individual subjectivity within

---

38. Sarah Stanbury, "Introduction," in *Pearl*, ed. Sarah Stanbury (Kalamazoo, MI: Medieval Institute Publications, 2001), 17.

the poem. The dreamer's turn toward the Eucharist is not a movement away from individual consciousness; it is a turn inward. The dreamer's decision to worship Christ in the sacrament is a direct result of his realization that he must firmly contain his emotions and desires. As in *Cleanness, Patience,* and *Sir Gawain and the Green Knight,* the poet argues in *Pearl* that the good aristocratic subject enacts his Christian devotion primarily through self-control and inner reform rather than external actions. In *Pearl,* the Eucharist is integral to individual reform because it forces the believer to accept the limits of his own subjectivity. Through Christ's simultaneous absence and presence in the Mass, worshippers encounter their desire and inability to identify with Christ. The good Christian acknowledges that there will always be a loss at the center of the self during earthly life because Christ is never fully present. For the *Pearl*-poet, rigid control of one's emotional state is essential if one is to accept the profound state of lack that defines human earthly life.

For the *Pearl*-poet, liturgical devotion is an internal act of textual interpretation of a figurative textual object: the consecrated host. *Pearl* uses metaphor in order to explore the limits of identification between believer and divine, between bread and Christ's body, between tenor and vehicle and to examine the reader's and believer's thwarted desire to bridge these categories. Like Mannyng's *Handlyng Synne, Pearl*'s presentation of the believer's inability to identify with Christ depends upon an Ambrosian understanding of the Eucharist as a sacred object. In the next chapter, I will explore a more Augustinian approach to the Eucharist and the challenges of constructing a community that identifies with and as the mystical body of Christ. For Middle English writers, this Augustinian focus necessarily demands the use of not metaphor but allegory.

CHAPTER 3

Christ's Allegorical Bodies and the Failure of Community in *Piers Plowman*

        ike *Handlyng Synne* and *Pearl,* William Langland's *Piers Plowman* aims to replace simplistic models of eucharistic devotion with more complex and identity-transforming ones. However, unlike those texts, the identity that *Piers Plowman* seeks to reform is communal rather than individual. In contrast to the more dominant Ambrosian eucharistic models, Langland draws on Augustine's presentation of the host as an allegorical sign of the Christian community. For Langland, as for Augustine, the Eucharist was paradoxically both reality and figure; it was a sign that both signified and contained the physical body of Christ, and signified Christ's mystical body, the community of the faithful. Langland treats the Eucharist in Augustinian terms in order to resist simple correlations between Christ's mystical body and the fourteenth-century earthly Christian church; he exploits the disjunction between literal and allegorical levels of his text precisely to invite readers to transform their social world.

    Though scholars have often examined Langland's theology and interest in religious practice, very few scholars have treated Langland's views on the Eucharist directly.[1] Indeed, until David Aers's recent treatment of the topic, to my knowledge there had not been a single scholarly article on the Eucha-

---

      1. In an important overview of *Piers Plowman*'s theology, Robert Adams remarks that Langland's views on the Eucharist are of little interest because "his attitude seems altogether conventional and pious; and since the Eucharist is not frequently mentioned in the poem, it seems unlikely that the subject holds much promise for extensive future research." Robert

rist in *Piers Plowman*.² Surveying the poem as a whole, Aers argues that, for Langland, the Eucharist cannot be separated from the context of its reception, the Christian community. He concludes by claiming that Langland's theology is somewhat radical in its avoidance of debates about the Real Presence. Aers is right to point to the importance of the Christian community within Langland's eucharistic theology, but his conclusion does not reflect the full complexity of Langland's treatment of the Eucharist. This chapter will present a detailed reading of the poem's penultimate passus—19 in the B Text, 21 in the C text, the one passus most centrally concerned with eucharistic theology.³ I want to reconsider Aers's crucial point, Langland's commitment to Christian community, in the light of another interest that has received ample scholarly attention: Langland's interest in allegory.⁴ By highlighting Passus 19's exploration of both allegory and the Eucharist, I show that Langland's interest in the corporate body of Christ is not a slight to belief in the Real Presence, but rather stems from his sense of the inseparability of the two as sacramentally related concepts.

Passus 19 begins and ends with instances of failed eucharistic reception: when Will falls asleep at Easter Mass immediately prior to the consecration, and when the Christians in the Barn of Unity reject Conscience's call to receive the Eucharist. Framed by these two eucharistic moments, the middle of the passus is an investigation of the way in which signs, particularly Christ's name and the Church as a sign of Christ's presence on earth, chal-

---

Adams, "Langland's Theology," in *A Companion to Piers Plowman*, ed. John A. Alford (Berkeley: University of California Press, 1988), 98.

2. David Aers, "The Sacrament of the Altar in *Piers Plowman*," in *Sanctifying Signs*, 29–51. This chapter is a revised version of an earlier article: David Aers, "The Sacrament of the Altar in *Piers Plowman* and Late Medieval England," in *Images, Idolatry and Iconoclasm in Late Medieval England: Textuality and the Visual Image*, ed. Jeremy Dimmick, James Simpson, and Nicolette Zeeman (Oxford: Oxford UP, 2002), 63–80.

3. Passus 19 and 20 of the B Text are virtually identical to Passus 21 and 22 of the C Text. I cite the B Text throughout. All citations are from Willam Langland, *The Vision of Piers Plowman: A Critical Edition of the B-Text*, ed. A. V. C. Schmidt, 2nd ed. (London: Dent/Everyman, 1995).

4. The scholarship on allegory in *Piers Plowman* is vast. Some of the most influential works include the following: David Aers, *Piers Plowman and Christian Allegory* (London: Edward Arnold, 1975); Mary Carruthers, *The Search for St. Truth: A Study of Meaning in Piers Plowman* (Evanston, IL: Northwestern UP, 1973); Lavinia Griffiths, *Personification in Piers Plowman* (Cambridge: D. S. Brewer, 1985); Jill Mann, *Langland and Allegory*, Morton W. Bloomfield Lectures on Medieval English Literature, II (Kalamazoo, MI: Medieval Institute Publications, 1992); Maureen Quilligan, "Langland's Literal Allegory," *Essays in Criticism* 28 (1978), 95–111; Pamela Raabe, *Imitating God: The Allegory of Faith in Piers Plowman B* (Athens: University of Georgia Press, 1990); D. W. Robertson Jr., and Bernard F. Huppé, Piers Plowman *and the Scriptural Tradition* (Princeton, NJ: Princeton UP, 1951).

lenge and enable the human community's access to Christ. Thus, I argue that the passus constitutes a direct engagement in discussions of the Eucharist as a sign. Langland examines the host as an allegorical sign of Christ's body, both Christ's historical body and the corporate body of all Christians. Like most students of the topic in the past thirty years, I agree that Langland's intense focus on materiality continually causes failures or breaks in the poem's allegorical structure, dramatizing the limits of both allegory and language. As Kathleen Hewett-Smith points out, Langland's use of concrete detail frustrates "the success of allegorical interpretation by forcing our attention to an historically immediate material world, to the literal level of the sign, by advertising the disparity between real and ideal, signifier and signified."[5] At the same time, by arguing that Langland sees the Eucharist as an instance of allegory, I aim to shift the emphasis of this and similar claims, suggesting that Langland does in fact regard the perfect reflection of a transcendent signified in the material signifier as potentially possible. The reason that such a reflection almost never occurs is not due to the inherent inadequacies of language but because of the human community's failure.[6]

THE ALLEGORICAL PRESENCE

Piers Plowman participates in an ongoing theological discussion about the relationship between allegory, ecclesiology, and the Eucharist. Since so much of modern literary scholars' attention has been to the writings of Wyclif and the Lollards, there has been a critical tendency to assume that late medieval orthodox writings about the Eucharist always collapse the division between sign and signified in the sacrament. However, as I outline in my introduc-

---

5. Kathleen M. Hewett-Smith, "Allegory on the Half-Acre: The Demands of History," *Yearbook of Langland Studies* 10 (1996), 1. See also Carruthers, *Search for St. Truth*; Laurie A. Finke, "Truth's Treasure: Allegory and Meaning in *Piers Plowman*," in *Medieval Texts and Contemporary Readers*, ed. Laurie A. Finke and Martin B. Shichtman (Ithaca, NY: Cornell UP, 1987), 51–68; Griffiths, *Personification*; Kathleen M. Hewett-Smith, "'Nede ne hath no lawe': Poverty and the De-stabilization of Allegory in the Final Visions of *Piers Plowman*," in *William Langland's* Piers Plowman: *A Book of Essays*, ed. Kathleen M. Hewett-Smith (New York: Routledge, 2001), 233–53; James J. Paxson, "Inventing the Subject and the Personification of Will in *Piers Plowman*: Rhetorical, Erotic, and Ideological Origins and Limits in Langland's Allegorical Poetics," in *William Langland's* Piers Plowman: *A Book of Essays*, ed. Kathleen M. Hewett-Smith (New York: Routledge, 2001), 195–231; Quilligan, "Langland's Literal Allegory."

6. I am building off the work of Lawrence Clopper and Pamela Raabe who both suggest that Langland does not necessarily see a great tension between figural and literal, universal and individual. See Lawrence M. Clopper, "Langland and Allegory: A Proposition," *Yearbook of Langland Studies* 15 (2001), 35–42; Raabe, *Imitating God*.

tory chapter, many texts in both Latin and the vernacular celebrate the Eucharist precisely because of the complex relationship between figure and truth that the sacrament enacts. Allegorical language actually became increasingly important to definitions of the Eucharist as the doctrine of the Real Presence and the later doctrine of transubstantiation began to become defining elements of mainstream thought.

Drawing on Augustine's theory of verbal signs—that Christ the Word redeemed language and therefore language provides partial access to the divine—many theologians believed that treating the Eucharist as a sign enhanced its sanctity. It is a critical commonplace that Western medieval theologians often focused their thinking around a common theory of verbal signs that derived much of its authority from the Incarnation of Christ. Since Christ is both the Word made flesh and the mediator between God and humanity, it made sense to regard verbal signs as the primary means of gaining knowledge of the divine. Christ the Word redeemed language, and it is therefore through signs that humans can come to know him. Augustine, the theologian largely responsible for formulating this theory of signs, argued that verbal signs "whether literal or figurative, truly, if partially, represent really existing things."[7] Even though Augustine draws a sharp distinction between sign and signified, he assumes that there is a real relationship between the two.

Eucharistic language afforded writers of Middle English with the opportunity to discuss the relationship of transcendence to language itself. Medieval theologians typically based their understanding of the Eucharist as a sign in theory that proposed a real but complex relationship between sign and signified. During the later Middle Ages, verbal sign theory became a way of explaining the mystery of Christ's presence in the Eucharist that did not diminish its sanctity. In *On Christian Doctrine*, Augustine argues that literal signification may be able to express fairly simple aspects of reality, but metaphorical signification and figurative language are better suited to expressing realities that are complex and difficult to understand.[8] Figurative language gives mystery and honor to its subject both by clarifying it and by suggesting the inherent difficulty of comprehending it. In this context, it is evident that medieval theologians' insistence that the Eucharist was a sign could often be an affirmation of the Eucharist's spiritual worth. Like a figurative sign in scripture, the Eucharist posed interpretive difficulties because its meaning was not readily apparent. However, the nature of Christ's presence as both beyond the

---

7. Marcia L. Colish, *The Mirror of Language: A Study in the Medieval Theory of Knowledge*, rev. ed. (Lincoln: University of Nebraska Press, 1983), 53.

8. Augustine, *De Doctrina Christiana. De Vera Religione*, Corpus Christianorum Series Latina, vol. 32 (Turnhout, BE: Brepols, 1962), II.vi, 8.

sign and a part of it simultaneously protected Christ's presence from the disdain of nonbelievers and led to the spiritual benefit of the faithful. Throughout the Middle Ages, theologians often strengthened their arguments for Christ's presence in the host precisely by insisting that the Eucharist be understood as an instance of figurative language.

In the ninth century, during what became the first major eucharistic debates of the Middle Ages, Paschasius and Ratramnus set the precedent for future definitions of the Eucharist by arguing that defining the relationship between figure and truth was the central challenge of understanding Christ's presence in the host. These two monks at Corbie wrote the first theological treatises devoted specifically to a doctrinal treatment of the Eucharist, and both defined the nature of Christ's presence by examining the relationship between the terms *figura* and *veritas*.[9] The major difference between the two treatises was that, unlike Ratramnus, Paschasius insisted on the real presence of Christ's true body and blood in the host. According to Paschasius, the figurative nature of the Eucharist pertains to the sensible elements of the sacrament—the bread and wine—while the truth pertains to Christ. In his formulation, figurative language functions as a sort of veil, masking the truth that is fully present. Paschasius argues that the Eucharist "is a figure or character which is sensed exteriorly, but the whole truth, and not a shadow, is perceived on the inside, and through this, nothing else is shown than truth and sacrament of the flesh itself."[10] Paschasius recognizes that any sacrament is essentially a sign but he suggests that within the sacrament of the Eucharist is contained the signified itself. Ratramnus, on the other hand, contended that the change in the host takes place on a spiritual level, and Christ is therefore only figuratively present in the host. For Ratramnus, there must always be a sharp distinction between figure and truth, sign and signified; by definition, a figure must signify a reality beyond and separate from itself.[11] The Eucharist therefore signifies Christ but is not Christ himself. Ratramnus's definition of Christ's presence in the Eucharist was simpler than Paschasius's insofar as it posited a clear separation between figure and truth, host and body. The fact

---

9. Celia Chazelle, "Figure, Character, and the Glorified Body in the Carolingian Eucharistic Controversy," *Traditio* 47 (1992): 1–36; Levy, *John Wyclif*, 126–37; Macy, *Theologies of the Eucharist*, 21–31.

10. "Est autem figura uel character hoc quod exterius sentitur, sed totum ueritas et nulla adumbratio quod intrinsecus percipitur ac per hoc nihil aliud hinc inde quam ueritas et sacramentum ipsius carnis aperitur." Paschasius Radbertus, *De Corpore et Sanguine Domini*, ed. Bede Paulus, Corpus Christianorum, Continuatio Mediaevalis XVI (Turnhout, BE: Brepols, 1969), 30. Translation is my own.

11. Ratramnus, *De Corpore et Sanguine Domini*, ed. J. N. Bakhuizen van den Brink (Amsterdam: North-Holland Publishing Company, 1954), VI–VIII.

that Paschasius's views on the Eucharist were the ones to become dominant over the next several centuries ensured that the relationship between figure and truth in the Eucharist remained fraught and therefore continued to incite controversy.

In the later Middle Ages, even as eucharistic doctrines became more insistent on Christ's literal physical presence in the host, theologians began to use a sacramental vocabulary that defined signifier (the appearance of bread) and signified (Christ's physical presence) as increasingly distinct.[12] The clear distinction between figure and truth was important even for theologians who insisted that sign (host) and signified (body) coincided in the Eucharist. In the twelfth century, Hugh of St. Victor reshaped eucharistic theology by redefining the term *sacramentum* in a way that collapsed figure and truth even as it emphasized the two categories as distinct. As Marcia Colish has shown, Hugh's greatest contribution to eucharistic theology is that he shifted the definition of a sacrament from a visible sign of invisible grace to a sign that contains and effects what it signifies.[13] The previous definition of *sacramentum* allowed for a variety of relationships between sign and signified, but Hugh's new definition depended upon the interweaving of truth and figure by suggesting that the sign has real effects. In his 1130 *De Sacramentis,* Hugh argues that the Eucharist is both truth and figure simultaneously: "Is the sacrament of the altar then not truth because it is a figure? Then neither is the death of Christ truth because it is a figure, and the resurrection of Christ is not truth because it is a figure."[14] According to Hugh, a strict separation between truth and figure is logically flawed because the Christian faith is rooted in events, Christ's death and resurrection, which are also truth and figure. Just as Paschasius did three centuries earlier, Hugh insists that the figural element of the Eucharist is the visible species since, through the consecration, the species appear present when, in reality, only the body of Christ is there. Hugh divides the Eucharist into three components: *sacramentum tantum* (the visible species), *sacramentum et res sacramenti* (the body and blood invisible beneath the species), and *res tantum* (spiritual grace). This language became tremendously influential. His terminology allowed orthodox theologians to argue that the Eucharist is a sign while at the same time insisting that there can be no sharp separation between sign and signified in the Eucharist. For Hugh and the

---

12. Ian Christopher Levy provides a useful overview of some of the major shifts in vocabulary in late medieval eucharistic theology. Levy, *John Wyclif,* 123–215.

13. Marcia L. Colish, *Peter Lombard,* vol. 2 (Leiden, NL: E. J. Brill, 1994), 564.

14. "Nunquid ideo sacramentum altaris veritas non est, quia figura est? Ergo nec mors Christi veritas est, quia figura est, et resurrectio Christi veritas non est, quia figura est." *Patrologia Latina* 176, Col. 466a. Translation from Hugh of Saint Victor, *On the Sacraments,* 308.

many medieval theologians who followed him, the power of the Eucharist as a mystery thus lay in the way it both maintained and confounded distinctions between figure and truth.

One way in which treatments of the Eucharist became explicitly allegorical was in discussions of the consecrated host as a sign of the Christian community. Starting in about 1050, theologians began to draw a sharp distinction between *corpus Christi* and *corpus mysticum*.[15] *Corpus Christi* referred only to the sacramental and historical bodies of Christ while *corpus mysticum* was the corporate body of Christ as manifest in the community of the faithful. While the sacrament both signified and contained the historical body of Christ, it only allegorically signified the corporate or mystical body of Christ. For many writers, both *corpus Christi* and *corpus mysticum* were signified in the host: the difference between the two methods of signification was that *corpus Christi* was literally present in the host while *corpus mysticum* was not. Communal readings of the Eucharist became more purely allegorical because they suggested a meaning for the host that was beyond the host itself.

Allegorical and communal readings persisted alongside literal, physical interpretations of the host in both Latin and vernacular literature throughout the late Middle Ages. For example, in his fourteenth-century poem, "De Septem Sacramentis," William of Shoreham explains that through eucharistic reception, the whole Christian community "o body beþe ine mystyke."[16] However, like many orthodox theologians, William is careful to distinguish between *corpus Christi* and *corpus mysticum*,

> Ac Þaȝ we be tokned þer
> Ine oure sauueoure,
> Ne lef þou nauȝt þe[t] we be þer,
> Ne forþe nauȝt of oure
>   þat were;
> Þaȝ þer be tokned þynges two,
> Þer nys bote o þyng þere;
> And þat hys swete ihesu cryst
> Ine flesche and eke ine bloude.[17]

Although the host signifies both Christ's physical body and the mystical body of Christ, William urges his readers to understand that only Christ's physical body is literally present in the sacrament; the mystical body is only figuratively

---

15. See my introductory chapter.
16. William of Shoreham, *Poems*, 23.
17. Ibid., 25.

present. Likewise, the fifteenth-century sermon that serves as the prologue to the ordinances of the York Corpus Christi guild draws on the allegorical meaning of the *corpus mysticum,* suggesting that guild members must honor the literal body in the consecrated host by becoming the mystical body, which the host allegorically signifies. The sermon's author tells guild members that "since our fraternity for the veneration of this same precious sacrament has been begun by rule, gathered together in the faith of the Church in peaceful unity, we will be a homogeneous part of the mystical body of Christ through our prayers, devotions, and acts of charity."[18] Several of Langland's contemporaries likewise extol the importance of the Christian community within their sermons' discussions of the Eucharist's signification.[19] In addition, as recent scholarship has shown, the documents surrounding the celebration and promotion of the feast of Corpus Christi particularly rely on an understanding of the Christian community as enacting the body of Christ, the body that Christians also worship in the consecrated host.[20] When Langland associates the Eucharist in his poem with both ecclesiology and allegory, in my view, he is not so much making a radical interpretive move, as Aers suggests, as participating in a continuing discussion about the relationship between the *corpus mysticum* and *corpus Christi.*[21]

EUCHARIST AS SOCIAL SIGN IN *PIERS PLOWMAN*

In Passus 19 of *Piers Plowman,* Langland repeatedly depicts the Eucharist as a sign in order to highlight the way in which this sacrament unites transcendent meaning and literal material reality. He links the seemingly disparate elements of the passus—the discussion of names, Christ's vita, Pentecost, the founding of the church, the invitation to and rejection of the Eucharist—through the concept of signification as it is elaborated in eucharistic theology. The two failed moments of eucharistic reception that frame Passus 19 are instances in

---

18. "cum nostra fraternitas in veneracione istius preciosi sacramenti sit regulariter incepta. erimus in fidei ecclesiae / vnitate pacifice congregati velut corporis Christi mistici in precibus votis et actionibus elemosinariis pars homogenia." Original and translation from Paula Ložar, "The Prologue to the Ordinances of the York Corpus Christi Guild," *Allegorica* 1 (1976): 104–5.

19. Woodburn O. Ross, ed., *Middle English Sermons,* EETS o.s. 209 (London: Oxford UP, 1940), 125–33; Mirk, *Mirk's Festial,* 129–32; D. M. Grisdale, ed., *Three Middle English Sermons from the Worcester Chapter Manuscript F.10,* (Kendal, UK: Titus Wilson, 1939), 50–80.

20. It is worth noting that these scholars present both the Eucharist and the very concepts of orthodoxy and heterodoxy as complex and multifaceted. Beckwith, *Signifying God*; James, "Ritual"; Rubin, *Corpus Christi,* 213–87.

21. Aers, "Sacrament of the Altar," 46.

which the material sign could have been united with its signified; the bread and Christ's physical body could have physically united with the corporate body of the faithful through the act of eating the host. This unification fails because the community does not act as the socially harmonious corporate body that the consecrated host signifies. Langland argues that proper eucharistic reception requires Christians to understand the Eucharist as a sign of both Christ's physical and corporate bodies, and to recognize their own ethical obligation to become one with that signified body.

In Passus 19, Langland argues that the Eucharist is a communal act with communal significance. At the beginning of the passus, Langland is deeply suspicious of modes of worshipping the Eucharist that disregard the social world. By describing Will as falling asleep in the middle of Mass, Langland highlights the disjunction between two models of eucharistic devotion: the Eucharist as an individual affective encounter with Christ and the Eucharist as a celebration of the Christian community. Langland never fully explains the significance of Will's sleep at this moment, but there are at least two provocative possibilities. The first is that Will's dream is a vision of Christ's Real Presence in the host. Like in sermon exempla that encourage individual affective devotion to the host through narratives of bleeding hosts or a mutilated Christ-child on the altar, Will dreams of a bloody Christ-like figure experiencing the tortures of the Passion.[22] Instead of participating in the Mass and seeing the host elevated, Will sees that "Piers the Plowman was peynted al blody, / And com in with a cros before the commune peple, / And right lik in alle lymes to Oure Lord Jesu" (B.19.6–8). If read as a fairly typical eucharistic vision, Will is seeing the Real Presence hidden behind the host: Christ, with his irreducible humanity emphasized by his representation as the earthly Piers Plowman, offering himself as a sacrifice before the people. However, this eucharistic vision is atypical because Will does not see the literal, historical body of the human Christ. He sees either Piers Plowman looking like Christ or, as Conscience will later suggest, Christ dressed as Piers Plowman. According to Will, Piers is "right lik in alle lymes" to Christ; he is not Christ himself. If this is a eucharistic vision, it is not one that transcends representation. Rather it emphasizes the truth of the host's representation through another act of representation.

A second possible interpretation of Will's sleep during Mass is that it allegorically signifies his lack of spiritual awareness. By not consciously participating in the Mass, Will fails to be part of the spiritual community and

---

22. On bloody eucharistic miracles in sermon exempla, see Bynum, "Seeing and Seeing Beyond"; Rubin, *Corpus Christi*, 108–47.

therefore fails to enact the corporate body of Christ that the host signifies. This interpretation of Will's sleep as a manifestation of his sinfulness is supported by the fact that his act is sinful on the literal level: most medieval Christians would consider falling asleep at Mass to be a sin.[23] However, since Will's dream is an exploration of the significance of the Eucharist in relation to the church, reading Will's slumber as a sign of moral failure is not a fully satisfying explanation either.

What these two explanations have in common is that both depict this attempted eucharistic reception as a moment dependent on allegorical representation—either Christ represented as Piers, or sin represented as sleep—and both create a division between Will's individual experience and his community's act of worship. Although Langland never fully articulates the precise significance of Will falling asleep at Mass, Will's sleep is clearly a move away from his immediate historical, physical community and therefore undercuts his initial motivations for going to Mass; he does not celebrate the Easter Mass with his family, and he sleeps through the Eucharist. Whatever spiritual truths he may encounter in his dream, he has had to sacrifice the communal aspect of worship in order to receive them. While Langland clearly believes that individual piety can be fruitful, he is very skeptical of any spirituality that totally neglects communal worship.

In this passus, individual devotion gains its importance from its social context. The poem's celebration of Easter starting at the end of Passus 18 is a return to the social world and, with it, the Eucharist, the sacrament that celebrates the unity of the church.[24] At the end of Passus 18, after witnessing the Harrowing of Hell and the reconciliation of Mercy, Truth, Justice, and Peace, Will wakes up and returns to his social community in order to celebrate Easter, the same event of which he has just been dreaming. Easter was the most important celebration of the church's liturgical year, marking the greatest event in Christian history—Christ's Resurrection—and Langland depicts this celebration as fundamentally social. Will awakens on Easter to two sounds that

---

23. Falling asleep at Mass was typically associated with sloth. For example, Robert Mannyng's *Handlyng Synne* begins its section on sloth with a long treatise against sleeping when one should be at Mass and not paying proper attention during the Mass itself. Mannyng argues that "he ys ful of slownesse / Þat may and wyle nat here hys messe." Mannyng, *Handlyng Synne*, 108. On sloth in *Piers Plowman*, see John M. Bowers, *The Crisis of Will in* Piers Plowman, (Washington, DC: Catholic University of America Press, 1986).

24. In this respect, I agree with James Simpson who argues that the final two passus "reimagine the whole of society as springing from and contributing to this renewed Church." James Simpson, *Piers Plowman: An Introduction*, 2nd rev. ed. (Exeter: University of Exeter Press, 2007), 194. On the poem's final outward turn, see also Malcolm Godden, *The Making of Piers Plowman* (London: Longman, 1990), 152.

blend into one another: the earthly church's bells and Love's heavenly singing from his dream. Earth and heaven join together as a community united in celebration and music. The song Love sings—"Ecce quam bonum et quam iocundum"—is from the first verse of Psalm 132, which announces "Behold how good and how pleasant it is for brethren to dwell in unity" (B.18.425a).[25] This song suggests that one of the primary reasons for joy at the Resurrection is the united Christian community, which the Resurrection created, and Will himself recognizes the bells and the singing as calls to communal celebration. As soon as he wakes, he "called Kytte my wif and Calote my doghter: / 'Ariseth and go reverenceth Goddes resurexion'" (B.18.428–29). Will knows that Easter is a communal event, and he must therefore celebrate it with his family and in a church. In Passus 19, the poem turns away from the more purely psychological dialogues of Passus 8–18 and toward Easter, a community celebration that ought to culminate in eucharistic reception.

After the Easter setting with which the passus begins and ends, the central biblical event in Passus 19 is Pentecost, an event that centers on the social manifestations of Christian spirituality. One reason that Pentecost plays such a central part in this passus, marking the transition from the discussion of the names of Christ to the foundation of the church, is that it allows Langland to explicitly place Will's individual spiritual quest within the broader context of the entire church's search for unity with God. As Langland describes it, Pentecost is an event that unites the Christian community throughout history. Pentecost, which traditionally marks the birth of the Christian church, was the moment at which the Holy Spirit descended upon the disciples and endowed each of them with individual gifts. It is significant, both for Langland's poem and for the Christian tradition more generally, that the Spirit bestows these gifts within a communal setting and for the benefit and production of a Christian community. In *Piers Plowman,* Pentecost is not a firmly historical event; the need for and availability of the Holy Spirit to the Christian people is constant. After Conscience tells Will about the crucifixion and resurrection, Will experiences the original feast of Pentecost as if he himself were present at that historical moment. He dreams that he hears hundreds of others praying to the Holy Spirit with him, suggesting that there are more people present at this dream-version of Pentecost than would have been present at the historical event. Conscience demands that Will not simply witness the coming of the Holy Spirit, but actually participate in it. In their communal prayer, all the people present sing Pentecost hymns, which necessarily postdate the original event. This anachronism functions in the same way that anachronism often

---

25. Translation is from the note in A. V. C. Schmidt's edition.

does within medieval devotional texts: it emphasizes the way in which spiritual events transcend history. The participation of both Will and Piers Plowman in the original Pentecost implies that the foundation of the church and the Holy Spirit's involvement in it is not a finite historical fact, but an ongoing process. In this poem, the church is not simply an institution, but a community of believers that transcends time and space.

In his description of Pentecost, Langland subordinates individual identity to group identity even as he celebrates individual abilities and works. Grace tells Conscience that, in order to defend the church from the Antichrist, he "gaf ech man a grace to gye with hymselven, / That Ydelnesse encombre hym noght, ne Envye ne Pride: / *Divisiones graciarum sunt*" (B.19.227–29a). Grace cites this passage from Paul's first letter to the Corinthians—"There are varieties of graces, but the same Spirit"—partly in order to invoke the famous metaphor that follows it: the community is the body of Christ, and each individual person is a member of that body. In explaining the reason for bestowing gifts, Grace suggests both that every individual is autonomous and therefore has a responsibility to defend himself against the attacks of the Antichrist, and that every individual's gifts serve a purpose in promoting and protecting the well-being of the entire Christian community. Grace advises Piers and Conscience, "Loke that noon lakke oother, but loveth alle as bretheren," because all gifts are essential to the functioning of the greater community, and all crafts, no matter how undignified, originate from a gift of Grace (B.19.256). Although Grace places particular emphasis on crafts rather than gifts and lists many professions that are more medieval than ancient, his instructions are otherwise a very direct application of Paul's directions to the Christian community in Corinth. For Paul as for Langland, individual gifts are very significant, but primarily insofar as they contribute to the greater Christian community: the corporate body of Christ. Individual identity and group identity are interdependent, but group identity, because it is essentially the identity of Christ, is the most important.

SIGNS OF CHRIST

Since, according to Langland, Christians ought to know and worship Christ within their own social context—and not primarily through direct, personal encounters with Christ—individuals must understand Christ through signs and language. When Passus 19 shifts from Will's eucharistic vision of Piers to Conscience's explication of the many names for Christ, the transition seems abrupt, but the two moments are thematically linked insofar as both are explorations of the immediacy of Christ through signs. The discussion of the names of Christ is an examination of the reliability of signs as objects of devotion, an issue that is central to medieval eucharistic theology, since transubstantiation simultaneously demands that believers disregard their faith in physical signs and that they direct their deepest devotion to a sign that proclaims the physical presence of Christ. In his explication of Christ's names, Langland shows that it is essential for every Christian to understand the complex ways in which signs provide access to the divine.

Through Will and Conscience's discussion of the identity of the bloody man in Will's vision, Langland suggests that recognizing Christ through signs is one of the greatest challenges of Christian devotion. When Will sees the bloody figure carrying a cross, he becomes confused and asks Conscience, "Is this Jesus the justere . . . that Jewes dide to dethe? / Or it is Piers the Plowman! Who peynted hym so rede?" (B.19.10–11). For Will, as for the reader, the identity of the bloody man is vitally important because it determines one's proper devotional response to the vision. If Will were to kneel down and worship this bloody figure, he might be performing proper religious devotion or he might be committing idolatry by worshipping Piers instead of Christ. Will cannot determine the relationship between physical signs and the identity they signify, and his inability to do so makes devotion very difficult. Conscience provides a solution to Will's quandary by informing him that the bloody man is Christ dressed in the colors and armor of Piers. Christ bears signs that represent Piers even though he is not Piers. This answer leads Will to question the stability of signs in worship, a problem he approaches by asking whether "Jesus" or "Christ" is the most appropriate name for the second person in the Trinity. The fact that this question directly follows a Mass-inspired vision of Christ strongly implies that the question itself is directly relevant to the Eucharist; in both eucharistic adoration and the worship of Christ's name, the object of worship is Christ as he is perceived through a sign. When Conscience tells Will that the figure who stands before the commons is Christ even though he looks like Piers, Conscience points to the challenges that worship through representation poses for belief.

In his explanation of Christ's names, Conscience argues that verbal signs of Christ are devotional tools that have a close relationship to that which they signify, but must not be mistaken for the signified itself. After Conscience identifies the bloody man as Christ, Will asks

> "Why calle ye hym Crist?" quod I, "sithen Jewes called hym Jesus?
> Patriarkes and prophetes prophecied before
> That alle kynne creatures sholden knelen and bowen

>   Anoon as men nempned the name of God Jesu.
>   *Ergo* is no name to the name of Jesus,
>   Ne noon so needful to nempne by nyghte ne by daye."
>   (B.19.15-20)

By asking this question, Will attempts to establish a firm relationship between signifier and signified. Will wants to determine both the proper way to worship Christ and the best way of understanding Christ's identity through language. According to his logic, if "Jesus" is a holy and accurate name for the second person of the Trinity, there must be a real relationship between the word "Jesus" and Jesus himself; Will takes the popular devotional tradition of reflecting ardently on the name "Jesus" a step further by implying that no other word can accurately represent Jesus.[26] Will believes that there should be one word that is a better representation of Jesus than all others, and so when faced with Conscience's reference to Jesus as "Christ," Will is more willing to concede that "Christ" is a better name than he is willing to admit that multiple names could equally refer to the same divine reality (B.19.24). Conscience responds to Will's question by asserting that both "Jesus" and "Christ" are accurate descriptions of the same person—Conscience himself often refers to Christ as "Jesus" in the course of the passage—but that the difference between the names is the different aspects of Christ to which they refer. He argues that, much in the same way that one person can be knight, king, and conqueror simultaneously, various names can accurately apply to Christ. Conscience claims that "Christ" corresponds to the word "conqueror," which "cometh of special grace, / And of hardynesse of herte and of hendenesse— / To make lords of laddes, of lond thathe wynneth, / And fre men foule thralles, that folwen noght his laws" (B.19.30-33). The name "Christ," which both Will and Conscience agree that Jews do not use, signifies Jesus' power over the Jews and demonstrates his spiritual authority over all others who do not believe in Christ. In this way, Conscience challenges Will's perception by showing that names are arbitrary to the extent that it is possible for one person to be accurately called many different names. However, Conscience does not therefore suggest that signs have no direct relationship to that which they signify. Like Augustine, Conscience regards signs as bearing a relationship to truth, but signs are not that truth itself.

Conscience explicates Christ's names through a retelling of the story of Christ's life and, in doing so, shows that names and appearances have the

---

26. On this tradition, see Stephen A. Barney, *The Penn Commentary on* Piers Plowman, vol. 5 (Philadelphia: University of Pennsylvania Press, 2006), 112.

power to reveal as well as conceal true identity. For example, when the Magi come to offer Christ gifts at the Nativity, Conscience emphasizes that their gifts have figural values that are hidden beneath their external appearances. The kings offer "Reson, covered under sense," "Rightwisnesse under reed gold," and "Pitee, apperynge by mirre" (B.19.86; 88; 92). In all three cases, Conscience implies that the gifts' true significance is internal and hidden; their physical qualities and appearance are almost entirely incidental. Conscience goes on to argue that signs, in themselves, do not provide reliable and complete access to truth by showing how Christ's name changes over time. He divides Christ's ministry into three parts, the three names that have been the objects of Will's searching since Passus 8: Dowel, Dobet, and Dobest. As in the rest of the poem, the distinction between these three terms is not particularly decisive, in the sense that Will is never able to arrive at a conclusive definition of the three terms apart from specific actions. It is therefore fitting that Conscience invokes these names here in the context of his discussion of the way in which names cannot fully describe Christ. The name "Jesus" does not provide complete knowledge of the nature of Christ, much in the same way that the word "Dobet" can never provide Will with a specific and complete path for Christian living.

The events of Christ's life necessitate a proliferation of names, names that Christ always exceeds. Unlike personifications in the poem, such as Conscience or Mede, whose actions can strain but never exceed or change the word that signifies them, Christ continually exceeds the signs that purport to contain him. Christ is a signified who can never be fully contained by any sign, although many signs accurately describe specific aspects of him. Conscience's retelling of Christ's life in Passus 19, in contrast to the version of Christ's life in Passus 18, focuses primarily on miracles of transformation: the Incarnation, the transformation of water into wine, miraculous healings, and the Resurrection. In this narrative, the relationship between signs and substance continually shifts. Conscience begins this narrative with the Incarnation and shows that this transformation of God into man brought about the name "Jesus." At the second major event in Conscience's narrative, the wedding feast at Cana at which Christ transforms water into wine, requires giving Christ another name. As Conscience tells it, this miracle is one of signification:

> In his juventee this Jesus at Jewene feeste
> Turnede water into wyn, as Holy Writ telleth,
> And there bigan God of his grace to do wel.
> For wyn is likned to lawe, and lif of holynesse.
> (B.19.108–11)

Conscience's interpretation downplays the importance of the transformation of the physical elements of water and wine; the fact that the people at the wedding feast had run out of wine, the biblical motivation for performing the miracle, does not even merit a mention. Instead, Conscience argues that the wine is only relevant because of what it signifies apart from the physical wine itself: law and holiness. Although the physical miracle is the transformation of water into wine, the importance of the miracle is the way in which it alters patterns of signification. From this miracle arises another of Christ's many names, "A fauntekyn ful of wit, *filius Marie*" (B.19.118). Jesus performs this miracle in front of his mother in order to show her his otherworldly nature, to ensure that she is fully aware that he "thorugh Grace was gete, and of no gome ellis" (B.19.121). Conscience calls Jesus "son of Mary" at the same moment that he reveals the extent to which Christ transcends that identity. The significance of the miracle is that it reveals that Christ is not just the son of Mary but fully the son of God.[27]

Langland depicts knowledge of the limits and powers of signs as a defining aspect of Christian identity and belief. In Conscience's narrative, the enemies of Christ, particularly the Jews, have him put to death in part because the proliferation of his names was too extensive. As Christ continues to perform miracles of transformation, his followers develop more names in their attempts to more accurately describe his identity in light of his transformative power. Because of his miraculous deeds:

> Forthi the contree ther Jesu cam called hym *fili David*,
> And nempned hym of Nazareth—and no man so worthi
> To be kaiser or kyng of the kyngdom of Juda,
> Ne over Jewes justice, as Jesus was, hem thoughte.
> (B.19.136–39)

Jesus' actions bring about public changes in the way in which those around him refer to him—he receives not only the name "*fili David*" but also the titles of kaiser, king, and justice—and it is precisely these changes in name, and the claims to power that such changes imply, that the Jewish high priests object to. Although the authorities undoubtedly fear the political power that these

---

27. It is worth noting that Langland significantly changes the emphasis of the biblical account in order to create this parallel between physical transformation and the limits of signification. First, given that Mary experienced the virgin birth firsthand, most medieval accounts of Mary's life involve her recognition that Jesus is fully the son of God. Second, in the biblical narrative, Mary demands that Christ perform the miracle; Christ does not demand that Mary be there to witness it.

new names imply, Langland arranges the narrative in order to suggest that it is in response to the names themselves "wherof hadde Cayphas envye, and othere of the Jewes, / And for to doon hym to dethe day and nyght thei casten" (B.19.140–41). As Conscience has explained, "Jesus" was the way in which the Jews first referred to Christ, and their ultimate rejection of Christ is signaled by their unwillingness to refer to him by any other name. According to Conscience, unlike the Jews, Christians are partly defined by their willingness to see beyond the one-to-one correspondence of sign and signified, Christ's name and Christ himself.

Through the doubting Thomas episode, Conscience claims that signs are the primary way in which contemporary Christians must come to understand Christ. Near the end of Passus 19's version of Christ's life, Conscience tells the story of doubting Thomas, the apostle who would only believe in the Resurrection once he had touched Christ's wounds. Christ presents Thomas with physical evidence of his transformation from death into life, and Thomas acknowledges this transformation by giving Christ yet more names, crying out "*Dominus meus et Deus meus*" (B.19.173). Christ then concludes the episode by proclaiming, "Blessed mote thei be, in body and in soule, / That nevere shul se me in sighte as thow seest nowthe, / And lelliche bileve al this—I love hem and blesse hem" (B.19.180–82). Although Christ approves of Thomas, he argues that he wants others to acknowledge him in the same way without requiring physical proof. While Thomas progressed from physical proof to belief in the resurrected Christ to the creation of verbal signs to describe Christ, future Christians ought to be able to believe in divine truth through those created signs alone. The truth of the words themselves ought to be enough to show that "Lord" and "God" are appropriate names for Christ. Although, as Conscience has shown, there is no single sign that will provide complete understanding of Christ, the collection of signs that the church makes available to Christians through scripture and liturgy offer essential access to divine truth.

COMMUNAL FAILURE

In his description of the foundation of the church in the second half of Passus 19, Langland argues that Christians must understand the Eucharist as a sign—of both Christ's historical and corporate bodies—in order to recognize their own obligation to become the harmonious body signified by the consecrated host. The community's failure to be that signified body is the focus of the conclusion of Passus 19. In contrast to Christ who always exceeds the signs that represent him, the Christian community struggles to live up to the name that ought to signify it: Unity. After his description of Pentecost, Langland narrates the foundation of the institutional church, with Piers as a figure for the papacy and his barn, Unity, as a figure for the institution itself. Unlike the many names for Christ, the name "Unity" does not describe the church as it is; it describes the church as it ought to be. Langland details how Piers builds Unity from scripture, the writings of the church fathers, and the cardinal virtues. The foundation of the church is perfect and has the potential to protect believers from the assaults of the Antichrist. However, the strength of the church depends not only on its foundational elements but also on the moral and spiritual integrity of the Christians within it. Once Pride plans to attack Piers and his barn, Conscience advises all Christians "to wende / Hastiliche into Unitee and holde we us there, / And praye we that a pees were in Piers bern the Plowman" (B.19.359–61). According to Conscience, the only way to defend Unity from outside attacks is to embody unity itself. Christians must bring their gifts together as the corporate body of Christ if they are to defend that corporate body from attack. Conscience's call to Unity is somewhat circular: Conscience assumes that, by attacking Piers and the foundation of the church, Pride attacks all Christians as if they were already united in the church. In order to defend Unity from attack, Conscience argues that Christians must form a unified body of believers that Conscience assumes already exists. In this passus, as in much of the poem, Langland suggests that there is a gap between what the church ought to be and the way it actually operates in the contemporary world.[28] Conscience's call to Unity is a call for recognition of a shared identity that has yet to be performed.

The ideal identity of the Christian community is one in which the Eucharist symbolizes the unity that the community embodies. Langland depicts the Barn of Unity as a place built to store grain, an object that allegorically signifies both the Eucharist and the Christian community. Grain was a common medieval image for the Eucharist.[29] Since, much like Unity's storage of grain, the medieval church's identity and authority rested on its control of the sacraments, the association of Piers's grains with the Eucharist is clear. The way in which the grains also signify the Christian community is twofold. First, theologians who regarded communal symbolism as a central part of the Eucharist, such as Alger of Liège and Hugh of St. Victor, often contended that the individual grains and grapes that compose the eucharistic species symbolize

---

28. As Stephen Barney points out, "Presenting the foundation of the Church as an elaborated allegory seems to distance it conceptually as well as temporally from the Church of the brewer and the vicar that we encounter later." Barney, *Penn Commentary*, 146.

29. For examples of eucharistic grain imagery, see Aquinas, *Summae Theologiae*, 3a.74, 3; Astell, *Eating Beauty*, 57; Rubin, *Corpus Christi*, 312–16.

individual Christians united with each other and with Christ in the church.[30] Second, this passage draws heavily on the biblical parable of the wheat and the tares that describe all of humanity as wheat and weeds growing in a field.[31] In this parable, the farmer, the parable's representative of divine judgment, cannot readily distinguish between the wheat and the weeds in his field until they are fully grown, and so he allows both to grow together. When both are grown, he gathers the wheat into his barn and sets fire to the weeds. The wheat represents the saved, the weeds represent the damned, and the barn represents the kingdom of heaven. Langland clearly draws on this parable in his description of gathering the grains into Unity. Unity is different from the barn in the parable because it exists in the temporal world, but it is like the parable's barn insofar as it is a place in which Christians are gathered together in preparation for their final judgment. In his description of Unity as the ideal church, Langland envisions the purpose of the church as the preservation of grain: the unification of individual Christians symbolized by the Eucharist.

Conscience regards eucharistic reception as both effecting and declaring the community's union with Christ. When Conscience calls all Christians to receive the Eucharist in Unity, he is inviting them to complete their identity as Unity, as united in the body of Christ. Once the Christians have dug a moat around Unity, they undertake the work of penance: "Some thorugh bedes biddynge and some thorugh pilgrimage / And othere pryvé penaunces, and somme thorugh penyes delynge" (B.19.379–80). Conscience believes these individual penitential acts demonstrate the moral and spiritual strength of the community as a whole and proclaims, "I care noght . . . though Pride come nouthe; / The lord of lust shal be letted al this Lente" (B.19.385–86). By virtue of every individual's Lenten devotion, Conscience thinks the Christian community is unified and now needs only to receive the Eucharist in order to fully realize its strength against sin. He explains that the Eucharist is the natural conclusion to their penitence: "'Cometh,' quod Conscience, 'ye Cristene, and dyneth, / That han labored lelly al this Lenten tyme. / Here is breed yblessed, and Goddes body therunder'" (B.19.387–89). According to Conscience, the community ought to receive the Eucharist because it has demonstrated its Christian unity in devotion and because the Eucharist also strengthens and effects that unity. The community can only fully achieve unity when it is physically unified with Christ's body in the sacrament of the Eucharist, when the

---

30. Colish, *Peter Lombard*, 561.
31. Lorraine Kochanske Stock has investigated the influence of this parable on *Piers Plowman* in "Parable, Allegory, History, and *Piers Plowman*," *Yearbook of Langland Studies* 5 (1991), 143–64.

sign—the consecrated host that both represents and is Christ's body—literally becomes one with the bodies of the signified, the Christian community.

For Conscience, the Eucharist does not merely symbolize social unity; the people must literally enact social justice in order to make the Eucharist's symbolism possible. After inviting everyone in Unity to receive the Eucharist, Conscience puts a single condition on eucharistic reception:

> Grace, thorugh Goddes word, gaf Piers power,
> Myght to maken it, and men to ete it after
> In helpe of hir heele ones in a monthe,
> Or as ofte as thei hadde need, tho that hadde ypaied
> To Piers pardon the Plowman, *Redde quod debes*.
> (B.19.390–94)

In many ways, Conscience's invitation is a fairly straightforward assertion of orthodox eucharistic theology. He affirms the Real Presence of Christ in the host and the sacramental power of the priesthood as represented by Piers. Even the penitential condition that he places on reception is typical insofar as theologians required Christians to participate in the sacrament of penance before receiving the Eucharist annually at Easter.[32] What is striking about Conscience's condition is not its emphasis on penitence but its contention that the performance of penance must be irreducibly social and material.[33] The command "*Redde quod debes*" (give back what you owe) demands social responsibility since it emphasizes one's material debts to other people rather than simply one's spiritual debts to God. Individual Christians must work toward unity if they are to properly receive the Eucharist, the sacrament of unity.

Conscience's condition suggests that, within the celebration of the sacrament of the Eucharist, there ought to be a union of literal reality and allegori-

---

32. Conscience recommends more frequent eucharistic reception than the required yearly reception, but this discrepancy is far from radical. After all, Conscience is calling for monthly communion in what he initially perceives to be a strong and ideal version of the institutional church. Theologians, such as Thomas Aquinas, typically agreed that more frequent reception is an ideal but is often not possible in a world corrupted by sin. Aquinas notes that Pope Innocent III recommended annual communion because he was living at a time when "wickedness was multiplied and love grew cold" (iniquitatis abundantiam refrigerescente caritate multorum). *Summa Theologiae*, 3a.80, 10. David Aers regards Conscience's recommendation as marking a sharper deviation from contemporary medieval practices. Aers, "Sacrament of the Altar," 48–49.

33. What makes the social nature of Conscience's condition striking is a matter of emphasis rather than a radical deviation from orthodox tradition. Several medieval sermons do emphasize the need for social reconciliation as a precursor to eucharistic reception. For example, see Ross, *Middle English Sermons*, 125–33; Mirk, *Mirk's Festial*, 129–32.

cal ideal, of social justice and the idea of the harmonious corporate body of Christ. The passus's conclusion explores the negative response of the three estates—represented by a brewer, a vicar, and a lord and a king—and their refusal to accept Conscience's condition; by showing how these representatives of the Christian community refuse to live up to this condition, Langland implies that they reject the Eucharist itself.[34] The community turns away from the Eucharist precisely because it does not want this unity of material and transcendent; the individuals in Unity want to separate their daily lives from abstract spiritual truth. The first to reject Conscience's call to the Eucharist is a brewer who recognizes that his practice of cheating his customers—by selling "bothe dregges and draf"—is forbidden by the cardinal virtue of justice (B.19.403). The brewer implicitly accepts Conscience's alignment of eucharistic reception with justice, but is unwilling to give up his unjust business practices. Conscience responds by defending and explicating the relationship between social justice and the Eucharist. He condemns the brewer, saying, "But Conscience be thi commune fode, and Cardinale Vertues, / Leve it wel, thei ben lost, both lif and soule" (B.19.410–11). In his defense of the cardinal virtues, Conscience unites these virtues with the Eucharist, referring to both as food. In order to be part of the mystical body signified by the Eucharist, every person must properly order his conscience around the cardinal virtues; a Christian life consists not solely of prayer but also of carefully discerned righteous actions toward one's fellow Christians. The brewer rejects the Eucharist because he does not want to enact the social unity that the host signifies.

As the "lewed" vicar—the representative of the second estate and the second person to protest Conscience's condition—demonstrates, the members of the community fail to realize that their daily lives could have allegorical or spiritual significance at all. They have become so focused on material things that they can no longer see the material world's connection to transcendent meaning. The vicar protests Conscience's condition because he refuses to recognize abstract ideals beyond his literal, physical reality. In particular, he cannot see the way in which the Eucharist signifies a divine, transcendent reality beyond the church hierarchy. He rejects Conscience's claim that the cardinal virtues are necessary to righteous living because "I knewe nevere Cardynal that he ne cam fro the Pope" (B.19.417). The vicar refuses to distinguish between the cardinal virtues—justice, prudence, temperance, and fortitude—and car-

---

34. David Aers makes a similar point when he suggests that the community rejects the Eucharist because reception requires ethical social behavior. He argues that this scene "suggests that Christians now want the Eucharist only if it has absolutely no entailments for their social practices." Aers, "Sacrament of the Altar," 50.

dinals, the high-ranked clergy who advise the Pope.[35] According to the vicar, when cardinals visit an area, the local clergy take the people's food in order to serve the cardinals. In contrast to Conscience's argument that the cardinal virtues will provide the commons with access to spiritual food, the Eucharist, the vicar claims that the cardinals of the church steal the commons' food, the necessities of daily life. Although Langland is no doubt sympathetic to the vicar's complaint that the cardinals and the Pope have strayed from Christian virtues by abusing the common people, Langland suggest that the vicar's argument is deeply flawed insofar as it is a response to Conscience's call to the Eucharist.[36] By listing the faults of others within the earthly church—rather than choosing to perform restitution for his own sins in order to build up Unity—the vicar rejects Conscience's invitation and therefore implicitly rejects the Eucharist itself. For Langland, the church does not solely consist of its hierarchy; the church is the entire Christian community. In contrast, the vicar only sees the church in its literal manifestation as the fourteenth-century ecclesiastical hierarchy. To some extent, the vicar recognizes literal-mindedness as a fault when he points out that the commons "counten ful litel / The counseil of Conscience or Cardinale Vertues / But if thei sown, as by sighte, somewhat to wynnyng" (B.19.455–57). However, the vicar places the blame for such materialism almost entirely on the church hierarchy's corruption rather than on individual Christians. The vicar refuses to recognize the ideal of Unity—the vision of what the church ought to be—and rejects the Eucharist along with the very idea of transcendent meaning. For the vicar, the Eucharist is virtually worthless because he does not value or recognize the possibility of allegorical, transcendent meaning within the fourteenth-century church.

According to Langland, proper eucharistic reception requires that Christians recognize their own role as the signified corporate body of Christ, a body in which all members are equally important. He argues for this allegorical interpretation of the Eucharist through his negative example of the king, the chief representative of the first estate and the only member of the Christian community who claims to meet Conscience's condition for eucharistic recep-

---

35. My reading is thus similar to Rosanne Gasse's understanding of the vicar. She argues that the vicar is "literal-minded, unable to distinguish the different meanings of cardinal." Rosanne Gasse, "Langland's 'Lewed Vicory' Reconsidered," *Journal of English and Germanic Philology* 95 (1996): 322–35.

36. In general, scholars have tended to be sympathetic to the vicar's argument because it contains valuable and valid social critiques. For example, see Barney, *Penn Commentary*, 167–79; Priscilla Jenkins, "Conscience: The Frustration of Allegory," in *Piers Plowman: Critical Approaches*, ed. S. S. Hussey (London: Methuen, 1969), 125–42; Robertson and Huppé, *Piers Plowman*, 227.

tion. The king argues that he is worthy of the Eucharist through reference to the body politic of which he is metaphorically the head. According to the king, although he takes from others, he only does so within the boundaries of the law: "I am heed of lawe: / For ye ben but members and I above alle. / And sith I am youre aller heed, I am youre aller heele, / And Holy Chirche chief help and chieftain of the commune" (B.19.473–76). The king claims that, because he is the source of laws, he always acts in accordance with the law and is therefore just and worthy to receive the Eucharist. Instead of being humbly penitent, the king believes his earthly authority makes it virtually impossible for him to be unjust and proclaims that he "may boldely be housled" (B.19.479). The passus ends before Langland tells us whether or not this king ultimately does receive the Eucharist, but there is good reason to suspect that this king does not live up to Conscience's standards. Most importantly, he ignores the metaphor of the community as the corporate body of Christ, a metaphor that the passus has been alluding to since its description of Pentecost, because that metaphor places Christ as the head of the body. Instead of focusing on Christ's body, the king speaks only about the body politic. The king fails to realize that his own authority is not absolute and therefore insists upon a single metaphor of the communal body and imagines that metaphor as totally authoritative.

When Conscience challenges the king's claim to the Eucharist, he demonstrates that proper eucharistic reception involves both the recognition of the host as a sign of the communal body and a commitment to literal justice within that social body. Although the king eagerly accepts that the host is intimately related to an abstract idea of the social body, Conscience insists that the king must also account for his daily actions toward others. In order to emphasize the importance of personal accountability, Conscience places specific conditions on the king's eucharistic reception: "That thow konne defende, / And rule thi reaume in reson, right wel and in truthe, / That thow [have thyn asking], as the lawe asketh: *Omnia sunt tua ad defendendum set non ad deprehendendum*" (B.19.481–83a) (The realm is yours for defending, not for plundering).[37] Conscience will permit the king to receive the Eucharist as long as he is willing to be accountable for his specific social actions, rather than rely on the metaphor of the body politic as his sole justification for his worthiness. For Conscience, the king's figural justice must have a basis in material reality. Although the king comes closest to eucharistic reception, the dream ends there, and when Will wakes, no one has received the Eucharist. None of the people in Unity have been able to reconcile their own actions with Conscience's condition for eucharistic reception. This failure to secure the identity

---

37. I am grateful to Stephen Barney for this translation.

of Unity through the sacrament of Unity contributes to Unity's vulnerability to the Antichrist in the poem's final passus. The community has failed to become the unified body of Christ signified by the consecrated host.

For Langland, the power of the Eucharist lies in its unification of the two halves of the allegorical sign: the material appearance of bread unites with Christ's body, and the consecrated host that signifies the Christian community becomes one with that community through eucharistic reception. He argues that the host's communal significance cannot be complete without communal participation. As he shows in his discussion of Christ's names, it is essential for Christians to understand the nature of the signs that signify Christ. In the case of the Eucharist, Christians must recognize their own obligation to enact the social justice and equality that the host signifies. The Christians in Unity fail to receive the Eucharist because they refuse to recognize their role in the Eucharist's signification and to transform their own divided social body into the perfect reflection of the unified body of Christ.

For Langland, the process of transforming the community into the body of Christ is a process of reading and interpretation of both his text and the consecrated host. Characteristically, Langland depicts such interpretation as a complicated and confusing process, but one that is vital to the shaping of the Christian community. In the next chapter, I will turn to Julian of Norwich, a writer who intently focuses on this process of devotional reading—of both host and written text—and shows how an understanding of devotional reading as socially transformative is essential to the mystical body of Christ.

CHAPTER 4

Julian of Norwich's Allegory and the Mediation of Salvation

The act of reading—much like the act of eating the Eucharist—has the potential to transform both the individual reader and the wider Christian community. In this chapter, I turn to Julian of Norwich's *A Revelation of Love,* a text that I argue engages in eucharistic poetics in order to present an intellectually and poetically ambitious model of devotional reading. In certain respects, such a claim may be surprising because scholars have tended to regard the eucharistic devotion of late medieval female mystics, including Julian, as primarily ecstatic and literalist. In her landmark *Holy Feast and Holy Fast,* Caroline Walker Bynum describes in persuasive detail a primarily continental tradition of female mystics who became empowered through their identification with the bleeding, suffering body of Christ, especially as that body is made manifest in the Eucharist.[1] In this chapter, I counter the critical tendency to accept Bynum's work as descriptive of English eucharistic piety and English women's mysticism.[2] Although Julian—who, along with Margery Kempe (the subject of my next chapter), is one of only

---

1. Bynum, *Holy Feast.*
2. Julian's long text has been published under various titles, but I use the title *A Revelation of Love* throughout both because it is the way in which she herself describes the text and because it is the title of the edition from which I cite: Julian of Norwich, *The Writings of Julian of Norwich: "A Vision Showed to a Devout Woman" and "A Revelation of Love,"* ed. Nicholas Watson and Jacqueline Jenkins (University Park: Pennsylvania State UP, 2005). All in-text citations will be by chapter and line number of this edition.

two known late medieval female mystics in England—draws on the continental female mystics and their writings, she consciously defies the continental model of eucharistic devotion.

In fact, I argue that Julian, like William Langland, deliberately chooses to explore the Eucharist through allegory. Through an analysis of Julian's treatment of "meanes," both linguistic signs and church mediation through rituals and symbols, I show that Julian understands the Eucharist in terms of language rather than direct affective encounter. Julian imagines eucharistic devotion as analogous to allegorical interpretation. Though scholars do not typically read *Revelation* as allegorical, I show that, for Julian, God's truth is only available through allegory, a division between sign and signified, earthly and transcendent that is more perceived than real. Drawing on the logic of transubstantiation, Julian makes a claim for the absolute unity between sign and signified while stressing the importance of holding those categories in tension as an aid to human comprehension.

In contrast to the vast body of scholarship that treats Julian as potentially subversive because of her gender politics and her salvation theology, I show how Julian's eucharistic poetics ultimately supports the institutional church by revealing the necessity of the church's role in creating the literal half of the allegorical sign—the bread, the images, the rituals, the prayers—that points to the divine reality, which could not be understood without reference to the literal.[3] Julian depicts the sacraments, and particularly the Eucharist, as essential to human devotion precisely because they are signs of a union with God that is not yet realized, but for which the human community ought to long continually. Thus Julian draws on the allegory inherent in medieval eucharistic theology in order to develop a model of devotional reading as simultaneously affective and intellectual. Ultimately, Julian encourages readers to imagine

---

3. Much of the scholarship on Julian of Norwich portrays her as radical, either through her valorization of femininity or through her reinterpretation of the doctrine of Original Sin. Though I do not necessarily disagree with such scholarship, my focus here is decidedly different. For scholarship on Julian of Norwich's distinctly feminine mysticism, see Alexandra Barratt, "'In the Lowest Part of Our Need': Julian and Medieval Gynecological Writing," in *Julian of Norwich: A Book of Essays,* ed. Sandra J. McEntire (New York: Garland, 1998) 239–56; Elizabeth Robertson, "Medieval Medical Views of Women and Female Spirituality in the *Ancrene Wisse* and Julian of Norwich's *Showings,*" in *Feminist Approaches to the Body in Medieval Literature,* ed. Linda Lomperis and Sarah Stanbury (Philadelphia: University of Pennsylvania Press, 1993), 142–67; Nicholas Watson, "'Yf women be double naturelly': Remaking 'Woman' in Julian of Norwich's Revelation of Love," *Exemplaria* 8 (1996): 1–34. For important scholarship on Julian's theology of salvation, see Denise N. Baker, *Julian of Norwich's "Showings": From Vision to Book* (Princeton, NJ: Princeton UP, 1994); Nicholas Watson, "Visions of Inclusion: Universal Salvation and Vernacular Theology in Pre-Reformation England," *Journal of Medieval and Early Modern Studies* 27 (1997): 145–87.

language itself as eucharistic because all signs propose the idea of a union of earthly signifier with transcendent signified that cannot fully take place until the afterlife. In doing so, Julian resists wholly affective and individualistic models of the Eucharist in favor of a vision of the Eucharist as building a community that bridges both time and individual identities.

REDEFINING THE MYSTICAL EUCHARIST

In *Revelation,* Julian deliberately thwarts audience expectations of women's mystical writings when she focuses on the mediated nature of reading practices rather than ecstatic eucharistic union. Like many of the continental women mystics, Julian draws extensively on eucharistic language and eucharistic theology; however, she transforms the mystics' focus on affective union by arguing that affective piety arises out of humans' sorrow at their perception of distance between themselves and God. This perception is fundamental to human nature, and humans therefore need the institutional church as a mediator in order to overcome this perceived distance. In doing so, she draws on the mystical tradition in order to avoid accusations of heresy while questioning and carefully redefining the importance of the sacraments and, more broadly, the entire institutional church to Christian life.

Julian pointedly invites readers to see her text in relation to the writings of the female continental mystics by, among other things, drawing on their use of highly eucharistic language. By the late fourteenth century when Julian began writing *Revelation,* English readers seem to have shown a significant interest in continental mystical writings, and texts such as Catherine of Siena's *Dialogo della divina providenzza* and Bridget of Sweden's *Liber Celestis* became available in Middle English.[4] Since Norwich had close economic and social ties to the continent, Julian was geographically placed to take early notice of such continental mysticism.[5] Although it is impossible to determine which particular texts Julian might have had direct access to, she was at the very least aware of this large and influential body of women's writing. As Bynum has shown so compellingly, such female mystical writers saw the Eucharist as

---

4. Nicholas Watson notes that such texts began to arrive in England by the 1390s at the latest. See Nicholas Watson, "The Composition of Julian of Norwich's *Revelation of Love,*" *Speculum* 68 (1993): 653. See also Norman P. Tanner, *The Church in Late Medieval Norwich, 1370–1532* (Toronto: Pontifical Institute of Mediaeval Studies, 1984), 58; Rosalynn Voaden, ed., *Prophets Abroad: The Reception of Continental Holy Women in Late-Medieval England* (Cambridge: D. S. Brewer, 1996).

5. Watson, "Composition," 656.

a point of entry into union with the divine.⁶ Like such continental mystics, Julian begins *Revelation* with a stated desire for identification with Christ's suffering body, and the idea, if not the realized experience, of a eucharistic union with Christ permeates the text. Throughout, Julian is fascinated by the power of Christ's blood and frequently links this blood to the act of drinking and to the rituals of the church. During her description of the fourth revelation, for example, Julian explains that Christ wants Christians to take his blood "for ther is no licour that is made that liketh him so wele to geve us" (12.11–12). And she describes how when Christians reach the afterlife they will endlessly be "swetly swelwing" him (43.43). Even her much-celebrated depiction of Jesus as mother is highly eucharistic because, in this text in particular and in the late medieval period more broadly, one of the major grounds of comparison between Christ and mothers was that both nursing mothers and Christ feed their children from their own bodies.⁷ Julian's emphasis on thirst and drinking as well as Christ's motherly feeding of humanity suggest that her desired union between Christ and humanity is one of mutual ingestion and bodily incorporation.

However, Julian's text differs radically from such continental writings in that she does not ultimately regard the Eucharist as a way to achieve personal union with Christ.⁸ Unlike Bridget of Sweden, for example, who sees Christ during the elevation of the host, Julian never describes the Eucharist or an experience at Mass. In fact, for a text that purports to retell Julian's experience of the sixteen revelations she received from God, it is surprisingly nonnarrative; her engagement with the Eucharist and the sacraments is on an abstract and theological level rather than a personal one. In this sense, Julian definitely does not conform to Bynum's model.⁹ The Eucharist is an almost silent presence in the text. Julian anticipates her reader's association of mystical experiences with the Eucharist and thwarts audience expectations.

By drawing on the continental mystical tradition but refusing to describe a moment of affective union with the divine, Julian carefully reflects on the role

---

6. Bynum, *Holy Feast*; Caroline Walker Bynum, "Women Mystics and Eucharistic Devotion in the Thirteenth Century," in *Fragmentation and Redemption: Essays on Gender and the Human Body in Medieval Religion* (New York: Zone Books, 1992), 119–50.

7. Caroline Walker Bynum, "Jesus as Mother and Abbot as Mother: Some Themes in Twelfth-Century Cistercian Writing," in *Jesus as Mother: Studies in the Spirituality of the High Middle Ages* (Berkeley: University of California Press, 1982), 153.

8. David Aers also notes that Julian's text consistently forecloses the possibility of affective identification. David Aers and Lynn Staley, *The Powers of the Holy: Religion, Politics, and Gender in Late Medieval English Culture* (University Park: Pennsylvania State UP, 1996), 77–104.

9. It is worth noting that, although Bynum includes Julian in her discussion of female mystics, she very rarely discusses Julian individually or directly.

of mediation, particularly ecclesiastical mediation, to an individual's experience of the divine. Since mystical experiences offer direct contact with the divine outside of an institutional context, they pose a potential threat to the ecclesiastical hierarchy's monopoly on access to Christ's body. Such is Julian's commitment to the Christian church, both in the sense of the Christian community and in the sense of the institutional church, that she explicitly subjugates her mystical experience to the textual experience of her readers:

> For sothly it was not shewde to me that God loveth me better than the lest soule that is in grace. For I am seker ther be many that never had shewing ne sight but of the comen teching of holy church that love God better than I. For if I looke singulery to myself, I am right nought. But in general I am, I hope, in onehede of cherite with alle my evencristen. (9.4–8)

According to Julian, the teachings of the church provide access to Christ for all Christians, and if she is to value the communal nature of redemption, she must also value the church itself. She repeatedly asserts that "in all thing I beleve as holy church precheth and techeth" (9.17–18). Though many scholars have read these statements as disingenuous defensive screens for a radical theology, I believe it is worth considering that such statements are a serious and integral part of Julian's text.[10] As Christopher Abbott contends, "Julian does not propose an anti-ecclesiological personal mysticism over against Catholic orthodoxy, but is looking (whether always wholly conscious of this or not) to the realization of possibilities already implicit in the sacramental culture of the official Church."[11] Like Robert Mannyng, the *Pearl*-poet, and William Langland before her, Julian focuses on the way in which textual and ecclesiastical mediation simultaneously thwart and enable the individual believer's access to the divine. Julian regards mediation of all sorts as central to her understanding of the divine, and the institutional church as an essential form of mediation between Christ and believers.

Julian diverges from this continental tradition in a distinctively English way, both in the sense that her work aligns itself with the larger tradition of Middle English eucharistic poetics, which emphasizes distance between the

---

10. The use of "screen" is Lynn Staley's. See Aers and Staley, *Powers of the Holy,* 107–78. By taking Julian's claims for her own orthodoxy seriously, I in no way intend to diminish the radical potential of her writings. Rather, I recognize that, to a certain extent, the definition of orthodoxy is always contingent and, since Julian regarded herself as working within the boundaries of orthodoxy, I believe it is worth examining the ways in which her text attempts to do exactly that.

11. Christopher Abbot, *Julian of Norwich: Autobiography and Theology* (Cambridge: D. S. Brewer, 1999), 142–43.

believer and the divine, and in the sense that it reflects her awareness of the Lollard heresy. Both a belief in the individual's direct access to the divine and an understanding of the Eucharist as sign rather than direct, physical presence have the potential to mark Julian out as a heretic. However, Julian avoids such links to heresy by using her mystical experiences and her exploration of the nature of signification to reinforce the importance of the institutional church. By the time Julian was writing *Revelation*, between roughly 1393 and 1415, Wyclif and the Lollards who followed him had adopted the language of signs for their own heterodox definitions of the Eucharist.[12] In contrast to the many theologians who describe the Eucharist as simultaneously sign and signified, they insisted that the consecrated host was *only* a sign.[13] In his 1379 treatise, *De Eucharistia*, Wyclif contends that the consecrated host does not contain the physical presence of Christ; instead, the substance of the bread remains in the host after consecration and the host merely signifies Christ.[14] Therefore, he argues, priests wrongly encourage the laity to engage in idolatry by telling them to worship what is, in reality, a piece of bread. When they denounced transubstantiation, the Lollards posed a direct threat to the church's authority by denouncing priestly sacramental power, as well as denying one of the most popular and lucrative modes of lay devotion. As I outlined in my introductory chapter, ecclesiastical authorities recognized that the Lollards' arguments against the Eucharist threatened the entire structure of the church and their opposition to the Lollards grew increasingly fierce.[15] From the late fourteenth century on, the vernacular discussion of eucharistic theology became progressively more dangerous because clerical authorities often perceived such discussions as a direct threat to the integrity of the church. By placing her text in the tradition of continental women's mysticism, Julian strategically demonstrates her belief in the literal divine presence in the sacraments and therefore her commitment to the institutional church.

Julian reframes the affective mystical tradition by denying the possibility of personal union with Christ and depicting the most affective moments of her text as arising from her failure to identify with him. My claim that Julian does not believe in the possibility of personal union with Christ may seem

---

12. On the dating of the text, see Watson, "Composition."

13. Almost all of the lengthy Lollard writings were composed between 1381 and 1413, and one of the most frequent subjects of these writings was the Eucharist. Hudson, *Premature Reformation*, 117–19, 208.

14. John Wyclif, *De Eucharistia Tractatus Maior*, ed. Iohann Loserth (London: Trübner & Co., 1892), 1–326.

15. Although church authorities ultimately declared a variety of Lollard beliefs heretical, the church's virulent and violent response to the Lollards was primarily a result of their teaching on the Eucharist. See Aston, "Wyclif and the Vernacular"; Catto, "John Wyclif."

counterintuitive because most recent scholarship has argued precisely the opposite. Scholars typically praise Julian for challenging conceptual boundaries, especially the boundary between Christ and believer.[16] Although Julian believes there is no real separation between God and the human soul, she repeatedly argues that such a perception of difference is absolutely essential to human spirituality.

According to Julian, the inner human soul in some sense already knows God, but it is necessary to search and struggle for that knowledge.[17] The inner, higher part of the soul is absolutely good and united with God's will. She explains that "in ech a soule that shall be safe is a godly wille that never assented to sinne, ne never shall" (53.9–10). Although the outer, lower part of the soul may consent to sin, it is impossible for the entire soul to be sinful because the inner soul is united with God and therefore always strives for good. Through the existence of the godly will, the soul always knows God because "thus is mannes soule made of God, and in the same pointe knite to God" (53.33). The difficulty that believers encounter in their struggle for union with God is not the intangibility of God since the soul and God are already united. Rather, the challenge lies in the human capacity to understand that union.

---

16. For example, Lynn Staley argues, "Rather than establish terms that seek to contain—and inevitably delimit—the objects they signify, Julian creates a system [of language] wherein identities flow almost imperceptibly into one another." Aers and Staley, *Powers of the Holy,* 178. Some recent examples of work that focuses on the dissolution of conceptual boundaries include Frederick Christian Bauerschmidt, *Julian of Norwich and the Mystical Body Politic of Christ* (Notre Dame, IN: University of Notre Dame Press, 1999); Maria R. Lichtmann, "'God fulfilled my bodye': Body, Self, and God in Julian of Norwich," in *Gender and Text in the Later Middle Ages,* ed. Jane Chance (Gainesville: UP of Florida, 1996), 263–78; Kevin J. Magill, *Julian of Norwich: Mystic or Visionary?* (London: Routledge, 2006); Jon Shickler, "The Cross and the Citadel: Reconciling Apophatic and Cataphatic Traditions in the *Showings,*" *Studia Mystica* 21 (2000): 95–125.

As an important recent exception to this critical trend, Michelle Karnes points out that Julian is, in fact, intently focused on difference, and her text "notably directs its energies more to the impediments that separate Julian from God than to their closeness." Karnes focuses more on difference as a philosophical and hermeneutic tool than as an aspect of affective piety or sacramental theology. Michelle Karnes, "Julian of Norwich's Art of Interpretation," *Journal of Medieval and Early Modern Studies* 42 (2012): 335. For another scholar who focuses on difference in *Revelation,* see Cynthea Masson, "The Point of Coincidence: Rhetoric and the Apophatic in Julian of Norwich's *Showings,*" in *Julian of Norwich: A Book of Essays,* ed. Sandra J. McEntire (New York: Garland, 1998), 153–81.

17. This idea that the soul already knows God is Augustinian in origin. On the godly will in Julian, see Denise N. Baker, "The Structure of the Soul and the 'Godly Wylle' in Julian of Norwich's *Showings,*" in *The Medieval Mystical Tradition in England: Exeter Symposium VII,* ed. E. A. Jones (Cambridge: D. S. Brewer, 2004), 37–49.

Julian begins *Revelation* by aligning herself with the continental mystics in her desire for an ecstatic union with Christ's suffering body, but very quickly depicts that union as impossible. When she witnesses the moment of his death, for example, instead of experiencing his pain as her own, Julian encounters a different kind of pain entirely: she sees Christ's pain without being able to share in it. At first, when she gazes upon Christ's dying body, she contends, "I felte no paine but for Cristes paines" (17.43) and believes that Christ has fulfilled her desire for affective union with him. However, she soon realizes that "my paines passed ony bodily deth" (17.46), implying that her pain is fundamentally different from Christ's experience of dying. When Julian sees Christ's body drying and growing limp on the cross, she does not identify that pain as something similar to her own. Instead, she compares his body to a sagging piece of cloth (17.20) and a dry piece of wood (17.29), objects that have no sensation whatsoever. She describes her pain as categorically different from Christ's. She reflects, "'But of alle paines that leed to salvation, this is the most: to se thy love suffer. How might ony paine be more then to see him that is alle my life, alle my blisse, and alle my joy suffer?' Here I felt sothfastly that I loved Crist so much above myselfe that ther was no paine that might be suffered like to that sorrow that I had to see him in paine" (17.48–52). A fundamental aspect of Julian's pain is her recognition that she can distinguish Christ's pain from her own. At the point of Christ's greatest suffering, she must stand apart from Christ and watch him suffer. The difference between her pain and Christ's is not, as one might expect, that her pain is emotional while his is clearly physical; Julian has no difficulty viewing both experiences as equally painful. The problem for Julian, the source of the intensity of her anguish, is that their two bodies are ultimately incommensurable. Though, drawing on the continental tradition, Julian initially expects Christ's Passion to be the moment in Christ's life when she will lose herself in the identity of Christ, it is at precisely this moment that Julian recognizes her inability to claim Christ's pain as her own.

Far from imagining this inability as a personal failure, Julian portrays her perception of difference between herself and God as a defining aspect of the relationship between humanity and the divine. Once she realizes that she cannot directly identify with Christ, Julian meditates on the figure of the Virgin Mary at the foot of the cross. Unlike her experience with Christ's pain, Julian claims that it is entirely possible for her to understand the precise nature of Mary's emotional suffering. She explains the source and nature of Mary's anguish by stating that "the higher, the mightier, the swetter that the love is, the more sorow it is to the lover to se that body in paine that he loved" (18.6–7). By placing this description in general terms, she implies that Mary's suffering is of a sort that is accessible to all humans. Julian regards her identification with Mary and the other disciples present at the crucifixion as almost effortless; she feels secure in articulating the depth of their emotional suffering solely on the authority of "my awne feling" (18.9). According to Julian, the reason that the pain that she, Mary, and the disciples endure is radically different from Christ's is because it is rooted in "kinde love" (18.3; 18.4). In this case, the word "kinde" particularly denotes the category of humankind and suggests that humans have a unique way of experiencing emotional pain. When Julian describes "kinde love" as the source of their sorrow, she suggests that their feelings are a direct result of their innate and distinctly human affection for Christ.

Humans are only capable of a partial identification with Christ because Christ, as both fully human and fully divine, surpasses human nature. During her vision of the crucifixion, Julian describes, "Here saw I a gret oning betwene Crist and us, to my understanding. For when he was in paine, we ware in paine, and alle creatures that might suffer paine suffered with him" (18.11–12). Although this description at first seems to suggest that all creation can experience emotional union with Christ through pain, Julian quickly reveals that the pain each creature feels is of a particular category, a category that Christ ultimately surpasses: everyone suffers "in ther kind" and "for kindnes" because "it longeth kindly to ther properte to know him for ther lorde" (18.14; 18.17; 18.15). Certainly every individual's pain is similar to Christ's insofar as Christ shares the individual's "kind" by virtue of his human nature, but Julian never forgets that Christ has two natures—both God and man.

Ultimately, Christ's divine nature makes full understanding of him impossible. Julian describes how, at the moment of Christ's greatest suffering, "the oning of the godhed gave strength to the manhed for love to suffer more than alle men might" (20.1–3). Christ's human nature is never separate from his godly nature; his union with the Trinity is always perfect and complete. However, it is Christ's divine nature that gives him a greater capacity for love, and this greater love in turn increases his suffering. The quantitative difference between each believer's pain and Christ's pain is therefore so large that "he sufferd more paine than all men of salvation that ever was, from the furst beginning into the last day" (20.4–5). Even when believers strive to increase their suffering in order to better understand the Passion, they do not decrease the difference between Christ's pain and their own. For example, when Christ sees Mary at the foot of the cross, "sufferde he for her sorowse, and more over" (20.19); Mary's sorrow for Christ's suffering actually increases that suffering itself. It is never possible for a human to experience the depth of Christ's suffering because, unlike Christ, humans are not fully divine.

Humanity's perception of its own distance from the divine is what makes the institutional church essential to human devotion in Julian's view. It is with regard to sin that the perspectives of humanity and Christ differ most radically. According to Julian's theology, an unchanging godly will resides in each person's soul, and sin arises not from willful disobedience but from overzealous actions committed out of desire for God. At one point, Julian remarks that she never saw sin during the course of her vision because sin has no being or substance unto itself (27). Although conventional Christian theology suggested that sin ought to be a source of guilt and shame, Julian's Christ views sin in a radically different way.[18] He shows her that, in heaven, "sinne shalle be no shame, but wurshipe to man" (38.1). Sin will ultimately be a source of honor to all who are saved because every time a person falls into sin it provides God with another opportunity to raise the sinner up by lavishing his love, mercy, and forgiveness upon him. Regardless of how liberating God's perspective on sin may initially seem, Julian urges her readers not to try to share this perspective during their earthly lives. By making this distinction, Julian is able to question conventional understandings of sin at the same time as she affirms church doctrines that emphasize guilt and repentance. According to Julian, one of the essential processes by which God shows his mercy is through the sacrament of penance, a process that requires believers to feel true contrition for their sins. Although God recognizes that every human soul possesses an unchanging godly will, every Christian ought to feel "with gret sorow and with gret shame that he hath so defouled the fair image of God" (39.8–9). God never sees his followers as unworthy, but they ought to view themselves in this way while living on earth. In heaven, all shame shall turn to honor and joy, but it is necessary for humans to first experience shame in order to allow God to reveal the depth of his mercy. Despite Christ's adoption of human flesh, the perspectives of human and divine must remain separate. Julian asserts that "otherwise is the beholding of God, and otherwise is the beholding of man" (52.58). Although it is important for humans to understand that God's perspective is different, they ought not to strive to hold that divine perspective during their earthly lives. Julian argues that divine and human perception must be split in two and operate together as a "doubil werking" (52.76–77). When Julian tells her readers that God does not view their sins as

---

18. Julian's deviation from conventional understandings of the nature of sin has received much scholarly attention. See Baker, *Julian of Norwich's "Showings"*; Sandra McEntire, "The Likeness of God and the Restoration of Humanity in Julian of Norwich's *Showings*," In *Julian of Norwich: A Book of Essays*, ed. Sandra J. McEntire (New York: Garland, 1998), 3–33; Watson, "Visions of Inclusion."

marks of shame, it is to increase their trust in God and not to alleviate their need to repent their sins.

According to most contemporary theology on Original Sin, every person, with the exceptions of Christ and the Virgin Mary, is a sinner, and so no one is capable of fully living within the bliss of God's love in this life. However, according to Julian, this experience of God's distance from humanity as a result of sin is an illusion. God's love and grace are always present in each person, even though they go unperceived. Julian argues: "For notwithstonding that oure lorde God wonneth now in us, and is here with us, and halseth us and becloseth us for tender love that he may never leve us, and is more nere to us than tonge may telle or harte may thinke, yet may we never stinte of morning ne of weping, nor of seeking nor of longing, till whan we se him clere in his blisseful chere" (72.19–23). It is of great comfort to know that God makes his home within every human's soul, but that knowledge should never alleviate the need to mourn one's own sinfulness because the pain that humans experience as a result of sin keeps them from fully understanding God. All souls naturally desire to know God and must therefore mourn that the pain of sin keeps them from fully seeing God in this life. For Julian, affective piety arises from humans' perception of their distance from the divine, a perceived distance that is essential to human belief and one on which the institutional church encourages believers to focus.

ALLEGORICAL READING

For Julian, any attempt to understand the divine is necessarily a process of devotional reading and proliferating textual interpretations. Julian understands the divided relationship between God and humanity through reference to allegorical signs, both in the sense that it is only through language that believers can come to know God and in the sense that this relationship itself is analogous to the separation of allegorical and literal meanings within an allegorical text. Allegorical language separates the categories of literal and transcendent even as it unifies them.

In Julian's formulation, humans primarily experience the literal human world and can only know God through signs and language. Scholars have not fully recognized Julian's reliance on allegory nor, until very recently, the degree to which Julian's theology is dependent upon her understanding of literary form. As Michelle Karnes has recently argued, Julian is an astute literary theorist who is uniquely concerned with exploring the nature of literary interpretation, particularly how "successful interpretation actually requires the association of apparently unlike things."[19] Extending Karnes's work, in this section I consider how Julian's interest in literary aesthetics and difference shape her understandings of both affective piety and eucharistic devotion. For Julian, allegory, broadly defined as seemingly independent literal signs that signify a transcendent meaning beyond themselves, is not simply an intellectual mode; it is a highly affective mode, revealing the difference between human and divine in literary form, a difference that Julian longs to overcome.

In her lord and servant parable in particular, earthly life is like an allegorical text; literal reading corresponds to human perception and allegorical reading corresponds to divine perception. In this way, Julian contributes to a long tradition of Neoplatonic Christian allegoresis, which regards the physical world as a book that reveals the invisible and spiritual secrets of God beneath its surface.[20] Unlike many Christian exegetes, Julian does not regard literal meaning as something that ought to be discarded or transcended just as someone would discard a shell in order to reach the kernel inside;[21] rather, Julian longs for the unification of the literal and allegorical levels of meaning. Like the literal level of an allegorical text, human lives always possess meaning beyond their own physical reality, even though humans may find it difficult or impossible to fully grasp that meaning. According to Julian, humans do not have full access to God's meaning in their earthly lives and so cannot see how the human and divine coincide, how the literal and allegorical can correspond to form a single unit. The work of human devotion in this life is interpreting signs whose full significance cannot be known and, in so doing, increasing the human desire for the fullness of knowledge that will come from union with God in the afterlife.

Allegory is perfectly suited to Julian's discussion of the immediacy of transcendent meaning because allegory functions by simultaneously inviting and blocking readerly interpretation. Within an allegorical text, the reader plays a central role in the production of meaning because the genre itself foregrounds

---

19. Karnes, "Julian of Norwich's Art," 333. Karnes's argument is similar to my own in its emphasis on difference and interpretation. However, her focus is primarily hermeneutics, rather than affective piety and sacramental theology.

20. This Neoplatonic allegoresis dates back at least to Plotinus and Augustine. For discussions of the effect of this tradition on late medieval literature, see especially David Aers, *Piers Plowman and Christian Allegory* (London: Edward Arnold, 1975); Maureen Quilligan, *The Language of Allegory: Defining the Genre* (Ithaca, NY: Cornell UP, 1979). For a more recent discussion, see Suzanne Conklin Akbari, *Seeing through the Veil: Optical Theory and Medieval Allegory* (Toronto: University of Toronto Press, 2004).

21. This tradition of regarding allegoresis as the task of separating shells from kernels is very fully discussed in Aers, *Piers Plowman*.

the text's status as signifying a meaning beyond the literal.[22] However, allegory also highlights the way in which such interpretive work can neither be definitive nor complete. As modern theorists of allegory have shown, allegory refuses the complete coincidence of representation and meaning, making visible the disjunction between literal sign and allegorical abstraction.[23] Nicolette Zeeman explains of medieval religious allegory, "If allegory always works by juxtaposing unlike terms, religious allegory seems especially often to foreground the unlikeness and the possible discrepancies between the terms it brings together."[24] Instead of offering a moment of identification with the divine, allegory invites the reader to participate in the creation of the text's meaning even as it highlights the fact that representation and transcendent reality fail to perfectly coincide. In contrast to such theorists, Julian, like Langland, believes that it is theoretically possible for representation and abstraction to coincide; however, such perfect coincidence can only occur in the mind of God. For humans, this coincidence is painfully just out of reach.

Through the parable of the lord and the servant, she examines the ways in which literal and allegorical meanings both coincide and threaten to pull apart from each other. The literal narrative of the parable is relatively simple: A lord sends a servant out to do his will. Out of love, the servant is so eager to obey his lord that he runs too fast and falls down in a ditch and hurts himself. Although the servant is too ashamed to look at the lord, the lord does not blame the servant for his fall, but instead plans to reward him since it was only good will and love that caused the fall in the first place. However, this narrative is never just a literal one. In her introduction to the parable, Julian explains that this "sight was shewed double in the lorde, and the sight was shewed double in the servant" (51.3-4). Even before it begins, Julian divides the narrative's significance into four parts by splitting it into discrete roles of lord and servant, and endowing each role with both literal and allegorical significance. As her exploration of the parable continues, Julian highlights the divisions between the literal and the allegorical, and the servant and the lord. She demands that readers regard this parable as a lesson in reading allegorically, a process she regards as perceiving two disparate but interrelated meanings at the same time.

---

22. One of the works to most fully explore the role of the reader in allegory is Quilligan, *Language of Allegory*.

23. Steven Mailloux provides a useful overview of allegory in postmodern theory. Steven Mailloux, "Hermeneutics, Deconstruction, Allegory," in *The Cambridge Companion to Allegory*, ed. Rita Copeland and Peter T. Struck (Cambridge: Cambridge, 2010), 254-65.

24. Nicolette Zeeman, "Medieval Religious Allegory: French and English." *The Cambridge Companion to Allegory*, ed. Rita Copeland and Peter T. Struck (Cambridge: Cambridge UP, 2010), 149.

Julian herself is initially reluctant to engage in allegorical interpretation of the revelations precisely because she recognizes that to do so would implicate her in the creation of their meaning. In fact, she claims that it took her over twenty years to interpret this parable, and she therefore omitted it entirely from her earlier short text. She confesses that she was initially inclined not to interpret the parable at all because she felt that it was "misty" and "indefferent" (51.75–76). The idea of engaging in extensive interpretation of it made her uncomfortable because she felt that her initial understanding of it was essentially incomplete, and "culde I not take therein full understanding to my ees in that time" (51.55–56). At least part of this reluctance stems from a hesitation to claim authorship of an allegorical reading. When she first received the revelations, she interpreted the parable as a narrative of humanity's fall from grace in which the servant represents Adam and the lord represents God. At this allegorical level, the parable is a radical reinterpretation of the doctrine of Original Sin because it attributes Adam's fall from grace to his sincere love for God, rather than willful disobedience. Even Julian's most basic interpretation seemed to challenge official doctrine and therefore would have called into question her capacity to interpret the revelations at all. Julian's ultimate decision to include the parable in her long text attests to her willingness to participate in the creation of the revelations' meaning and her acceptance that such interpretation will always be incomplete. Although Julian's presentation of the parable is extensive and almost mathematically precise in its interpretation of detail, Julian does not suggest that her interpretation is final. As she points out in her concluding chapter, "This boke is begonne by Goddes gifte and his grace, but it is not yet performed" (86.1–2), suggesting that her interpretation does not complete the revelations' meaning. By including this parable in *Revelation*, Julian argues that God wants her to engage in allegorical interpretation and, by extension, that such interpretation can be an important way for humans to understand God.

Throughout this text, allegorical interpretation necessarily involves the proliferation of meaning and the recognition that such interpretation is never finished. Once she accepts the reading of the servant as Adam, Julian discovers that the allegorical meaning of the parable expands. Although one of the ostensible purposes of a parable is to illustrate doctrine, Julian instead finds herself in a state of "unknowinge" when she begins her work of interpretation (51.59). Upon fixing the identity of the servant as Adam, she is troubled to discover that "I sawe many diverse properteys that might by no manner be derecte to singel Adam" (51.57–58). The details in the parable—expressions, clothing, gestures, and colors—all suggest to Julian that simple interpretations will not be possible, and she may never fully understand it. This realization leads her to recognize that this vision is not unique among the revelations with regard to its allegorical significance because "I sawe and understode that every shewing is full of privities" (51.61–62). Every one of her visions is full of signs, signs that point beyond their literal meaning to the secrets of God.

The difference between divine and human perception of these signs is that God understands the allegorical and literal simultaneously while humans find it difficult to see how the two fit together. When the lord sees the servant fall into the ditch, he beholds his loving servant "with a doubil chere" (51.34), the outer expression of pity and the inward joy at the knowledge that he will now be able to restore his servant into grace. Throughout the text, the inner or allegorical meanings correspond to God's view of the world. Like the lord of the parable, only God is able to hold this double perspective in which he understands both human and divine perception of the same event. In contrast, the servant, whom Julian eventually understands as representing all of humanity, cannot look at his lord because of his fallen state; he is limited to his own perspective. One exception to this division between human and divine perception is Julian. On account of her visions, Julian *does* briefly understand God's perspective, and it is almost beyond her comprehension. She exclaims, "Methought it might melt our hartes for love and brest them on two for joy" (51.110). Even for Julian, full understanding of the true nature of the relationship between God and humanity is something that, from a human perspective, is always divided, always split into two parts. Halfway through her explication of the parable, Julian discovers that the servant not only signifies the first Adam but also the second Adam, Christ. Through Christ's incarnation, God chose to be inextricably bound to humanity through human flesh and so, "when Adam felle, Godes sonne fell. For the rightful oning which was made in heven, Goddes sonne might not be seperath from Adam, for by Adam I understood alle man" (51.185–187). Christ is always part of humanity, and so the union between human and divine has already taken place; human beings are just unable to fully recognize that union. Julian describes humanity as God's crown, "which crowne is the faders joy, the sonnes wurshippe, the holy gostes liking" (51.270–71). Humanity is as close to the Trinity as it is possible to be without being part of the Trinity itself, but humanity's fallen state prevents humans from seeing the double perspective of human and divine at once.

This split between divine and human perception is ultimately a separation within the self, between the substantial and sensual parts of the soul. In Julian's theology, the individual human soul consists of substance and sensuality.²⁵ The sensuality is humanity's nature as it knows itself in the physical world and the substance contains the godly will. In this formulation, humanity does not see the link between substance and sensuality, and only God can link the two: "Oure faith is a vertu that cometh of oure kinde substance into oure sensual soule by the holy gost" (54.22–23). Only God unites the two parts of the soul that correspond to the perspectives of God and humanity, the substantial and the sensual, the allegorical and the literal. Since God dwells in the substantial soul, the union of the soul with God at the end of time will also be a recognition of the soul's unity within itself.

During their earthly lives, humans are unable to understand the union of substance and sensuality that has already taken place. Through his incarnation, Christ united substance and sensuality by uniting divinity and flesh: "Theyse two perties were in Crist, the heyer and the lower, which is but one soule" (55.40–41). According to Julian, Christ exists in the human soul "in the same point that oure soule is made sensual, in the same point is the cite of God" (55.21–22). Christ dwells at the meeting point between substance and sensuality in the human soul, holding them together when human logic often wants to pull them apart. Although Julian recognizes that substance and sensuality are fundamentally inseparable, she continually speaks about them as though the soul were made up of two separate elements. For example, she argues that, through Christ's sacrifice on the cross, God saved humankind from a "doubil deth," the death of both body and soul (55.38). Christ has already united substance and sensuality, but the very fact that Julian still speaks of them as two distinct parts reveals that it is difficult for humans to perceive them as a single unit.

Although the substantial/allegorical/divine and the sensual/literal/human are ultimately inseparable, humans can only understand the soul if it is split into these two parts. In the fifty-sixth chapter, Julian claims that understanding God is necessary if one is to understand one's own soul, and understanding one's own soul is necessary if one is to understand God.²⁶ Although these

---

25. Barbara Newman helpfully defines these two nonstandard terms unique to Julian's theology. Substance is actual union with God "already given by the fact of creation," and sensuality is "humanity's empirical being in time—embodied, limited in perception, fallen, yet still united with the human nature of Christ through the Incarnation." Barbara Newman, *God and the Goddesses: Vision, Poetry, and Belief in the Middle Ages* (Philadelphia: University of Pennsylvania Press, 2003), 228. Caroline Walker Bynum defines "substance" as what is essentially human and "sensuality" as referring to humanity's fallen state. Bynum, *Wonderful Blood*, 205.

26. This explanation draws very heavily on Augustine's explication of the Trinity. In *De Trinitate*, Augustine argues that knowing oneself and knowing God are interdependent endeavors. Every individual's innermost soul contains the image of God and is a tripartite structure analogous to the Holy Trinity; the soul is capable of recognizing and loving God because it already knows God through the image of God inside itself. The Trinity and the human soul are

statements suggest that knowledge of the self and knowledge of God are identical, Julian presents them as if they were two separate activities. The goal of attempting to know either God or the human soul is the same, but Julian holds these two ideas in tension even though she realizes that they ultimately bleed into each other. The complete collapse of boundaries does not aid human understanding. Rather, humans need to see distinct categories and boundaries before it is possible to contemplate the ways in which those categories are united. Julian concludes this chapter by asserting that God "in his endlesse wisdom wolde that we were doubil" (56.50–51). Rather than suggest that the human soul is a union of body and soul, Julian describes the soul as "doubil," suggesting that substance and sensuality must be perceived as two discrete, distinct elements of the human soul.[27] Perhaps most intriguingly, Julian does not argue that this human propensity to see the soul as double rather than united is somehow sinful. She argues that this double vision is precisely how God designed humans to be: God wants believers to be allegorical readers.

READING SIGNS AND SACRAMENTS

The difficulty that believers encounter in their struggle for union with God is not the intangibility of God since the soul and God are already united. Rather, the challenge lies in the human capacity to understand that union. As Julian's own attempts to understand the revelations through writing demonstrate, the human soul must struggle for knowledge of God through language, a system of signs that is incapable of entirely conveying the true nature of God. For Julian, the human process of understanding God is always one of interpreting signs, especially what Julian calls "meanes"—the church's sacraments, prayers, rituals, and images—that draw the believer toward contemplation of the divine.

She presents signs as gaining their spiritual power from their seeming insignificance; the fragility of the sign's physical reality reveals the sharp contrast between the unstable nature of the earthly world and the stability of the divine reality it signifies. During the first revelation, Christ shows Julian an object—"a little thing the quantity of an haselnot" (5.7)—which is only signifi-

---

distinct entities, but from a human perspective, it is impossible to know one without knowing the other. Augustine, *De Trinitate libri XV*, Corpus Christianorum Series Latina Vol. 50 (Turnhout, BE: Brepols, 1968).

27. As Karnes notes, "As Julian describes it, heavenly bliss consists in the bringing together both of the parts of an individual and of the individual and God. The human condition before that time is defined by doubleness." Karnes, "Julian of Norwich's Art," 342.

cant insofar as it leads to the understanding of God. The object is so small and fragile that Julian is amazed that it is able to exist at all because "methought it might sodenly have fallen to nought for littlenes" (5.11). Rather than ask Christ the significance of this object, Julian understands that it is a sign that demands her own interpretation and concludes that this object signifies "all that is made" (5.10). The object's miraculous continued existence proves that God made it, loves it, and protects it, and it is on the basis of this observation that Julian argues that its allegorical referent is God's devotion to all of creation. After reflecting on this object as a sign, Julian realizes that all created things are also fragile, tiny objects that could easily collapse into nothingness if it were not for God's love. The object itself—whether or not it is a hazelnut— is inconsequential for Julian's purposes. What matters is that it functions as a sign, pointing to a greater meaning beyond itself.

Julian argues that earthly attachments, such as an attachment to a hazelnut for its own sake, are ultimately unfulfilling because humans can only find true rest in God. She warns, "For this is the cause why we be not all in ease of hart and of soule: for we seeke heer rest in this thing that is so little, wher no reste is in, and we know not our God, that is al mighty, all wise, and all good" (5.21–24). The hazelnut may signify God, but Julian urges her readers not to regard signs of God as the presence of God himself. The hazelnut teaches Julian about God, but she understands that "no soule is rested till it is noughted of all thinges that is made" (5.26). The soul can only rest in God once it has rid itself of all outside attachments, even attachments that signify God. Signs are worldly things that are no longer necessary once one has experienced total union with God in the afterlife.

Since God is ultimately indescribable in human language and signs are, by definition, part of a system of language, signs must inevitably fail to express the true nature of God. Before discussing the power of the hazelnut as sign, Julian constructs a metaphor that she initially regards as clear and convincing: Christ is human clothing. She explains, "He is oure clothing, that for love wrappeth us and windeth us, halseth us and all becloseth us, hangeth about us for tender love, that he may never leeve us" (5.3–5). Initially, Christ as clothing is a comforting metaphor for Julian, implying assurance in the union of Christ with humanity. However, after her discussion of the hazelnut and the limitations of signs, Julian realizes that all metaphors are incapable of describing God. At this point, she reintroduces the metaphor as a simile: "For as the body is clad in the cloth, and the flesh in the skinne, and the bones in the flesh, and the harte in the bowke, so ar we, soule and body, cladde and enclosedde in the goodnes of God" (6.35–37). She moves from outer coverings of the body to inner containers within the body, increasing the sense of containment of the self by God. She ultimately suggests that no matter how internally oriented her descriptions of the human body and its various enclosures become, she will never be able to explain God through signs because God is "more nere to us without any likenes" (6.39). The shift from metaphor to simile itself suggests Julian's increasing lack of confidence in the comparison to definitively convey divine reality. Language may aid believers in coming closer to understanding God's love for humanity, but it ultimately fails to communicate the true nature of God because signs remain only means rather than ends in themselves. However, Julian does not suggest that attempts to understand God through signs are fruitless. Indeed, barring direct mystical experiences, signs are the only way to encounter God during one's earthly life. Julian argues that it is necessary to worship God through signs and mediation, but believers must also understand that God's goodness and love surpass all earthly significations.

Julian presents unmediated access to Christ as an ideal, but ultimately argues that the mediation of signs, especially church mediation, is the way in which God wants humanity to come to an understanding of him. While Julian was reflecting on the meaning of the hazelnut, "the custome of our prayer was brought to my mind: how that we use, for unknowing of love to make meny meanes" (6.3–4). At this moment, she deliberately opposes the church's methods of worship and proper love of God by implying that the church's dependence on mediation stems from its own misunderstanding of God's true nature. After arguing that all "meanes" are ultimately unworthy of God and contending that believers ought to worship God directly, she begins a long list of the various sorts of mediation that believers use in praying to God, including devotion to his flesh and blood, prayer to Mary, prayer to the saints, and devotion to the true cross. After completing this list, Julian reverses her earlier position and proclaims that "God of his goodnes hath ordained meanes to helpe us full faire and fele" (6.19). For Julian, the abstract idea of mediation is initially distasteful, but the reality of some of the most common mediators present in the prayers of the church is not. Worshipping God through signs is worthwhile precisely because God himself has chosen them as means by which he ought to be worshipped.

Despite her initial aversion to mediation between God and the individual soul, Julian believes that the mediating effects of signs are central to even her most direct, intimate visions of Christ. In her description of the first revelation, Julian sees Christ's bleeding head "without any meane" (4.5) and initially believes that the lack of mediation assures her of Christ's intimate love for her. However, within a few sentences, Julian recognizes that even this experience is itself a sign that needs to be interpreted. She explains that, although her visions only show Christ, their real subject is the entire Trinity: "For wher Jhesu appireth the blessed trinity is understand, as to my sight" (4.11). The significance of Christ's body is neither self-evident nor self-contained; it is a sign pointing beyond itself to the reality of the triune godhead. It is noteworthy that Julian authorizes her claim that Christ's body signifies the Trinity by reference to her "sight," particularly since her claim is precisely for that which she does not see. Her visions give her the authority to interpret signs, not to move beyond them.

It is only through focus on individual signs and "meanes" that believers can begin to grow in their knowledge of the much larger reality of God. At the start of the third revelation, Julian "saw God in a pointe—that is to say, in my understanding" (11.1). In this instance, the word "pointe" denotes a specific location in space that, like the hazelnut image from the first revelation, invites Julian to derive spiritual meaning from a discrete physical space with carefully defined boundaries. Like the hazelnut, this point ultimately signifies that God "is in al thing" (11.2). Paradoxically, it is through ascribing Christ's presence to a single place that Julian recognizes the impossibility of fixing Christ's location. This third revelation ends when Christ proclaims to Julian: "See, I am God. See, I am in all thing. See, I do all thing. See, I never lefte my hands of my works, ne never shalle without ende. See, I lede all thing to the end that I ordaine it to, fro without beginning, by the same might, wisdom, and love that I made it with" (11.42–45). Christ repeats the word "see" several times, but Julian has not physically seen anything. Instead, she has understood the presence of Christ in all things and all times through her own intellectual understanding of God in one particular point in space. Nevertheless, Christ emphasizes Julian's vision in order to suggest the importance of that singular point to human understanding. For God, the particular point itself holds no particular significance except insofar as it represents the equal significance of all other things. For Julian, however, the point is essential because it acts as a sign. Without focusing on God in a particular point, it would be impossible for her to understand God's presence in all things. When Christ repeats the word "see," he emphasizes the importance of physical sight and moments of physical focus to human understanding. The word "see" eventually fades from meaning physical sight to meaning understanding, but its repetition continually calls the reader's attention back to that particular point in space, showing that humans cannot understand the broader goodness and love of God without first seeing it through a sign: whether that sign is a hazelnut, a saintly image, or a point in space. It is necessary to localize God before one is able to understand that such localization is ultimately impossible.

EUCHARISTIC LONGING AND THE CHURCH

For Julian, the Eucharist is the most important of "meanes" because, through transubstantiation, the Eucharist confounds the distinction between sign and signified, thus inviting a highly affective yet literary mode of reading. Julian defines the Christian community's relationship to Christ's body in profoundly eucharistic terms: the communal desire to drink Christ's blood and thereby become one with him. This imagery implicitly affirms the centrality of the sacrament of the Eucharist at the same time as it defines the relationship between Christ and his church as one of longing for a full physical union that is not yet realized. Julian's focus on signs, especially the sacraments, as markers of difference highlights this longing that defines the relationship between Christ and believers. Although the image of God dwells in every soul, Christians must seek God as if they did not already possess his presence because the perception of difference increases desire, and God wants humans to ardently desire union with him.

Julian depicts the fulfillment of this desire for union as a eucharistic process of mutual bodily ingestion. At the end of time, both Christ and believers will consume each other. When the soul finally achieves full union with God, "than shall we alle come into oure lorde, oureselfe clerely knowing and God fulsomely having" (43.40–41). In this context, the word "having" has a primarily bodily and sensual connotation, increasing the emphasis on the physical incorporation of Christ's body into the body of the believer. Julian goes on to highlight the sensual aspects of this incorporation by explaining how, at the end of time, "we endlessly be alle had in God, him verily seyeng an fulsomely feling, and him gostely hering, and him delectably smelling, and him swetly swelwing" (43.41–43). The union with Christ at the end of time will be a perfect Eucharist; rather than seeing Christ's body through the sign of bread, the human soul will consume Christ's body while seeing him face to face.

Throughout the text, Christ's blood acts as a particularly powerful sign of this desired eucharistic union. His blood signifies the potential for union with him, and the lack of it represents the impossibility of that union. During the first revelation, Julian describes the sight of Christ's blood as "most comfort to me" and believes that this vision demonstrates God's desire to give humans solace (7.25; 40). Even though she knows that the source of the blood is Christ's dying body, she still finds this vision joyful and reassuring. In contrast, during the eighth revelation, Julian focuses intently on the drying of Christ's crucified body and finds this vision horrifying. When she describes how all "the precious blode was bled out of the swete body that might passe therfro," she focuses almost exclusively on pain (16.11–12). Her horror directly stems from the realization that Christ's body is losing the blood that she regards as so wonderful and redemptive. As Christ's body dries, Julian realizes that identification with Christ has become increasingly impossible. Christ's skin is so inexplicably dry and broken that it falls in disparate mismatching pieces that look "as a cloth and sagging downward, semin as it wolde hastely have fallen for hevines and for loosenes" (17.20–21). As the skin on Christ's head loosens, it forms a ring of flesh around the thorns so that the two become indistinguishable. Likewise, the rest of Christ's body becomes so dry and brown that it begins to match the cross itself—"like a drye bord whan it is aged" (17.29). As he dries, Christ is barely recognizable as human, and there is a complete lack of emotional connection between the human and the divine. Christ's blood is important to Julian precisely because it signifies the possibility of her eventual union with him.

Julian depicts the desire for this eucharistic union and the resultant unification of literal and allegorical meaning as a thirst for Christ's blood, a thirst that both Christ and believer experience. When she sees Christ's body drying on the cross, Julian describes Christ's need for his own blood as a thirst, explaining how "I sawe in Crist a doubille thurst: on bodely, and another gostly" (17.2). It is immediately apparent that Christ's bodily, literal thirst is his physical need for moisture, but after suggesting that his thirst also possesses allegorical meaning, Julian delays a partial explanation of this spiritual thirst for fourteen chapters and a full explanation for over fifty. This delay itself signifies what Julian eventually defines as Christ's spiritual thirst: the ongoing desire for the union between human and divine, a union in which the spiritual meanings of God will finally be fully understood. Christ's thirst is a thirst for the collapse of the allegorical sign, in which bodily and spiritual meanings fold into each other. In the middle of the text, Julian declares, "Therfore this is his thurste: love-longing to have us all togeder, hole in him to his endlesse blisse" (31.14–15). At this moment, Christ's thirst for union with humanity is no longer a "gostly thirst" but is simply "his thurste," collapsing the physical, literal sign and the spiritual, allegorical one.

Christ's thirst signifies the divide between Christ and believers and the force of love by which that divide will cease to be. As long as Christ thirsts, it means that the union between Christ and humanity has not taken place. Julian explains, "For the thurst of God is to have the generalle man into him, in which thurst he hath drawen his holy soules that be now in blisse. And so getting his lively membris, ever he draweth and drinketh, and yet him thursteth and longeth" (75.3–6). Just as Christ longed for moisture on the cross, he thirsts for all souls to join together with him in heaven. His thirst did not end with his death and resurrection; since humanity is not yet united with him, Christ still thirsts in heaven and, in order to quench his thirst, he must continually be "us drawing uppe to his blisse" (31.40–41). By describing Christ as drawing his bodily "membris" to himself, Julian depicts this thirst as a longing to have his own physical body return to him. Near the end of *Revelation*, Julian argues that Christ "shall al besprinkil us in his precious blode" and regards this pouring out of his blood as an expression of his thirst (63.16–17). Even as Christ pours out his blood for humanity, he thirsts to have it return to him through his followers. His followers receive his blood and, through their reception of it, long to fully unite themselves with his body. Rather than suggest that Christ's thirst will exist only until *he* is satiated, Julian says that Christ's thirst will be "lasting in him as long as we be in need" (31.40). Christ's thirst is therefore the force by which the human thirst for God is quenched. Christ will only cease to thirst when humanity's desire for union with him is fulfilled.

Ultimately, the quenching of Christ's eucharistic thirst would also mean the collapse of literary signification, the moment at which literal and allegorical unite. Julian repeatedly uses forms of the verb "drawen" to describe how Christ's thirst pulls souls toward him (31.40; 43.29; 75.3). Her use of this particular word is a pun that suggests both that Christ "draws up" and "drinks" human souls. Through using this single word to signify both a bodily and a spiritual action, Julian reveals the collapse of allegorical and literal that Christ's thirst ultimately aims to accomplish. At the end of time, all those who are saved will receive a new bliss "which plentuously shalle beflowe oute of God into us and fulfille us" (75.16–17). At the moment when Christ's thirst is finally quenched, he shall pour more of himself into his people, and the effects of this bliss will fulfill the human desire for knowledge by uncovering the "privetes" of God's meaning that were hidden during earthly life. Upon receiving this bliss, humans will understand the full meaning and causes of all God's acts, and "the blisse and the fulfilling shalle be so depe and so high that, for wonder and merveyle, all creatures shalle have to God so gret reverent dred . . . that the pillours of heven shulle tremelle and quake" (75.22–25). When Christ's thirst ceases to exist, the saved will be completely fulfilled because they will have full knowledge of God's meaning; they will understand the significance of all God's works. Julian reinforces the connection between the slaking of Christ's thirst and the union of literal and allegorical by recalling the image of the hazelnut from the first revelation. She describes how, upon receiving this new bliss, the saved will be "endlessly merveyling of the greatnesse of God the maker, and of the litilhede of all that is made" (75.28–29), echoing the earlier description of the hazelnut as a tiny object that represents "all that is made" (5.10). The small object, the created sign of God's all-powerful love, is an object of marvel alongside that which it signifies: God himself. In summing up her depiction of Christ's thirst, Julian argues that Christ's thirst and the thirst of all believers is for the end of signification, where there is no gap or confusion between the signifier and the signified. Julian describes this thirst for complete signification as a distinctly communal desire, a desire in which the entire church participates.

The church itself is a sign and, as such, it is a sensual, literal institution, incomplete without the spiritual substance of Christ. At one point during the revelations, Julian has difficulty reconciling the relationship between God and the church because she perceives that, while God assigns no blame for sin, the church teaches that each person must be ever mindful of her own sinfulness (45.10–27). Out of her initial confusion, Julian asks "that I might se in God in what manner that the dome of holy church herein techeth is tru in his sight, and howe it longeth to me sothly to know it, whereby they might both be saved, so as it ware wurshipfulle to God and right wey to me" (45.23–26). Julian struggles to uphold both views on sin and ultimately succeeds in doing so by aligning the church's stance with sensual and earthly perception. In response to her request for a way of reconciling her visions with church doctrine, Julian receives "no nother answere but a marvelous example of a lorde and of a servant" (45.26–27). The solution that the parable offers is to designate the church the role of the servant, a figure who, because of his limited perspective, believes that sin makes the sinner unworthy of redemption. She explicitly aligns the church's judgment with sensuality, the lower, earthly part of the human soul (45.21–22). While the servant's viewpoint is not accurate, neither is it sinful or wrong. It is a necessary position for humanity to hold in order to experience the glory of redemption through Christ. The sensual and earthly are not sinful and are not to be discarded; it is simply necessary to recognize that the substantial and the godly take precedence over earthly things. The church maintains a human perspective on God, a perspective that will ultimately be surpassed but never condemned. It is a sign of God's continued presence in the human world, but it is not that presence itself.

The church plays a vital role in the human search for salvation by providing Christians with the most important signs of all, the seven sacraments. As even Thomas Aquinas points out, humans need sacraments as a way to experience and understand God's grace because they are not yet in the full state of grace they will reach in heaven, and they therefore perceive God through signs rather than reality.[28] Early in the text, Julian explains that Christ is delighted

---

28. *ST* 3a.61, 4.

when people obey the church because "he it is, holy church. He is the grounde, he is the substance, he is the teching, he is the techer, he is the ende, and he is the mede wherefore every kinde soule traveleth" (34.13–15). At this point, her claim is somewhat general in nature: the church provides a series of signs and actions that ultimately lead to Christ. As the text continues, Julian becomes more explicit and definitive in her interpretations of the revelations, and she reinterprets this statement to refer particularly to the sacraments. She argues that Christ means to tell all Christians that "all the helth and the life of sacraments, alle the vertu and the grace of my worde, alle the goodnesse that is ordained in holy church to the, I it am" (60.30–32). The most important objects of spiritual interpretation are the church's sacraments and the rituals that produce them.

The sacraments offer believers the opportunity to participate in acts in which the earthly and spiritual perfectly coincide. Since sacraments are signs of the sacred, they function in a way very similar to the hazelnut image from the first revelation. Through a focus on a discrete physical object or action, believers are able to begin to contemplate the divine. However, the sacraments are superior to such arbitrary signs because sacraments are the divine reality that they signify. A sacrament is therefore a moment in which the allegorical and literal, human and divine, fold into each other. For Julian, this collapse of the earthly and the spiritual is a moment in which the individual briefly experiences the union with God that has already taken place in every human soul. God gives each person virtues through the substantial soul, and it is through the sacraments that "the same vertuse that we have received of oure substance, geven to us in kind of the goodness of God, the same vertuse by the werking of mercy be geven to us in grace, throw the holy gost renewed" (57.32–34). Julian describes the sacraments as providing the individual with the grace that, in some sense, that individual already possessed. The sacraments invite the believer to see, for a brief moment, the coincidence between human and divine that only God sees.

The Eucharist is the most important sacrament because it promises an intense physical intimacy that it does not fully provide; it therefore heightens the believer's desire to go beyond the sign and enter into union with God. The ingestion of Christ's body and blood in the form of a sign increases the believer's thirst to leave the sign behind. In order to show the potential for intimate contact with Christ in the Eucharist, Julian compares a Christian receiving the Eucharist to a baby being breastfed by its mother. Through this comparison, she argues that Jesus is even more physically and emotionally generous than a mother because, while earthly mothers only give their children milk, he "may fede us with himself, and doth full curtesly and full tenderly with the blessed sacrament that is precious fode of very life" (60.26–27). At the moment of eucharistic reception, Christ does not hold humans against his breast as a nursing mother would, but is instead more intimate because "he may homely lede us into his blessed brest by his swet, open side" (60.34) By immediately following these descriptions of eucharistic intimacy with explanations of the importance of the church and its rituals, Julian implies that the believer can only experience this intense intimacy with Christ through the mediation of another mother: the church. The Eucharist promises physical union with God, but simultaneously thwarts the full realization of that union because the Eucharist is always a mediated experience, marked by separation. Through the use of the sign of bread, the Eucharist produces a desire for Christ that cannot be fulfilled until after death.

To argue, as I have, that *A Revelation of Love* uses eucharistic language is to make two distinct but interrelated claims: on the most basic level, the text's vivid descriptions of Christ's blood and Julian's desire for physical union with Christ use language and imagery typically associated with the Eucharist. Perhaps more importantly, however, Julian imagines language itself as eucharistic. The Eucharist, like other signs, invites the reader to imagine the collapse of signifier and signified even as its very existence indicates their separateness. In worshipping or trying to understand the Eucharist, the believer simultaneously expresses a desire for union with God and admits that that desire remains unfulfilled. For Julian, signs are imperfect ways of understanding God precisely because they fail to provide full understanding. However, understanding through language, the process of seeing "double" and recognizing that there is a spiritual meaning behind the literal one, is a necessary aspect of the human condition. In this sense, all signs are eucharistic because they invoke the idea of a union with a transcendental signified, a union that never fully takes place.

For Julian, the importance of the Eucharist lies in its function as a sign that helps believers to strive to understand the relationship between God and humanity. Unlike many of the continental female mystics, Julian does not see the Eucharist as a site of potential ecstatic union, an opportunity to become one with the suffering of Christ. The sacraments are not objects and actions that are important for their own sake; they are significant insofar as they are signs that encourage believers to grow ever closer to union with God. Because humans are primarily confined to the realm of the earthly, literal, and sensual, the church's "meanes" are one of the few ways in which believers can begin to understand their relationship with Christ. According to Julian, the entire Christian church ought to value and interpret sacred signs because such signs reveal that Christians must long for the completion of meaning, even though they know that such completion is ultimately impossible in their earthly lives.

Julian depicts the institutional church's role in the formation of a Christian community of readers as powerfully and positively transformative. In the next chapter, I examine two texts that depict the church in a very different light. Nicholas Love's *Mirror of the Blessed Life of Jesus Christ* and *The Book of Margery Kempe* both regard the institutional church as systematically limiting the lay believer's contact with and intellectual knowledge of Christ's body. However, as we will see, such limitations enable these two writers to imagine new relationships between lay reading and the creation of a spiritual community on earth.

CHAPTER 5

The Willful Surrender of Eucharistic Reading in Nicholas Love and Margery Kempe

Nicholas Love and Margery Kempe invite their lay audiences to take pleasure in submission. Drawing on the Eucharist as their central devotional object, *The Book of Margery Kempe* and Nicholas Love's *Mirror of the Blessed Life of Jesus Christ* discourage theological thought and instead encourage readers to suffer with and for Christ. The *Mirror* and the *Book* set forth specifically lay models of affective eucharistic reading, and both frame these models within the context of the institutional church's increasingly extreme restrictions on lay education in the first decades of the fifteenth century. Love's text, a series of meditations officially endorsed by Archbishop Arundel, encourages the laity to engage in an unthinking emotional devotion to Christ's crucified body, especially as that body was physically present in the consecrated host. In *The Book of Margery Kempe*, Margery herself engages in ecstatic eucharistic devotion—weeping loudly during the Mass—and Arundel personally approves her practice of frequent eucharistic reception.

Rather than offer affective piety to Christ's suffering body as simple, both texts suggest that affective devotion involves both the involvement of the will and an intellectual engagement with ideas about what it means to read a devotional text affectively. Neither text dismisses lay readers as being incapable of higher contemplation or even argues wholeheartedly that lay people are more suited to affective piety because of their feminized status; instead they invite lay readers to choose affective piety out of obedience. They suggest that the lay community's willful refusal of contemplation produces spiritual pleasure. For the *Mirror* and the *Book,* the Eucharist is a symbol of the Christian community's pleasurable surrender of the will both to Christ and to the institutional church; both regard the Eucharist as essential to lay devotional reading precisely because of the affective union with Christ it does not fully provide. Neither text offers simple eucharistic promises of individual fulfillment in the Eucharist; rather, they encourage willed, disciplined acceptance of powerlessness and a lack of knowledge as necessary preconditions for spiritual and communal transformation.

My argument proceeds in four stages. First I demonstrate how the *Mirror* and the *Book* share an interest in affective eucharistic devotion that is particularly characteristic of fifteenth-century English piety. Next, I examine how Nicholas Love constructs a model of lay devotion centered on a eucharistic and pleasurable surrender of the will to ecclesiastical authority. I then show how the *Book of Margery Kempe* extends the *Mirror*'s model of eucharistic reading by revealing how this inward-looking lay piety shapes the *corpus mysticum*. Finally, I argue that, through the deliberately alienating figure of Margery, the *Book* invites readers to embrace eucharistic reading as an intellectual and emotional challenge.

DEVOTIONAL READING IN THE FIFTEENTH CENTURY

The eucharistic devotion that lies at the center of the *Mirror* and the *Book* is in many ways representative of a fifteenth-century inward affective trend in devotional writings that demanded both self-reflection and submission to the institutional church. In fifteenth-century England, vernacular religious writings shifted toward the affective and devotional both because of the increasing restrictions on vernacular writing and because of a growing lay interest in the "mixed life." Through the increased production of books of hours, translations of Continental religious texts into English, and original Middle English writings that urged readers to look "inward," it is evident that fifteenth-century Middle English writings demonstrate a proclivity to focus on affect and the reform of the self.[1]

---

1. Near the end of the fourteenth century, lay people, particularly the wealthy, began to develop an increased interest in more inward-looking devotional practices, practices that involved a focus on one's own emotions and the state of one's own soul rather than more specifically communal devotion. On this inward turn and the turn toward the mixed life, see Bryan, *Looking Inward*; Rice, *Lay Piety*.

Both texts contribute to the growing body of fifteenth-century religious works that encourage believers to turn inward, to be concerned with the state of one's own soul. Love names his text a "mirror" precisely in order to contribute to this body of literature. As he explains, the life of Christ cannot be fully described and so must be shown "in a maner of liknes as þe ymage of mans face is shewed in þe mirrroure" (11).[2] Through his use of the mirror image, Love suggests that Christ always exceeds linguistic representation and places his text alongside other medieval works that call themselves a "mirror" or "speculum" in order to indicate that the text is meant to reveal readers to themselves.[3] Love tells his readers that, during the reading process, they must imitate St. Cecilia, who bears the story of Christ's life "in þe priuyte of her breste" (11). For Love, reading is an imaginative process and one that must remain fundamentally private. Margery Kempe later draws on Love's meditations to take up this practice of devout imagination, particularly through her visions of Christ's Passion, events that she willfully imagines and that become her own private encounters with Christ's life. Fifteenth-century meditative texts are often simultaneously restrictive to and enabling of individual lay devotion through their focus on providing what Sarah McNamer has usefully called "intimate scripts": "quite literally scripts for the performance of feeling—scripts that often explicitly aspire to performative efficacy."[4] For those committed to the institutional Church, affective devotion to the suffering body of Christ provided a powerful link to the divine, a link that the ecclesiastical hierarchy actively encouraged the laity to believe truly existed. Such intimate scripts are particularly important to worship of the Eucharist because many religious lyrics provided lay readers with scripts for how to feel and imagine Christ during the Mass.[5]

Through their shared emphasis on and imitation of the monastic reading practice of *lectio divina,* the *Mirror* and *Book of Margery Kempe* draw on the growing lay interest in the mixed life and present themselves as texts aimed at generating intimate scripts. Love himself directly invokes the practice of *lectio divina*—with its emphasis on repetitive "rumination" over textual pas-

---

2. All quotations of Love are from Nicholas Love, *The Mirror of the Blessed Life of Jesus Christ, A Full Critical Edition,* ed. Michael G. Sargent (Exeter: University of Exeter Press, 2005).

3. On this literary tradition, see Anna Torti, *The Glass of Form: Mirroring Structures from Chaucer to Skelton* (Cambridge: D. S. Brewer, 1991).

4. McNamer, *Affective Meditation,* 12.

5. Elevation prayers and lyrics are particularly good examples of this phenomenon. See *Lay Folks Mass Book.* Versions of elevation prayers are scattered in modern editions. For a complete listing, see Robert R. Raymo, "Works of Religious and Philosophical Instruction," *A Manual of the Writings in Middle English,* ed. Albert E. Hartung, vol. 7 (New Haven: Connecticut Academy, 1986), 2559–61.

sages read aloud—when he describes how St. Cecilia "with a likyng & swete taste gostly chewyng in þat manere þe gospell of crist" (11).[6] Love thus advises readers to behave like monks in their religious devotion, not seeking new material but always rereading and remeditating on familiar passages. Since he believes lay people must not translate the Bible into the vernacular, Love suggests that readers may use his text in the way that monks use scripture itself. Although Love, following the Latin *Meditations,* divides his text into meditations ascribed to the seven days of the week, he tells his readers near the end of the text that "it semeþ to me beste þat euery deuout creature þat loueþ to rede or to here þis boke take þe partes þerof as it semeþ moste confortable & stiryng to his deuocion, sumtyme one & symtyme an oþere" (220). By placing this instruction near the end of the *Mirror,* Love indicates that he wants his readers to read the entire text at least once, but after that, they ought to read the text selectively, depending on which passages produce the most fervent affective response. Likewise, the *Book of Margery Kempe* begins by presenting the text as "a schort tretys and a comfortabyl for synful wrecchys, wherin thei may have gret solas and comfort to hem" (41).[7] As Rebecca Krug has suggested, there is much to be gained in our understanding of late medieval reading practices if we take the *Book* at its word and regard it as a text intended for spiritual education rather than an autobiography.[8] Near the conclusion of the proem, the *Book* tells us, "Thys boke is not wretyn in ordyr, every thing aftyr other as it wer don, but lych as the mater cam to the creatur in mend whan it schuld be wretyn," (49). While it is certainly possible that this description simply indicates the way in which the *Book* was dictated, it also is an indication to readers that the order of the *Book* is not of much importance.[9] The *Book* deliberately models itself on other devotional works—silently drawing on Love's text while explicitly naming Walter Hilton, Bridget of Sweden, Richard Rolle, and the *Stimulus Amoris*—and suggesting that it was written in

---

6. On the *lectio divina* tradition, see Jean Leclercq, *The Love of Learning and the Desire for God,* trans. Catharine Misrahi (New York: Fordham UP, 1961); originally published in French as *L'Amour des lettres et le désir de Dieu* (Paris: Edition du Cerf, 1957).

7. Margery Kempe, *The Book of Margery Kempe,* ed. Barry Windeatt (Woodbridge, UK: D. S. Brewer, 2004). All further quotations of the *Book* are cited by book, chapter, and page number from this edition.

8. Rebecca Krug, "Margery Kempe," *The Cambridge Companion to Medieval English Literature 1100–1500,* ed. Larry Scanlon (Cambridge: Cambridge UP, 2009), 217–28.

9. I am grateful to Sarah Noonan for this suggestion. Though she does not focus on *The Book of Margery Kempe,* Noonan provides an excellent analysis of selective reading practices in her recent article: "'Bycause the redyng shold not turne hem to enoye': Reading, Selectivity, and *Pietatis Affectum* in Late Medieval England," *New Medieval Literatures* 15 (2013): 225–54.

a meditative manner tells readers that it can also be read in such a way, reading whichever parts of the *Book* are most likely to stir the reader to devotion.[10]

For all these inward-looking texts, there is a disjunction between looking inward for religious meaning and accepting the decidedly external authority of ecclesiastical authorities. This disjunction is heightened when texts discuss the Eucharist because the political and theological stakes surrounding the sacrament were particularly high. Although they present their meditations in strikingly different ways, both texts offer a self-consciously orthodox model of lay eucharistic piety as central to the practice of devout reading and to religious devotion more generally. Since Love asserts that the *Mirror* is meant to serve as a "lollardorum confutacionem" (confutation of the Lollards; 7), the Eucharist is central to both his antiheresy agenda and his model of piety. Although Love elsewhere cuts and condenses large amounts of his source text's material, he adds a substantial amount of material on the Eucharist, adding approximately 2,500 words to the treatment of the Last Supper and appending the text with the "Treatise on the Sacrament," which deals directly and exclusively with the Eucharist. Love intertwines his instruction that lay people feel instead of think with eucharistic devotion. Likewise Margery's piety centers on eucharistic devotion. She receives special permission to receive the sacrament weekly and experiences her most frequent and dramatic bouts of weeping and roaring during the Mass. For both texts, affective reading means eucharistic piety and this sort of eucharistic piety demonstrates obedience to the ecclesiastical hierarchy.

LOVE AND AFFECTION

In the *Mirror,* Love presents a model of lay affective reading that is dependent upon eucharistic piety. The Eucharist lays the foundation for two essential elements of his model of lay reading: affective devotion to Christ's body and submission to the ecclesiastical hierarchy through belief in the doctrine of transubstantiation. Love encourages his readers to use his written meditations as intimate scripts, which produce "affeccion" for Christ's body in the Eucharist—a term that, for Love, demands the intervention of a disciplined will. Love recognizes that in order for lay people to read affectively, they must deliberately will themselves away from intellectual or contemplative encoun-

---

10. The *Book* twice names these four texts, in chapter 17 and 58. Scholars have long recognized the *Book*'s debt to Love or, at the very least, another translation of the *Meditationes*. For an influential example, see Gail McMurray Gibson, *The Theater of Devotion: East Anglian Drama and Society in the Late Middle Ages* (Chicago: University of Chicago Press, 1989), 47–66.

ters with the divine. He argues that this paradoxical willful surrender of the intellect, far from being a detriment to the affective lay reading experience, is an essential and appealing element of it.

Scholarship on the *Mirror* has tended to focus on the degree to which the text is spiritually and politically oppressive.[11] In contrast, I want to suggest that one of the reasons that Love's intended lay audience may have found the text attractive is precisely because of the intellectual limitations his model of affective piety demands.[12] Love's vernacular translation of the pseudo-Bonaventuran *Meditationes Vitae Christi* actively encourages its lay readers to submit silently and obediently to ecclesiastical authority, but it was one of the most well-read vernacular books in fifteenth-century England.[13] Though Love's model of devotional reading may not appeal to modern scholars, it certainly held the interest of many medieval readers.

In developing his model of lay affective reading, Love draws heavily on the Eucharist and eucharistic imagery throughout the text, not only turning repeatedly to the sacrament itself but also depicting lay learning as a process of ingestion. Along with adding material that directly discusses transubstantiation, as Sarah Stanbury notes, throughout his narrative of Christ's life, Love urges readers to "behold" Christ's body in a manner evocative of a cleric holding the consecrated host aloft during the Mass.[14] In the proem, when Love first explains his belief that lay people should imagine and engage in simple affective devotion to Christ's body rather than theological inquiry, he compares religious learning to eating, contending that lay people are only able to ingest particular forms of divine knowledge. Love explains that his lay readers are

---

11. Much of the scholarship on Love up until this point has detailed the ways in which Love's attempt to convince his lay readers to be satisfied with lower levels of contemplation and submit their own wills to the power of the ecclesiastical hierarchy is oppressive. David Aers, *Sanctifying Signs*, 1–28; Sarah Beckwith, *Christ's Body: Identity, Culture and Society in Late Medieval Writings* (Florence, KY: Routledge, 1996); Michelle Karnes, "Nicholas Love and Medieval Meditations on Christ," *Speculum* 82 (2007): 380–408; Nicholas Watson, "Censorship." As an exception, Ian Johnson argues that the *Mirror* is an empowering text. Ian Johnson, "The Non-Dissenting Vernacular and the Middle English Life of Christ: The Case of Love's *Mirror*," *The Medieval Translator: Lost in Translation?*, ed. Denis Renevey and Christiania Whitehead (Turnhout, BE: Brepols, 2009), 223–36.

12. I am building off the work of Sarah McNamer and Sarah Stanbury, both of whom examine the affective and aesthetic impact of Love's text despite and because of its oppressive aims. McNamer, *Affective Meditation*, 128–49; Stanbury, *Visual Object*, 172–90.

13. As Michael G. Sargent points out in the introduction to his critical edition, Love's *Mirror* survives in fifty-nine originally complete manuscripts (1).

14. On the eucharistic focus of the text, see Stanbury, *Visual Object*, 172–90. See also Richard Beadle, "'Devout ymaginacioun' and the Dramatic Sense in Love's *Mirror* and the N-Town Plays," *Nicholas Love at Waseda*, ed. Shoichi Oguro, Richard Beadle, and Michael G. Sargent (Cambridge: D. S. Brewer, 1997), 1–17.

"symple creatures þe whiche as childryn hauen nede to be fedde with mylke of ly3te doctrine & not with sadde mete of grete clargye & of hye contemplacion" (10). Love thus compares lay believers to infants and the basic points of doctrine to breast milk. His comparison transforms the lay desire for religious education into an unthinking physical appetite and, by contrasting milk with meat, highlights the fluidity and insubstantial nature of the doctrine that Love believes they should be offered.[15] Love uses eucharistic imagery such as breastfeeding throughout the *Mirror* in order to connect directly the affective devotion to the physical body of Christ and the official doctrines of the institutional church.

Love argues that the goal of his book is to help the individual reader shape the inward self in the image of Christ. As in *Handlyng Synne*, among others, this invisible inner transformation is evocative of transubstantiation. Love immediately follows his description of the *Mirror* as educational milk with his explanation of his choice of *Mirror* as a title, directly linking ingestion and self-reflection as essential to the knowledge of the divine. In doing so, Love, like such writers as Julian of Norwich and Walter Hilton, draws on an Augustinian tradition that regards the soul as a reflection of God. For Love, becoming like Christ is a process of highly literal ingestion. Reading his text should not only lead believers to transform their inner lives in the image of Christ's life; it should also lead to the literal ingestion of Christ's physical body in the Eucharist.

Love tells his readers to base their devotion on direct physical affection for Christ and avoid figurative interpretation. According to Love, readers must approach both the *Mirror* and the Eucharist itself with an affection that does not seek to go beyond the literal. In his discussion of the Last Supper, Love presents the apostles as models of lay readers who must restrict their interpretation of signs as much as possible even as Love himself recognizes exegesis as an essential component of eucharistic doctrine. Love explains that he has lengthened the meditation on the Last Supper because it is the most fruitful of all the meditations, "principaly for þe passyng tokenes & shewyngis in dede of his loue to mankynde" (145). In this meditation, Love does not ask readers to identify with the suffering of Christ or the apostles. Rather, Love asks readers to understand what the events signify, in the sense of pointing to a meaning beyond themselves. He offers the apostles' reactions to the Last Supper as models of both devout lay reading and of proper eucharistic recep-

---

15. Love's presentation of religious knowledge as breast milk is also eucharistic, reminiscent of the many images of Christ as a mother feeding his believers from the open wound in his side. Such imagery is discussed most fully in the work of Caroline Walker Bynum. See especially Bynum, *Holy Feast*; idem, *Jesus as Mother*.

tion. The apostles "laft all hir kyndely reson of manne, & onely rested in trew byleue to alle þat he seide & dide" (149). The apostles refuse natural reason in deference to the authority of Christ, an authority to which Love has just compared a medieval priest's. He moves rapidly from historical Last Supper to the medieval Mass in order to show how the two events signify each other across history. Love explains that "þis is þat swete & precious memoriale þat souereynly makeþ mannus soule worþi & pleisyng to god, als oft as it is dewely receyuede, ouþere by trewe & deuout meditacion of his passion or elles & þat more specialy in sacramentale etyng þerof" (149). Love indicates that the Last Supper was a historical event that is memorialized in the sacrament of the Eucharist. But it is an historical event that has the unique power to transform the individual human soul through reverence toward the power of the sacrament both in the present day and during the historical Last Supper.[16] For Love, this event is the most important meditation partly because it is central to the goal of refuting the Lollards but also because it is the most full of signs; it is the meditation in most need of exegesis, which, despite the fact that Love has argued against exegesis, makes it significant. Because of the requirement that lay people be aware of the exegetical basis for the Eucharist and then refuse to reason with it, the Eucharist has the power to transform lay devotion and the way in which individual believers see themselves.

Interpretation of signs and texts remains essential to Love's model of eucharistic piety, even as he circumscribes the limits of such interpretation. Love's explicit turn to the Eucharist in the "Treatise on the Sacrament" foregrounds the disjunction between complex exegesis and a physical, intimate, and emotional piety directed at the literal body of Christ in the host. In contrast to the "mylke of lyȝte doctrine" he promised in the proem, Love turns his attention to "þat preciouse gostly mete of þe blessede body of oure lorde Jesu in þe sacrament of þe awtere" (223). By using the word "mete" repeatedly throughout the treatise instead of "flesh"—a word that would emphasize the flesh of the human body and that frequently appears in Middle English writings on the Eucharist—Love emphasizes the meaning of "mete" as solid food, in opposition to "drink."[17] The term "mete" itself becomes both literal and figurative. With his shift from the literal "mylke" to the both literal and figurative "mete," Love reveals the difficulty of fitting the Eucharist under the umbrella

---

16. As Kantik Ghosh points out, Love's use of "reason" in relationship to the Eucharist often doubles back on itself because Love both argues that the doctrine of transubstantiation is reasonable and that in order to believe you must leave behind your reason. Kantik Ghosh, *Wycliffite Heresy*, 164.

17. "Flesh," 1.d., *Middle English Dictionary*. Ann Arbor: University of Michigan Press, 2001. See also: "mete," n.1.

of "ly3te doctrine." In order to justify the specific details of transubstantiation to lay readers, Love cannot depict the physicality of Christ as something simple and outside the realm of intellectual interpretation.[18] Love resists figurative language by insisting that Christ's "hoc est corpus meum" is and was literally true—the bread literally is Christ's flesh—but he must explain the difference between substance and accidents, and precisely why the Lollards' reliance on Aristotle is wrong but the church's use of Aristotle is right.[19] With his transition from "mylke" to "mete," Love cannot maintain a strong connection between physicality and simplicity because, as Love points out, the Lollards are the ones who insist on simple physicality with regard to the Eucharist; it is the Lollards who see only bread during the Mass (151). Paradoxically, the Eucharist is the cornerstone of Love's model of lay affective reading, but it is precisely on the topic of the Eucharist that he cannot maintain his insistence on "ly3te doctrine." As Love recognizes, it is impossible to describe the Eucharist as only literal since the sacrament itself troubles the boundary between the material world and signification.

Lay devotion to the Eucharist necessarily involves both affective worship of the material body of Christ and an intellectual understanding of how that body is present in the consecrated host. Love overcomes this difficulty by suggesting that, once readers have understood the Eucharist as "mete," as substantial theological learning, they should no longer seek to understand it. Love argues that the Lollard belief that the Eucharist is still bread after the consecration "wiþout doute springen of gostly pride & presumpcion of kyndely witte, in defaut & lakke of lowely drede" (225). The obedient lay person's belief in the Eucharist must be a combination of reason—in order to understand the precise definition of transubstantiation and to recognize that God's omnipotence is capable of overcoming the laws of nature—and submission to the knowledge of ecclesiastical authorities through "drede." As Love explains, "It is moste sikere namely to a symple soule, & sufficeþ to sauacion touchinge þe foreside merueiles & alle oþer of þis blessed sacrament, to þenke & fele in þis manere, þus hauen holy doctours tauht, & holi chirch determined, & þerfore þus I trowe & fully byleue þat it is in soþenes, þouh my kyndely reson a3eyn sey it" (227). Love baldly asserts that Christians need to believe in transubstantiation simply because the ecclesiastical hierarchy tells them to. For lay readers as well as for Love himself, devotion to the Eucharist as "mete"

---

18. Love encounters a logical problem because, although he is committed to plain language, he needs to go into complex language in order to defend the Eucharist since the doctrine has little basis in the narrative of Christ's life. Aers, *Sanctifying Signs*, 1–28.

19. According to Love, the Lollards do not recognize that Aristotle only teaches about natural law, but according to holy church, transubstantiation is "aboue kynde" (236).

demands thinking and feeling in a way that is firmly bound by willing submission to the superior knowledge of the ecclesiastical hierarchy.

Love wants readers to experience an intense emotional reaction to the Eucharist, a reaction that involves the will to restrict their own capacities for reason. This particular combination of controlled thinking and feeling is what Love calls "affeccion": not strictly emotion but particularly willed and controlled emotional reactions. For Love, as for many Middle English writers from Walter Hilton to John Lydgate, "affeccion" refers not simply to emotion but to the faculty of the soul concerned with emotion and volition.[20] In Thomas Aquinas's "Treatise on the Passions," for example, even though the passions are movements of the nonrational appetites, there is a moral value to them insofar as they are subject to the control of the reason and the will.[21] For Love, affection for Christ is essential to eucharistic devotion and that emotional response to the sacrament must be willed. Love ends the "Treatise" with an elevation prayer that is to serve as an intimate script for lay people to perform inwardly when they see the host elevated during the Mass. The prayer requests that "Myn affeccion be enflaumede with fire of þi loue" through the encounter with the sacrament (238). Love urges his lay readers to pray both with affection and for affection to be generated through the Eucharist. Though Love invokes Richard Rolle's model of affective and ecstatic divine contemplation through using the phrase "fire of love," Love overtly restricts his readers from attempting to engage in a contemplative life.[22]

Like Archbishop Arundel, Love recognizes that the independent thinking of lay people poses a potential threat to the institutional church, and he asks for lay participation in the avoidance of such thought. "Affeccion" toward the Eucharist becomes both an emotional desire for union with Christ and an obligation to believe in the doctrine of transubstantiation. Love urges readers that the Eucharist "be prentede euer in oure mynde, & to be bisily kept in þe inwarde affeccion of þe herte" (224). Much as the *Pearl*-poet regards ritual repetition as essential to spiritual reform, Love suggests that through the repetition of the liturgy, Christ's sacrifice ought to become imprinted on the hearts of believers and then finally move to believers' hearts. In doing so, Christ's memory will be "prentede in þe herte" (224). Far from being the first

---

20. "Affeccion," *MED*.

21. Aquinas, *Summa Theologiae*, 1a.2ae.24, 1.

22. The phrase "fire of þi loue" appears to be original to Love's version of the prayer. His source, the *Seven Poyntes of Trewe Love and Everlastynge Wisdome*, asks that "myne affeccyone be flawmed and kyndelyd." Cited in Sargent's introduction to the *Mirror*, 72.

step or the simplest in producing piety, the proper emotion has to be consciously produced and produced in response to church rituals.[23]

For Love, the Eucharist is a tool for the control and containment of both lay affect and lay cognition, but significantly, he believes that lay people must choose this discipline; such containment cannot happen exclusively by restricting access to sacred or controversial texts. Love encourages repetition and emotion as ways for the laity to think about the divine, even as he recognizes that repetition and emotion are not entirely distinct from the rational and the new. Repetition always involves the potential for change, and as Love's use of "affeccion" shows, feeling is never fully distinct from thinking.[24] Love tells readers that their "affeccion" for the host must remain private, not interfering with the social world or the hierarchy of the church. In order to convince readers of this idea, he provides two exempla—one of Edward the Confessor and one of Hugh of Lincoln—of holy men who had miraculous encounters with the consecrated host but decide to keep the experience "priuey" and away from "þe comune knowing" (230, 229). In order to preserve the holiness of the experiences of the host, such experiences must be individual and internal. Even moments of ecstatic union with Christ must be disciplined and contained.

Love presents this lay "affeccion" for the Eucharist as a sort of masochistic pleasure, derived from the laity's consent to their own submission. Affective devotion to the host includes not only attempts to identify with the crucified body of Christ in the host but also a paradoxically willing surrender of will to the ecclesiastical hierarchy.[25] For all of its condescension, Love's model of eucharistic piety is surprisingly dependent upon the will of lay readers. Throughout the *Mirror*, Love encourages readers to "behold" imagined events of Christ's life and consider them "inwardly," placing his reader as audience to the events he describes, watching and feeling but not interacting with events as they unfold.[26] The language of beholding is much less frequent in the "Trea-

---

23. Although "affeccion" is a state of thinking and feeling rather than an utterance, Love's version of "affeccion" is much like William Reddy's "emotives": emotional expressions that are "an attempt to call up the emotion that is expressed in an attempt to feel what one says one feels." Jan Plamper, "The History of Emotions: An Interview with William Reddy, Barbara Rosenwein, and Peter Stearns." *History and Theory* 49 (2010): 237–65.

24. As Sarah McNamer notes, in opposition to scholarship that regards Love's writing as wholly oppressive, "Is feeling really so innocent, so unproductive, so distinct from the rational? Do 'rounds' always lead nowhere or always back to tradition? Not always." *Affective Meditation*, 148–49.

25. As Sarah Stanbury puts it, "Central to the pleasure of the text is a forfeiture of will." Stanbury, *Visual Object*, 187.

26. On Love's use of "behold," see Stanbury, *Visual Object*, and McNamer, *Affective Meditation*, 119–49. On Love's emphasis on inwardness, see Bryan, *Looking Inward*, 49–54.

tise," largely since the lay reader already knows to "behold" the Eucharist because it is exactly what the individual lay believer does during the Mass—stands back and beholds the host at the elevation. Unlike the events in the text that must be imagined, the Mass is an event that Love's readers presumably see at least once a week. Thus, the "Treatise," as the conclusion to the *Mirror,* reaffirms the indispensability of the clergy as the public displayers of Christ's body and the role of the laity as audience.[27] Just as the host contains Christ's body, lay believers are meant to contain their own spiritual experiences, willing themselves to feel and feel silently. Love offers a model of lay reading centered on the deliberate choice to focus on the literal level of both text and sacrament; in doing so, Love provides readers with the opportunity to choose a surrender of the will to the ecclesiastical hierarchy.

CORPUS MYSTICUM AND MARGERY KEMPE

The Book of Margery Kempe is both an enactment and an extension of Love's eucharistic model of lay devotional reading. Not only is the *Mirror* a primary source for many of Margery's meditations, but she also embodies many of Love's ideals: throughout the *Book,* Margery expresses a strong preference for emotional and physical forms of devotion in opposition to more intellectual and contemplative forms, and she intently structures her spiritual practice around the Eucharist. Like the *Mirror,* the *Book* focuses on such devotional issues as the relationship between the Eucharist and lay intellect, the relationship between the Eucharist and the lay community as a whole, and the importance of bodily, affective devotion to the consecrated host.

However, the *Book* enlarges Love's focus on the laity to consider more directly the communal nature of eucharistic piety. Though Margery views her own eucharistic devotion as a primarily individual encounter with the divine, the *Book* progressively depicts her piety as having communal significance. Margery's dramatic eucharistic piety reveals to readers the separation between Christ's physical body and the flawed, fragmented community of believers that is supposed to signify the body of Christ. The *Book* critiques the medieval English community's failure to follow its own beliefs—by engaging in sloth or lechery, for example—and therefore its failure to fulfill its role as the corporate body of Christ. In a manner more akin to Langland than Love, the *Book* examines the social problems that create a gap between the *corpus Christi* (the

---

27. According to Sarah Beckwith, the *Mirror* reaffirms the indispensability of the clergy—and the role of the laity as blind believers—by reaffirming the Mass as "the public, clerically controlled means of manipulating Christ's body." Beckwith, *Christ's Body,* 64.

physical body of Christ present in the consecrated host) and the *corpus mysticum* (the Christian community which that body should allegorically signify), but the *Book*'s solution to this gap is essentially Love's: lay submission to both divine and clerical authority.

Despite widespread acknowledgement that Margery's piety centers on the Eucharist, there is not to my knowledge any scholarly work focused on this important feature of the text.[28] One of the lasting aftereffects of the feminist recovery of Margery Kempe beginning in the 1980s has been that scholars tend to predominately read the *Book* as autobiography or even a sort of autohagiography rather than the genre that the *Book* explicitly asserts that it is: a religious treatise.[29] I do not wish to deny the importance or value of such scholarship, nor Margery Kempe's real historical existence and authorship. However, by reading the *Book* in this way exclusively, we risk missing not only how the *Book* imagines itself as being read, as Krug has persuasively argued, but we also leave unexamined the central object of Margery's piety: the Eucharist.[30] Throughout this chapter, in order to eschew controversies about authorship as well as to avoid focusing on the *Book* as autobiography, I refer to the voice and inscribed intention of the text as simply "the *Book*" and refer to the Book's protagonist as "Margery."[31]

When we read the *Book* as a devotional treatise, we see that although Margery is certainly audacious in the manner in which she promotes her model of piety—reclaiming her virginity after fourteen children, publicly criticizing lay person and cleric alike—that model is itself profoundly and explicitly in line with the orthodox model outlined by Love. My interpretation of the *Book*

---

28. I wish to take up Christopher Bradley's challenge that scholars attempt to read religious texts for how they "made sense to those persons who created or read them; along with a conviction that the ways in which they made sense to those individuals, not just rationally but emotionally, culturally, and practically, are worth scholarly attention." Christopher G. Bradley, "Censorship and Cultural Continuity: Love's *Mirror*, the *Pore Caitif*, and Religious Experience before and after Arundel," *After Arundel: Religious Writing in Fifteenth-Century England*, ed. Vincent Gillespie and Kantik Ghosh (Turnhout, BE: Brepols, 2011), 119.

29. The vast majority of criticism on the *Book* has focused on the person of Margery Kempe as a real historical figure or as a woman writer. Some of the most influential studies include Clarissa W. Atkinson, *Mystic and Pilgrim: The* Book *and the World of Margery Kempe* (Ithaca, NY: Cornell UP, 1983); Karma Lochrie, *Margery Kempe and Translations of the Flesh* (Philadelphia: University of Pennsylvania Press, 1991); Lynn Staley, *Margery Kempe's Dissenting Fictions* (University Park: Pennsylvania State UP, 1994).

30. Krug, "Margery Kempe."

31. The conventional distinction in scholarship on the *Book* has generally been Lynn Staley's: to distinguish between "Kempe," the author, and "Margery," the character. Sarah Salih has productively argued for using the name "Margery" without drawing any sharp distinctions between these roles. Sarah Salih, *Versions of Virginity in Late Medieval England* (Cambridge: D. S. Brewer, 2001), 171.

as fundamentally conservative thus differs radically from the many scholarly interpretations of it as a work of religious and political dissent.[32] Although heresy and orthodoxy are in the eye of the beholder, it is clear that the *Book* uses the Eucharist as a way of structuring, for both Margery and the reader, a piety that views itself as orthodox. Throughout the *Book,* Margery criticizes individual members of the ecclesiastical hierarchy for their sinful behavior, but she does not criticize either the structure of the medieval church or its theology in any fundamental way.

Margery models a self-consciously orthodox version of lay piety and lay reading centered on the Eucharist. Margery's devotion to the Eucharist is central to the *Book*: Christ instructs her to receive special permission to receive the Eucharist weekly (I.5), she has a vision of the consecrated host fluttering like a dove (I.20), her violent sobbing episodes occur most frequently during the Mass, she puts out a fire in St. Margaret's Church by requesting that the sacrament be brought before the fire (I.67), she frequently observes processions of the sacrament, and she engages in a pilgrimage to see hosts miraculously transformed into blood at Wilsnack (II.4–5). When Margery is accused of heresy and brought before the Archbishop of York, Margery utters a quintessentially orthodox statement of belief in transubstantiation when she explains how the consecrated host "is hys very flesch and hys blood and no material bred, ne nevyr may be unseyd, be it onys seyd" (I.48, 235). The *Book* does not go on to narrate all the questions—"as many as thei wolde askyn hir" (I.48, 235)—but instead lets her clear description of transubstantiation stand in as evidence of her orthodoxy. Her response not only affirms her personal eucharistic piety but also represents her complete adherence to the teaching of ecclesiastical authority.[33] As John Arnold notes, Margery's answer "is exemplary in its orthodoxy—one might even say strenuously exemplary—and cer-

---

32. Scholarship that has emphasized Margery Kempe's dissent includes the following: Carolyn Dinshaw, *Getting Medieval: Sexualities and Communities, Pre- and Postmodern* (Durham: Duke UP, 1999), 143–82; Lochrie, *Margery Kempe*; Ruth Shklar, "Cobham's Daughter: *The Book of Margery Kempe* and the Power of Heterodox Thinking," *Modern Language Quarterly* 56 (1995): 277–304; Claire Sponsler, "Drama and Piety: Margery Kempe," in *A Companion to the Book of Margery Kempe,* ed. John H. Arnold and Katherine J. Lewis (Cambridge: D. S. Brewer, 2004), 129–43; and Staley, *Margery Kempe's Dissenting Fictions.*

33. Scholars who also view Margery Kempe as presenting herself in an orthodox albeit unconventional manner include the following: John H. Arnold, "Margery's Trials: Heresy, Lollardy and Dissent," *A Companion to the Book of Margery Kempe,* ed. John H. Arnold and Katherine J. Lewis (Cambridge: D. S. Brewer, 2004), 75–93; David Lawton, "Voice, Authority, and Blasphemy in *The Book of Margery Kempe,*" in *Margery Kempe: A Book of Essays,* ed. Sandra J. McEntire (New York: Garland, 1992), 93–115; Felicity Riddy, "Text and Self in *The Book of Margery Kempe,*" in *Voices in Dialogue: Reading Women in the Middle Ages,* ed. Linda Olson and Kathryn Kerby-Fulton (Notre Dame, IN: University of Notre Dame Press, 2005), 435–53.

tainly informed by a knowledge of what one should *not* say and where no doubt should be left."[34] Although she will go on later in the same chapter to criticize priests who do not properly respect their own priestly offices, she does not launch a critique of the priestly role. For Margery, any corruption within the church stems from individuals' failures to fulfill their proper roles; there is not a systemic problem with the roles themselves.

The tension between Margery's inward devotion to Christ's physical body and the community's failure to practice similar devotion is sharpest in Book II. As Margery undertakes various travels as an older woman, she is frequently rejected by different groups of pilgrims and communities that find her either embarrassing or annoying. When Margery is offered the opportunity to travel on the feast of Corpus Christi to visit the Holy Blood of Wilsnack—miraculously bleeding hosts that became a site of pilgrimage in the late fourteenth century—she accepts on the condition that she have "good felaschep" (II.4, 400), a condition that implies both a practical concern for her physical well-being and the importance of fellowship to the experience of the Eucharist. After most of her traveling companions abandon her because of her weeping, Margery's guide forces her to walk too quickly, without regard for the fact that she is both aged and ill. Eventually, some generous women have to bring Margery in a wagon so that she can see the Holy Blood. Throughout this episode, the *Book* emphasizes the disjunction between the feast of Corpus Christi, the presence of Christ in the Eucharist, and the startlingly cruel behavior of Margery's fellow Christians.[35]

Margery's piety consistently points out to readers the separation between Christ's physical body and the flawed, fragmented community of believers that is supposed to signify the body of Christ. According to the *Book,* Christ purposefully uses Margery's exceptional and highly individual eucharistic piety to reveal the Christian community's need to reform itself into the just and orderly body of Christ, allegorically signified by the Eucharist. In its opening chapters, the *Book* depicts Margery's initial eucharistic devotion as individual, internal, and centered on identification with the crucified Christ. When, in the fifth chapter Christ tells Margery that he wants her to receive the Eucharist weekly, he presents eucharistic reception as an inward sacramental alternative to an outward and social meal. Christ demands that Margery give up eating meat and "instede of that flesch, thow schalt etyn my flesch and my blod, that is the very body of Crist in the sacrament of the awter" (I.5, 71–72). Not only

---

34. Arnold, "Margery's Trials," 84.

35. As Catherine Sanok argues, Margery's social critique lies in challenging "important fictions of community: the possibility of reconciling spiritual and social priorities and the existence of a community defined by shared religious ideals." Sanok, *Her Life Historical,* 116–44.

is Christ's flesh a spiritually superior food, but her weekly reception also sets her apart from members of the wider community, who receive the Eucharist much less frequently. And indeed, directly after commanding her frequent eucharistic reception, Christ explains, "Thow schalt ben etyn and knawyn of the pepul of the world as any raton knawyth the stokfysch" (I.5, 72). Margery's inward and private reception of the Eucharist will not bring her closer to the *corpus mysticum*, the corporate body of Christ; rather, it will bring her into closer identification with the suffering of Christ at the crucifixion, rejected and humiliated by his community. Christ wants Margery to eat his flesh so that she, too, can be devoured by her community. If the *Book* suggests any identification with the community at all here, it is that she eats Christ in the same way that her community eats her. The identification with the community is thus an identification based on shared sin, not on shared community.

Margery's devotion to the Eucharist is often a marker of her own individual sanctity, setting her apart from the wider Christian community. When Margery has a vision of the sacrament fluttering like a dove at the consecration and desires to have more eucharistic visions, Christ tells her that, although she will not see any more than she has already seen, she should be satisfied because, "My dowtyr, Bryde, say me nevyr in this wyse" (I.20, 129). Christ explicitly tells Margery that her vision ought to satisfy her, not for any specific or rich spiritual meaning it contains, but because Margery's vision is different and superior to even the visions of St. Bridget of Sweden. For Margery, the Eucharist's importance stems partly from her exclusive access to it. Far from representing communal unity here, it represents exclusion. When Margery asks what the significance of this vision is, Christ goes on to explain to her that it foretells an earthquake that will occur out of his own vengeance for the people's sins. The vision signifies the sins of the people and how Christ has deliberately set Margery apart from others. In fact, "The mor envye thei han to the for my grace, the bettyr schal I lofe the" (I.20, 130). Christ initially asks Margery to seek suffering in the form of the human community's rejection in order to receive more of his love.

However, Margery's piety is never private; Christ ensures that her performance of eucharistic devotion is a public sign of the community's need to reform itself. Margery's obtrusive and self-righteous eucharistic piety becomes a call for the community's repentance and, ultimately, the instrument of Christ's mercy. Immediately after hearing about the upcoming earthquake, Margery begs Christ for mercy and asks what she can do to protect the people. When Christ replies, the *Book* details that "owyr merciful Lord seyde: 'I may no mor, dowtyr, of my rytfulnesse do for hem than I do'" (I.20, 130). The *Book* describes Christ as merciful at the very moment at which he is apparently refusing to be merciful and then suggests that he has already offered his people all that he can for their conversion. It becomes clear that the instrument of God's mercy is in fact Margery herself. Margery's status as having a unique claim to holiness is itself a sign of the community's sinfulness and therefore a sign that they need to turn to God for forgiveness. It is noteworthy that Margery never has a bloody vision of the Eucharist as we might expect, such as a child or a Man of Sorrows rising from the host; the visible sign of Christ's body in this text becomes Margery's body, weeping and wailing. When, later in the *Book,* priests try to give Margery the Eucharist privately so that she does not disturb the rest of the community with her sobbing, her weeping becomes even more dramatic so that she needs two men to hold her up while she receives the Eucharist. According to the *Book,* God does not send her these ecstatic outpourings simply for the sake of her own spiritual benefit and her feelings of "the habundawns of lofe" (I.56, 273). Rather God tells her, "Dowtyr, I wil not han my grace hyd that I yeve the, for the mor besy that the pepil is to hyndryn it and lette it, the mor schal I spredyn it abrood and makyn it knowyn to alle the worlde" (I.56, 273). Margery's dramatic reaction to the Eucharist is a result of the public rejection of her. In this way, her piety is not just a sign of her own holiness but also of the community's need for redemption.

The *Book* depicts Margery's singular holiness as a spiritual benefit to the greater community. During a Corpus Christi procession in which the clergy process the consecrated host through the town, Margery follows the procession with what is initially a primarily inward devotion, "wyth holy thowtys and meditacyon" (I.45, 222). The nature of the eucharistic encounter changes, however, once a woman comes "be this creatur and seyd: 'Damsel, God yef us grace to folwyn the steppys of owr Lord Jhesu Crist'" (I.45, 223). It is unclear what this woman's intention is in approaching Margery, whether it is to give Margery a spiritual exhortation to follow Christ or whether she regards Margery as a holy woman who will help her in her own attempts to follow Christ. Both women at this moment are literally following Christ because they are following the consecrated host, so the woman's plea is both for an *imitatio Christi* in the sense that they ought to try to be more Christ-like in their actions and a literal acknowledgement that they are graced to be following the host on Corpus Christi day. Regardless of the woman's intention, her comment highlights the social and physical surroundings in which Margery is engaged, and it is this social circumstance that prompts Margery's ecstatic response. The *Book* narrates how "that worde wrowt so sor in her herte and in her mende that sche myth not beryn it" (I.56, 223). Margery's recognition of the immediacy of

Christ's body renders her physically unable to contain her feelings. Although she is overcome with emotion to the extent that she needs to leave the procession and go inside, she does not leave the Christian community. Rather, eating in the houses of strangers becomes an opportunity for her emotional displays to inspire those who host her to transform their own lives with contrition. Likewise, when Margery asks for the Eucharist to be brought out to stop a fire at St. Margaret's church, she does so because she believes that the presence of the Eucharist will save not just the building, but will be an act of mercy on the people (I.67). Here, Margery's devotion to the Eucharist literally saves a church, a building that metonymically stands in for the parish community. Margery's eucharistic piety is beneficial to the community, both because of and despite how her piety shows her superior holiness.

At the end of Book II, Margery's piety begins to look increasingly individual and contemplative, but through her prayer, she provides a script for readers to perform in imagining a communal intimacy with Christ. The *Book*'s closing prayer offers a vision of a union of Eucharist, Christian community, and Margery, specifically describing how Margery says the prayer in church "knelyng beforn the sacrament" (421). After saying the hymn, "Veni creator spiritus," a Pentecost hymn that marks the historical birth of the Christian church and, as discussed in *Piers Plowman,* celebrates the presence of the Holy Spirit in the Christian community, she begins her own prayer. She first thanks God for the miraculous events of her life and then prays that her weeping will transform the lives of both laity and clergy to make all the world "for to han the mor sorwe for her owyn synnys, for the sorwe that thu hast yovyn me for other mennys synnys" (423). Margery's weeping becomes a good work for the spiritual community. She goes on to pray for mercy for a variety of groups of people and concludes by placing her prayer and life in the context of the lives of saints and biblical figures, such as Lazarus and Mary of Egypt. The *Book* closes by inviting readers to pray with Margery for the union of *corpus mysticum* and *corpus Christi,* a union made possible through eucharistic devotion and the very process of reading the *Book* itself.

READING MARGERY KEMPE AS READER

Margery's plea for communal unity at the end of the *Book* may initially seem disjunctive, shifting from her self-glorification to a prayer for Christian unity. The *Book* invites readers to pray along with Margery for Christian unity; however, this prayer is a particularly challenging one: Margery is a woman who is difficult to like. Indeed, one of the most distinctive elements of Margery's piety for both modern readers and for those figures who encounter her in the *Book* itself is that she is often disruptive, self-righteous, annoying, unsettling, or embarrassing. By presenting Margery as an alienating figure and one with whom it is difficult to identify, the *Book* challenges readers to see Margery as part of the *corpus mysticum*. If readers can do that, they can begin to pray with her for the community and pray for a corporate body of Christ that more closely resembles the community of saints that her closing eucharistic prayer projects. In this section, I argue that Margery's dramatic behavior allows the *Book* not only to show Margery as a model for pious reading but also to ask readers to focus on what it means to read devotionally. The *Book* imagines devotional reading as a process modeled on the Eucharist: it is a process of inward transformation that invites readers to hold in tension the categories of individual and communal, worldly and divine, even as readers work hard to imagine those categories as unified. Following Love's model, the *Book* depicts eucharistic reading as a difficult willed process. For the *Book*, eucharistic reading is a process of willing to be unified with a body that will always to some extent be inaccessible. Such a reading practice requires readers to engage in the often alienating and painful struggle to become one with the body of Christ, both *corpus Christi* and *corpus mysticum*.

The figure of Margery encourages readers to reflect on the purpose and method of devotional reading. As many scholars have noted, the *Book* draws heavily on hagiography, particularly the life of St. Bridget of Sweden, in its depiction of Margery.[36] Although such self-conscious saintly modeling certainly demonstrates a sense of Kempe's own self-importance, I believe that it should also call our attention to how the *Book* was meant to be used, providing a model of a lay person modeling herself on the devotional literature to which she has access.[37] Margery Kempe was almost certainly a real historical figure, but the depiction of her in the *Book* is clearly an amalgamation of a variety of devotional models and, as such, provides a valuable model for show-

---

36. Julia Bolton Holloway, "Bride, Margery, Julian, and Alice: Bridget of Sweden's Textual Community in Medieval England," *Margery Kempe: A Book of Essays*, ed. Sandra J. McEntire (New York: Garland, 1992), 203–22; Christine F. Cooper-Rompato, *The Gift of Tongues: Women's Xenoglossia in the Later Middle Ages* (University Park: Pennsylvania State UP, 2010); Gibson, *Theater of Devotion*; Sanok, *Her Life Historical*, 116–44.

37. Jackie Jenkins has noted that Kempe presents devotional reading as a self-fashioning practice. Jacqueline Jenkins, "Reading and *The Book of Margery Kempe*," in *A Companion to the Book of Margery Kempe*, ed. John H. Arnold and Katherine J. Lewis (Cambridge: D. S. Brewer, 2004), 113–28.

ing lay readers how they are to read.³⁸ *The Book of Margery Kempe* is both a response to books of religious devotion and itself one of those books.³⁹

By repeatedly depicting itself as a devotional book about devotional reading, the *Book* encourages readers to think about how reading might be a transformative process modeled on the Eucharist. In particular, in Margery's exemplum of the bear and the pear tree, the *Book* explores the disjunction between *corpus mysticum* and *corpus Christi*, and suggests that personal transformation through devout reading is fundamental to bridging that gap. Devotional reading is essential in helping the individual believer and the wider Christian community understand and embody the *corpus mysticum*. When Margery is arrested and brought before the Archbishop of York, she tells the story of a priest who sees a hideous bear eat the beautiful flowers off a pear tree, and then "whan he had etyn hem, turnyng hys tayl-ende in the prestys presens, voydyd hem owt ageyn at the hymyr party" (I.52, 254). A hermit then interprets this apparently disturbing event for the priest, explaining how the pear tree represents the priest himself, and the flowers are the beauty of the sacraments and his priestly office. However, because of the priest's lack of devotion, "be thy mysgovernawns, lych onto the lothly ber, thu devowryst and destroist the flowerys and blomys of vertuows levyng" (I.52, 255). The priest particularly represents the bear because he says his mass without devotion and then receives "the frute of evyrlestyng lyfe, the sacrament of the awter, in ful febyl disposicyon" (I.52, 255). The fruit of the pear tree represents the Eucharist, the fruit of everlasting life. This exemplum's clever attack on clerical sin and excess is effective partly because of its central image, an image that has eucharistic implications. If the pear blossoms represent the sacraments, the Eucharist foremost among them, and if the bear's visible defecation represents the priest's performance of the sacraments, Margery seems to be comparing the Eucharist to excrement.⁴⁰ This comparison is evocative of Lollards who questioned the sacred nature of the host by pointing out that

---

38. Barbara Newman argues Margery Kempe's "piety is pure imitation." As Nicholas Watson aptly describes Margery, "Passionate pilgrim, part-time pauper, proponent of purgatory, self-proclaimed martyr, honorary virgin, spouse of two persons of the Trinity and vehicle for the third, she could easily be seen as a chameleon saint: a little bit of this and a little bit of that." Barbara Newman, "What Did It Mean to Say "I Saw"? The Clash between Theory and Practice in Medieval Visionary Culture," *Speculum* 80 (2005): 32. Nicholas Watson, "The Making of *The Book of Margery Kempe*," in *Voices in Dialogue: Reading Women in the Middle Ages*, ed. Linda Olson and Kathryn Kerby-Fulton (Notre Dame, IN: University of Notre Dame Press, 2005), 416.

39. Clarissa Atkinson contends that "Margery's book is especially valuable because it is a *response*" to other vernacular religious writings. Atkinson, *Mystic and Pilgrim*, 218.

40. Lynn Staley also discusses the eucharistic nature of this exemplum. Staley, *Margery Kempe's Dissenting Fictions*, 83–126.

the Eucharist ultimately ends up in "sepibus turpiter fetentibus" (foul stinking privies).[41] However, the excrement is the one element of the exemplum that Margery does not interpret; she leaves the connection between feces and Eucharist unspoken. Rather than focus on what has happened to the flowers/sacraments, Margery forces listeners to focus not on the bear's excrement but on the visible and disgusting act of defecation. In this way, the exemplum suggests that the priest is treating the sacrament *as if* it were feces. It is the priest's performance of the sacrament that is scandalous and revolting, not the sacrament itself. In this way, Margery's exemplum creates a sharp opposition between the sacramental body of Christ and the human body through which that body is produced.

In short, the tale centers on the apparent disjunction between the *corpus Christi* and *corpus mysticum*. In this way, the priest comes to stand for all priests, and indeed all Christians, questioning their worthiness to receive the Eucharist at all. The opposition between the beauty of the pear blossoms and the bear, between sacrament and priest, reveals one of Margery's fundamental points throughout the *Book*: fifteenth-century Christians are not worthy of the body of Christ, and they do not embody Christ's corporate body. Rather, they have transformed the corporate body of Christ into a loathly bear.

Even as the exemplum contrasts the corporate and sacramental bodies of Christ, it provides a eucharistic model of devotional reading, including a model for how the reader is meant to approach the *Book* itself. After Margery finishes the exemplum, a clerk who had previously questioned Margery exclaims that "this tale smytyth me to the hert" (I.52, 256). Although Margery had deliberately not mentioned any particular priest in the tale, the clerk recognizes himself in the tale and later begs Margery for her forgiveness.[42] Margery explains that such an interpretive practice is her intent when she details how a priest that she knows "seyth many tymes in the pulpit, 'Yyf any man be evyl plesyd wyth my prechyng, note hym wel, for he is gylty'" (I.52, 256).

---

41. For example, one Norfolk Lollard, Margery Baxter of Martham, ridiculed the way in which the doctrine of transubstantiation seems to posit that there are thousands of gods eaten by thousands of priests every day and then "comedunt et commestos emittunt per posteriora in sepibus turpiter fetentibus" (consumed and excreted through their rears into foul stinking privies). Norman P. Tanner, ed. *Heresy Trials in the Diocese of Norwich, 1482-31* (London: Royal Historical Society, 1977), 45. Translation from Windeatt's edition of *Book*, 254 n. 4228.

42. Edwin Craun notes that Margery's use of an exemplum here places her social criticism within the category of clerically sanctioned fraternal correction, since she is correcting others' actions without personally attacking them. Edwin D. Craun, "*Fama* and Pastoral Constraints on Rebuking Sinners: *The Book of Margery Kempe*," in *Fama: The Politics of Talk and Reputation in Medieval Europe*, ed. Thelma Fenster and Daniel Lord Smail. (Ithaca, NY: Cornell UP, 2003), 187-209.

According to Margery, the proper way to listen to preaching and spiritual teaching is to avoid looking for the personal flaws of a particular individual, and instead look to see yourself and your own sins reflected. Listeners and readers are supposed to be cut to the heart so that they can begin a process of transformation. When read in this way, the exemplum is not just an exemplum for the priest in the *Book*, it is an exemplum for every Christian who engages in church ritual and receives the Eucharist. The exemplum thus asks readers to transform their inward states and their outward actions toward the community in order to transform the loathly bear into the corporate body of Christ. Just as Margery challenges the clerk, the *Book* challenges readers to look beyond Margery's personal characteristics and to see what her behavior and her words reveal about their own spiritual failings.

The *Book* frequently depicts both Margery and her ecstatic eucharistic piety as alienating to the community around her, and the *Book* thus challenges readers to accept the alienation and distance that is so often at the heart of even the most fervent eucharistic devotion in Middle English texts. Throughout the *Book*, the spiritual identification between individual and Christ, and the unity between individual members of the Christian community, seem to be goals at odds with one another. Numerous scholars have pointed out a tension in the *Book* between spiritual transcendence and Margery's self-identification with the sinful physical world, between metaphor and literal reality.[43] While some scholars have suggested that the text aims to redeem the world and the flesh, others have argued that the text is fundamentally contemplative and rejecting of the social world.[44] I would argue that part of the challenge that scholars have had in determining whether the *Book* is encouraging readers toward a fully embodied piety or a contemplative piety that rejects the physical world is that Margery's piety is fundamentally eucharistic. She loves Christ who is both her real and metaphorical lover and whose blood she really does physically drink on a weekly basis. The Eucharist does not ultimately demand that believers reject either category, nor does it suggest that they are blurred together. Rather, the Eucharist holds these ideas in tension and their

---

43. For example, Nicholas Watson argues that, "Kempe presents her life as following two, apparently contradictory, trajectories: towards ever greater perfection on the one hand, and towards ever closer identification with the sinful world around her on the other." Watson, "Making of *The Book of Margery Kempe*," 418.

44. In contrast to the many scholars who have noted Margery's concern with the physical world, Sarah Salih and Felicity Riddy argue that Margery's ideal is a contemplative one. Riddy, "Text and Self"; Sarah Salih, "Margery's Bodies: Piety, Work and Penance," in *A Companion to the Book of Margery Kempe*, ed. John H. Arnold and Katherine J. Lewis (Cambridge: D. S. Brewer, 2004), 161–76.

irreconcilability is part of what provides the sacrament's ultimate appeal. The Eucharist represents a unity between the world and the divine, but it is a unity that is uncomfortable and difficult for believers to imagine.

Like Nicholas Love's *Mirror*, the *Book* depicts this contradictory and alienating eucharistic devotion as a willed process. As Jessica Barr has shown, Margery Kempe's religious practices are predominately affective, but that affective piety is predicated upon a volitional union with the divine.[45] Despite the often seemingly uncontrollable nature of Margery's weeping, the *Book* depicts her form of bodily affective piety as a choice. For example, Margery is initially unwilling to marry God the Father because she so intently chooses to focus on the physicality of Christ's body (I.35). Although Margery does gradually move toward a somewhat more contemplative model by the conclusion of the *Book*, her piety remains resolutely bodily and affective. In this way, her piety is what Nicholas Love imagined lay piety should be. In the sixty-fourth chapter, Christ tells Margery that he wants a volitional union with her: "Yyf thu wilt be buxom to my wyl, I schal be buxom to thy wil. Wher is a bettyr token of lofe than to wepyn for thi Lordys lofe?" (I.64, 301). Christ defines his relationship with Margery as a chosen mutual loving submission, and he explains that her weeping is a sign of that perfect union of wills. Like Nicholas Love's reader, Margery is a willing participant in her own affective suffering in service of God.

For Margery, this eucharistic reading practice centers on identification with the Virgin Mary. Mary is the perfect image of affective devotion through suffering in many medieval texts and images. She is also a model of willing submission to God in her response to Gabriel's announcement that she is to give birth to Christ: *fiat mihi* (let it be done to me). Margery much more frequently identifies with Mary in her Passion meditations than she does with Christ himself.[46] Part of this tendency to identify with the mother rather than the son comes directly from Love's text's influences on the *Book*. When Margery travels to Jerusalem and stands on Calvary, the place of the crucifixion, she

> fel down that sche mygth not stondyn ne knelyn, but walwyd and wrestyd wyth hir body, spredyng hir armys abrode, and cryed wyth a lowed voys as

---

45. Barr, *Willing to Know God*, 208–31.

46. Gibson, *Theater of Devotion*; Lisa Manter, "The Savior of Her Desire: Margery Kempe's Passionate Gaze," *Exemplaria* 13 (2001): 39–66; Liz Herbert McAvoy, *Authority and the Female Body in the Writings of Julian of Norwich and Margery Kempe* (Cambridge: D. S. Brewer, 2004), 28–63; Tara Williams, "Manipulating Mary: Maternal, Sexual, and Textual Authority in *The Book of Margery Kempe*," *Modern Philology* 107 (2010): 528–55.

thow hir hert schulde a brostyn asundyr, for in the cite of hir sowle sche saw
veryly and freschly how owyr Lord was crucifyed. Beforn hir face sche herd
and saw in hir gostly sygth the mornyng of owyr Lady, of Sen John and Mary
Mawdelyn, and of many other that lovyd owyr Lord. (I.28, 162–63)

Margery's dramatic actions on Calvary are certainly in response to Christ's pain, both remembered and in her vision. However, she does not identify with Christ at this moment. Rather, she imagines herself in Mary's place, gazing on Christ from the foot of the cross. She sees Christ crucified; she does not imagine it being done to her. She is identifying with Mary identifying with Christ. It is the interplay of identifications between Margery, mother, and child that makes this episode so sensational. Christ experiences pain, Mary identifies with him, Margery identifies with her, and the emotion is so powerful that it overflows Margery's body and marks the start of her dramatic public weeping. When Margery later has another vision of the Passion, she wonders how Mary was able to endure witnessing Christ's suffering and exclaims, "Lord, I am not thi modir. Take awey this peyn fro me, for I may not beryn it. Thi Passyon will sle me" (I.67, 309). Although Margery eventually recognizes that her visions are a spiritual gift, she associates Mary with an enlarged capacity for emotional suffering. This sort of suffering, according to the *Book,* is a form of devotion that lay readers should desire and that both Love and the *Book* spend much of their time asking readers to imagine. It is spiritually productive to emotionally identify with the Virgin Mary at her moment of greatest emotional suffering: when she is witnessing Christ's suffering.

This *imitatio Mariae* becomes a eucharistic reading practice, a process of willed suffering in order to become one with Christ. The *Book* positions Margery as a spiritual mother, drawing on and superseding Margery's physical motherhood of fourteen children. In the eighty-sixth chapter of the first book, Christ directly thanks Margery for her devotion to him and particularly and repeatedly thanks her for her devotion to the Eucharist. At the same time, he thanks her that "thu clepist my modyr for to comyn into thi sowle, and takyn me in hir armys, and leyn me to hir brestys and yevyn me sokyn" (I.86, 372). As Liz Herbert McAvoy argues, Margery's insistence on receiving the Eucharist weekly allows her to transform her earthly role as mother into a more spiritual category and

> to assert that the child who will fulfil her will not be that born of her own body, but is the divine child who will *enter* her body as sustenance in the form of the Host and keep her as its figurative mother in a perpetual state of grace. In effect, she will enter a state of perpetual pregnancy, but the progeny

will be a grace which she will hold within herself and which will direct her on her desired path towards perfection.[47]

Here, Christ explicitly links the Eucharist with breastfeeding, but it is Margery who is helping Christ to be fed. Christ feeds Margery through his own body in the Eucharist, and Margery nurses Christ in her soul. Both of these models of ingestion are metaphorical to a certain extent, but they represent the exchange of identities and bodies that the *Book* sets up as the eucharistic ideal. Immediately after Christ tells Margery early in the *Book* that she should begin receiving the Eucharist weekly, an anchorite confirms the legitimacy of Christ's message by referring to Christ as lactating: "Dowtyr, ye sowkyn evyn on Crystys brest" (I.5, 74).[48] When the anchorite describes how Margery nurses at Christ's breast, he conveys that not only is her vision divine but that Christ wants to be intimately physically connected to Margery, and he makes that physical connection through the Eucharist. For the *Book*, the Eucharist provides a physical intimacy with Christ that is both metaphorical and real. The Eucharist troubles the boundary between reality and metaphor, between physical and spiritual maternity, between community and solitary devotion. Christ as mother and as Eucharist brings together the intimacy of affective devotion with submission to a parental figure.

This interplay between intimacy and disciplined submission in eucharistic devotional reading is most fully realized in the *Book*'s retelling of the *noli me tangere* episode from John's gospel. The episode demonstrates that affective piety is a desire to long for a body that is primarily available through mediation, imagination, and figuration. In the *Book*'s retelling of the episode, when Margery witnesses Christ telling Mary Magdalene not to touch his resurrected body, Margery is amazed that Mary Magdalene rejoiced "for yyf owr Lord had seyd to hir as he dede to Mary, hir thowt sche cowed nevyr a ben mery. That was whan sche wolde a kissyd hys feet and he seyd, 'Towche me not.'" (I.81, 356). When Margery refuses to relinquish a physical connection with Christ, she insists on a fully physical form of piety in what is fundamentally a rejection of Christ's command. She recognizes that her desire for Christ's body can never be fulfilled, but she nevertheless will go on desiring Christ's body with an insatiable appetite. Of course, her refusal of distance is in some ways futile

---

47. McAvoy, *Authority and the Female Body*, 49.

48. As Caroline Walker Bynum explains, the image of Jesus as a mother reflected a move in the late Middle Ages toward a more personal and emotional version of God: "It was peculiarly appropriate to a theological emphasis on an accessible and tender God, a God who bleeds and suffers less as a sacrifice or restoration of cosmic order than as a stimulus to human love." Bynum, *Jesus as Mother*, 133.

because Margery is not physically present at the resurrection; she is having a vivid meditation on the scene as suggested by Nicholas Love. In the *Mirror*, Love emphasizes that lay readers should insist on physical devotion to Christ and concludes his version of the gospel narrative by suggesting that "afterward he suffrede hir to touch him, & to kysse boþe hands & feete, or þei departeden" (198). And just as Love imagines that Christ ultimately did let Mary touch him, Margery imagines that, if she were present as Mary is present at the resurrection, she *would have been* miserable to have been refused by Christ. However, what is notable about this scene is that Mary Magdalene has a much more immediate physical connection with Christ than Margery does because Mary is literally in the same historical time and place as Christ. What Margery imagines is that she herself would feel miserable if she were so close to Jesus but unable to touch him. Watching Jesus does not have quite the same effect on her.[49] Margery's insistence on touch ultimately supports precisely Love's version of lay piety: a recognition that there are other modes of piety beyond the physical and emotive, but an active refusal of those forms. By insisting on physical closeness, Margery recognizes that a degree of metaphor and distance will always be between herself and Christ's body. In her influential analysis of this episode from the *Book*, Carolyn Dinshaw argues that "Margery's whole story is a record of her inability to will that tactile contact or accept its inaccessibility—she is unable finally to write herself out of her earthly community and into a spiritual one."[50] On the contrary, I want to suggest that this scene demonstrates Margery's choice to consistently long for a body she knows is to some extent always inaccessible, always treading a fine line between literal presence and metaphorical comparison. Margery is actively refusing a possibility for contemplation offered by scripture and instead choosing to long for a body that she must always regard as at some distance.

The Book of Margery Kempe and Nicholas Love's *Mirror of the Blessed Life of Jesus Christ* emphasize the centrality of the Eucharist to lay devotion and show how the Eucharist functions as a symbol of willing subjection before the divine. In his *Mirror*, Love presents his written text as a tool for lay people to engage in a pleasurable surrender of the will to the ecclesiastical hierarchy, a surrender dependent on the intangible nature of Christ's presence in the Eucharist. *The Book of Margery Kempe* not only enacts Love's model of devo-

---

49. As Audrey Walton argues in her analysis of the tradition of medieval writings on the *noli me tangere*, "Margery's commitment to 'towche' does not merely limit her spiritual self-awareness, but serves to express and deepen her practice of affective piety." Audrey Walton, "The Mendicant Margery: Margery Kempe, Mary Magdalene, and the *Noli Me Tangere*," *Mystics Quarterly* 35 (2009): 5.

50. Dinshaw, *Getting Medieval*, 164.

tion but asks readers to consider the eucharistic nature of their own reading practices by depicting devotional reading as a transformative but often difficult process that does not provide the easy avenue toward affective union that it seems to promise. Both texts ask readers to submit to the Eucharist, desire physical contact with Christ, and recognize that there is pleasure in this perpetual state of longing for knowledge of Christ that they cannot have. Both texts ask lay readers to recognize that this willful submission is not just the best path for their own salvation but also the duty of the lay community as a whole in maintaining the *corpus mysticum* and preserving the holiness of the Eucharist, an allegorical meaning that they should embody but never question. In celebrating the simultaneous alienation and intimacy of encountering Christ through the inscribed material object—both text and Eucharist—Nicholas Love and Margery Kempe draw on and shape the English eucharistic poetic tradition.

CHAPTER 6

John Lydgate and the Eucharistic Poetic Tradition

The Making of Community

More than any other writer of the Middle Ages, John Lydgate purposefully draws on and engages with eucharistic poetics as an English literary tradition. As a monk and a self-proclaimed poet laureate, John Lydgate, the central poet of England's fifteenth century, frequently depicts himself as an authority on both poetry and religious devotion.[1] In Lydgate's poetry on the Eucharist, he deliberately draws on the tradition of Middle English eucharistic poetics in order to reflect on the importance of the Eucharist to devotion and on the way in which he imagines poetry itself to be eucharistic. As Lydgate scholarship has come into its own over the past two decades—moving forward from defenses of Lydgate's "dullness" to historicist explorations of his complex engagement in English politics through poetry—there has been a small but growing critical interest in Lydgate's specifically religious writings.[2] Such scholarship has effectively dem-

---

1. On Lydgate's laureate status, see Robert J. Meyer-Lee, "Lydgate's Laureate Pose," in *John Lydgate: Poetry, Culture, and Lancastrian England*, ed. Larry Scanlon and James Simpson (Notre Dame, IN: University of Notre Dame Press, 2006), 36–60; Larry Scanlon, "Lydgate's Poetics: Laureation and Domesticity in the *Temple of Glass*," in *John Lydgate: Poetry, Culture, and Lancastrian England*, ed. Larry Scanlon and James Simpson (Notre Dame, IN: University of Notre Dame Press, 2006), 61–97.

2. On Lydgate's dullness as poetic strategy, see David Lawton, "Dullness and the Fifteenth Century," *ELH* 54 (1987): 761–99. The recent surge in Lydgate studies and its historicist bent is clear, for example, in the two recent essay collections on Lydgate: Lisa H. Cooper and Andrea Denny-Brown, eds. *Lydgate Matters: Poetry and Material Culture in the Fifteenth Century* (New

onstrated the ways in which Lydgate's poetry makes careful interventions in fifteenth-century religious debates, particularly those surrounding heresy and iconoclasm.³ Extending this important work, my aim in this chapter is not so much to historicize Lydgate as to show how the Eucharist enables Lydgate to explore the spiritual power of poetic form. Rather than suggest that Lydgate's definition of eucharistic poetics is wholly unique, or that his theology, or indeed even some of the individual works themselves, are original or radical, I argue that Lydgate's poetic treatment of the Eucharist is significant because he recognizes and purposefully builds upon Middle English eucharistic poetics by showing how the Eucharist and the poetic have a reciprocal relationship: not only is poetic language a powerful tool for understanding the Eucharist, but the Eucharist is also fundamental to Lydgate's understanding of poetry.

For Lydgate, the Eucharist is central to both his own poetry and the English literary tradition because it is the highest form of figuration, containing and unifying the multiple meanings of "figure"—from physical representation to allegorical sign—in a way that no worldly linguistic sign can do. In one of the only studies on Lydgate's treatment of the Eucharist, Andrew Cole asserts that Lydgate is extraordinary in relation to many other contemporary poets because "Lydgate displays a sacramental way of thinking that always approaches Christ's bodily, sacramental presence . . . through language, metaphor, allegory, and, above all, poetry."⁴ Although I share Cole's view that Lydgate's eucharistic theology is decidedly figurative, I strongly disagree that Lydgate is therefore extraordinary. Far from being anomalous or subversive, Lydgate is deliberately contributing to a vibrant vernacular eucharistic poetic tradition that invites engagement in a process of intellectual interpretation of signs, a reflective and transformative reading process that is both textual and poetic. Through an analysis of Lydgate's poetic treatments of the Eucharist, particularly *Pilgrimage of the Life of Man* and *A Procession of Corpus Christi*,

---

York: Palgrave Macmillan, 2008); Larry Scanlon and James Simpson, eds. *John Lydgate: Poetry, Culture, and Lancastrian England* (Notre Dame, IN: University of Notre Dame Press, 2006). For scholarship specifically on Lydgate's religious writings, see Cole, *Literature and Heresy*; Lisa H. Cooper, "'Markys . . . off the workman': Heresy, Hagiography, and the Heavens in *The Pilgrimage of the Life of Man*," in *Lydgate Matters*, 89–111; Shannon Gayk, *Image, Text, and Religious Reform in Fifteenth-Century England* (Cambridge: Cambridge UP, 2010), 84–122; Fiona Somerset, "'Hard is with seyntis for to make affray': Lydgate the 'Poet-Propagandist' as Hagiographer," in *John Lydgate: Poetry, Culture, and Lancastrian England*, 258–78; Ruth Nissé, "'Was it not Routhe to Se?': Lydgate and the Styles of Martyrdom," in *John Lydgate: Poetry, Culture, and Lancastrian England*, 279–98.

3. See especially Cole, *Literature and Heresy*; Gayk, *Image, Text, and Religious Reform*; James Simpson, "John Lydgate," in *The Cambridge Companion to Medieval English Literature, 1100–1500*, ed. Larry Scanlon (Cambridge: Cambridge UP, 2009), 205–16.

4. Cole, *Literature and Heresy*, 135.

I will show how the Eucharist provides a model for Lydgate's own spiritual poetry. Poetry and the Eucharist share the social function of illuminating the Christian church by drawing the believer into an interpretive relationship mediated by the authority of both the poet and the ecclesiastical hierarchy that leads the reader from figurative language to divine truth. For Lydgate, poetic language both assists believers in coming to an understanding of the Eucharist and, at the same time, is itself a reflection of eucharistic theology insofar as it demands a level of intellectual engagement and self-reflection that has the power to transform the Christian community into the corporate body of Christ signified by the consecrated host.

LYDGATE'S LITERARY EUCHARIST

Lydgate's poetic treatments of the Eucharist demonstrate his belief that poetic language—defined broadly as figurative language which self-consciously engages in literary tradition—is essential to devotion because it demands readers' intellectual engagement.[5] As recent scholarship has shown, throughout his poetic corpus, Lydgate self-consciously represents his poems as highly aesthetic literary artifacts, purposefully cultivating an ornate and syntactically difficult style.[6] His often explicit emphasis on figurative language and literary tradition, specifically Chaucerian tradition, distinguish him as a poet uniquely concerned with defining the categories of the literary and the poetic.[7] Throughout his many discussions of the Eucharist, Lydgate repeatedly emphasizes the Eucharist as a sacrament understood through figurative language and draws on the polysemy of the Middle English word "figure" to explore the ways in which the Eucharist draws on and informs literary aesthetics. In Lydgate's poetry, the term "figure" can, and frequently does, refer to a whole range of meanings, including a person's bodily form, a material representa-

---

5. Gayk makes a similar point, focusing on Lydgate's use of images rather than figurative language specifically. In her reading of one of Lydgate's lyrics on the pieta, she points out that Lydgate's "democratic insistence on the capacity of 'folkys all' to read complex visual figures with the exegetical skill of 'doctors' is surprising given the frequent infantilization of the laity by Lydgate's clerical contemporaries." Gayk, *Image, Text, and Religious Reform*, 85. My definition of the poetic here draws on Maura Nolan's definition of the category of the literary in relation to Lydgate: she offers "two main assumptions about what the term literary means: first, that a text is literary if it uses figurative language, and second, that the idea of the literary implies a notion of 'tradition,' of a group of texts joined together somehow by a common theme or purpose." Maura Nolan, "Lydgate's Worst Poem," in *Lydgate Matters*, 72.

6. On Lydgate's style, see especially Phillipa Hardman, "Lydgate's Uneasy Syntax," in *John Lydgate: Poetry, Culture, and Lancastrian England*, 12–35; Maura Nolan, *John Lydgate*.

7. Nolan, *John Lydgate*.

tion, a written character, a sign, a symbol, a prefiguration, or even a poem itself.[8] His emphasis on "figure" in his writings on the Eucharist is both a theological choice emphasizing the Eucharist as sign rather than invisible bloody flesh as well as an argument for his own cultivated poetic style as essential to understanding the Eucharist.

Lydgate's poetry frequently draws the reader's attention to the textual and figurative nature of Christ's eucharistic presence. Rather than focus on bloody, literal images of the host as Man of Sorrows or chunks of flesh, one of Lydgate's preferred ways in which to describe Christ's earthly body is metaphorically as bread.[9] The metaphor of Christ as bread that is kneaded and baked through the process of the Incarnation and Passion is certainly not original to Lydgate, but his preference for this particular metaphor demonstrates his emphasis on figurative explanations of transubstantiation.[10] In *An Exposition of the Pater Noster*, for example, Lydgate explicates "panem nostrum cotidianum da nobis hodie" (give us today our daily bread) by explaining that "our daily bread" refers to the body of Christ "Knoden afforn Pilat, baken in thy passioun."[11] By describing the Passion as a bread-baking process, this poem implies not that bread is a vehicle for understanding Christ but that Christ's life is a vehicle for understanding the sacramental bread. Thus Christ's physical earthly existence becomes an historical prefiguration of his physical presence in the Eucharist. Although biblical narratives trace the institution of the Eucharist to the Last Supper, Lydgate's explication of the Eucharist and the Passion depends upon the idea that the bread that medieval Christians receive was not fully baked until after the resurrection. Far from trying to undermine familiar narratives of sacred history, Lydgate emphasizes that Christ's historical body is only accessible to medieval Christians through figuration; the bread, not Christ's historical body, is believers' most direct access to Christ. Even in this brief mention within his poetic explication of the *pater noster*, Lydgate does not attempt to simplify the Eucharist's figurative status but rather demands that readers understand the Eucharist as metaphor, prefiguration, and literal presence at the same time.

In his Passion meditation, *The Fifteen Oes*, Lydgate elaborates on his understanding of Christ's eucharistic presence by suggesting that the ingestion

---

8. "figure," *MED*. Cole and Gayk also note the importance of the slippery nature of "figure" for Lydgate's religious poetry and theology. See Cole, *Literature and Heresy*, 150; Gayk, *Image, Text, and Religious Reform*, 101.

9. This metaphor appears, for example, in *An Exposition of the Pater Noster, The Fifteen Oes of Christ, The Virtues of the Mass*, and *Pilgrimage of the Life of Man*.

10. On Christ as bread, see Rubin, *Corpus Christi*, 145–47.

11. John Lydgate, *An Exposition of the Pater Noster* in *The Minor Poems of John Lydgate*, Part 1, EETS e.s. 107, ed. Henry Noble MacCracken (London: Oxford UP, 1911), line 212.

of the Eucharist parallels the act of reading a poetic text: through intellectual rumination over figurative language, the reader can gain access to truth much in the same way that, through the ingestion of consecrated bread, the believer ingests and literally internalizes Christ's body. This meditation, Lydgate's version of a popular English prayer in which the Eucharist often features prominently, refers to the Eucharist both explicitly and implicitly throughout, for example calling Christ "our eternall ffoode" (217) and comparing Christ's body on the cross to a grape pressed in a wine press (315).[12] Lydgate further draws on eucharistic discourse when he asks Christ to transform him internally with knowledge of the Passion:

> Mercyful Iesu! of grace do adverte
> With thilke lycour wich þou dedyst bleede,
> By remembraunce to write hem in myn herte
> Ech day onys that I may hem reede,
> Close þe capytallys vnder þi purpil weede
> With offte thynkyng on thy bloody fface,
> Thorugh myn entraylles let þi passioun sprede,
> Marked tho karectys whan I shal hens passe.
> (281–88)

In a twist on the motif of the charter of Christ—in which Christ's promise of redemption takes the form of a metaphorical legal document written on Christ's body in wounds—Lydgate asks for Christ's Passion to be invisibly inscribed on his own body.[13] As Shannon Gayk suggests, the "stigmata that Lydgate seeks here are internal texts, inscribed in blood on the heart and meant to be read daily."[14] Unlike a literal manuscript on which the writing is intended to be legible and seen, Lydgate asks for Christ to "Close þe capytallys / . . . / Thorugh myn entraylles," thus inviting the Passion to transform his internal sense of his own emotions and thoughts.[15] This writing of the Passion

---

12. All in-text citations of *The Fifteen Oes* are from John Lydgate, *The Fifteen Oes of Christ* in *The Minor Poems of John Lydgate*, Part 1, 238–50. On the tradition of the Fifteen Oes as well as their frequent eucharistic emphasis, see Rebecca Krug, "The Fifteen Oes," in *Cultures of Piety: Medieval English Devotional Literature in Translation*, ed. Anne Clark Bartlett and Thomas H. Bestul (Ithaca, NY: Cornell UP, 1999), 107–17.

13. On the charter of Christ motif, see Emily Steiner, *Documentary Culture and the Making of Medieval English Literature* (Cambridge: Cambridge UP, 2003), 193–228; Rubin, *Corpus Christi*, 306–8.

14. Gayk, *Image, Text, and Religious Reform*, 112.

15. The word "entrailles" often refers to the internal organs as the seat of emotions and thoughts. See: "entraille," *MED*.

on his heart parallels the spiritual effects of the Eucharist: an ingestion and internalization of the suffering body of Christ that transforms the spiritual condition of Lydgate and, presumably, readers of the poem.

Through figurative references to the Eucharist as well as allusions to the Eucharist as figure, Lydgate depicts Christ as actively involved in forming his own body into a poetic text for readers to ingest. When, in the *Fifteen Oes*, Lydgate refers to Christ as the "plentyvous grape and vyne, / Wich on the cros for our Redempcyoun / In a pressorye pressid with gret pyne" (313–15), he makes the image of Christ's blood more vivid by imagining it as flowing juice and implies that the Eucharist was the primary purpose of the crucifixion. The cross is like a wine press specifically designed to produce physical and spiritual sustenance for believers.[16] When Lydgate describes how Christ operates the wine press with "gret pyne," he emphasizes the intensity of both Christ's pain and Christ's labor in working to operate the metaphorical wine press; Christ's body is both producer and product of the crucifixion. Lydgate suggests that Christ's body in the Eucharist is a text produced for the reader's consumption when he describes Christ as the son "of his [the Father's] substaunce the ffygure truely" (307). On the most basic level, this line refers to Christ as the true bodily presence of the Father's divine essence, but the mention of both "substance" and "figure" in this context alludes to eucharistic discourses centering around the relationship between the Eucharist as figure and the Eucharist as the substantial presence of Christ's body.[17] To be "ffygure truely" implies that Christ is a true human form who is also essentially figurative in nature, a sign pointing beyond himself toward a divine truth. Lydgate asks readers to see a unification of figure and truth in the Passion and the Eucharist. As in many Middle English texts from *Handlyng Synne* to *The Book of Margery Kempe*, both figure and truth are essential for the believer's spiritual transformation.

Multiple modes of figuration, far from detracting from Christ's Real Presence, highlight the Eucharist as a site for spiritually transformative acts of literary interpretation. In Lydgate's *Virtues of the Mass*, he particularly highlights multiple meanings of the word "figure" as well as its synonyms in order to define different kinds of figuration and to show how the Eucharist challenges the distinctions between them. The poem begins its detailed examination of the Mass, as well as its spiritual and worldly benefits for believers, with an invitation to reflect on the priest's vestments. Instead of immediately launching into a moralization or allegory of the priest's liturgical garments, Lydgate

---

16. Like Lydgate's discussion of Christ as bread, this metaphor is traditional. On the mystical wine press motif, see: Rubin, *Corpus Christi*, 313–14.

17. I discuss these debates in detail in my introductory chapter.

asks readers to turn inward, a turn that for Lydgate requires a focus on figurative language. He instructs readers to consider "with all your inward contemplacion, / As in a myrrour presenting in fygure / The morall menyng of that gostly armure" (3–5).[18] By using the term "myrrour," Lydgate depicts the Mass as a process of inward contemplation and an opportunity for self-reflection.[19] However, unlike Love's *Mirror* or texts from the Mirror for Princes tradition, Lydgate does not argue that the poem itself functions as a mirror. Rather, it is the priest's physical appearance that is meant to inspire this self-reflection. Lydgate asks readers to imagine that the priest's physical body or "fygure" is a symbol or allegorical sign for a greater moral meaning. Indeed, it is even possible that Lydgate is not actually describing the priest's vestments at all here since he only speaks about the priest's "gostly armure," which could equally suggest the priest's spiritual preparations for the Mass. In this case, Lydgate invites his readers to imagine the priest's inward state from looking at his body and use that as a text for their own spiritual reflection, which will lead to a higher moral meaning. In this poem, the process of understanding the Mass is a careful act of literary interpretation.

Lydgate complicates his definitions of the word "figure" by introducing the near-synonyms "sygne" and "token" into his explication of the Mass. When Lydgate begins his moralization of the priest's vestments in earnest, over a hundred lines after introducing them in his opening stanza, he describes the priest's amice as "a sygne, a token, and a fygure, / Owtward a shewyng, groundyd on the feythe" (146–47). Lydgate's use of these three words is in some respects redundant since all three mean "representation," surely the primary meaning of the line: the amice is an outward representation of the priest's inward faith. However, by placing these words directly beside each other, Lydgate foregrounds the differences between them. His use of "sign" highlights the priest's actions at Mass as meaningful bodily gestures, and his use of "token" emphasizes the way in which the amice is metonymic: a concrete, physical representation of a related spiritual reality beyond itself.[20] During the elevation prayer that Lydgate inserts after his discussion of the consecration, Lydgate places particular emphasis on the word "figure" rather than the other near-synonyms in order to highlight the way in which the Eucharist implies historical prefiguration. In this devotional script, Lydgate invites readers to express their personal love for Christ, their need for Christ's forgiveness,

---

18. All in-text citations of the *Virtues of the Mass* are from: John Lydgate, *The Virtues of the Mass* in *The Minor Poems of John Lydgate*, Part 1, 87–115.

19. On the use of mirrors as figures for self-reflection, see Torti, *Glass of Form*.

20. I am referring to the ways in which these two words' definitions differ from those of "figure." See "signe" and "token," *MED*.

and their desire for Mary's intercession.[21] The prayer then very abruptly shifts from being a relatively conventional affective elevation prayer to focusing on the ways in which the Old Testament prefigures the Eucharist. Specifically, Lydgate directly addresses Christ in the Eucharist as "pascall lambe in Isaac fyguryd, / Owre spirytuall Manna" (361–62), referring to Christ's eucharistic body as prefigured by the lamb eaten at the Passover, Abraham's willing sacrifice of his son Isaac, and the heavenly bread the Israelites ate during the exodus from Egypt. This jarring shift from affective piety to Old Testament prefiguration encourages readers to see how figurative language is essential to any understanding of Christ's presence.

For Lydgate, as for many of the authors I have considered in this study, the spiritual power of the Eucharist stems largely from its literary nature. At the climax of the elevation prayer in *Virtues of the Mass*, Lydgate brings together affective direct address and historical prefiguration by declaring, "Thow art in fygure, O blessyd lord Iesu!" (369).[22] Although many theologians argue that the miracle of Christ's presence is that it is truth rather than merely figure, Lydgate chooses to emphasize the opposite side of the equation. For Lydgate, the power of the sacrament comes not despite the element of figuration that it necessarily involves but precisely because of the figuration. At the moment of elevation, during which the believer is supposed to come into close contact with Christ's physical presence and imagine his crucified body, Lydgate asks readers to celebrate the multiple figurations that such an encounter with Christ's body entails.[23] At the conclusion of the elevation prayer, Lydgate refers to Christ as "myne aduertence, my mynde, and my memory" (386), three near-synonyms that parallel his earlier sign, token, and figure. These three

---

21. By referring to a "devotional script," I am drawing on McNamer's work on "intimate scripts." By this term, I mean poems or prayers that aspire to guide readers into the performance of devotional or affective states. McNamer, *Affective Meditation*.

22. Cole also emphasizes how this line reveals Lydgate's investment in the Eucharist as figurative. However, Cole suggests that the implications are much more theologically radical than I propose here when he says that "the sequence of lines indicates a phenomenological thought process, always associative and authentically disinterested in essences, substances, or fleshly bodies." Cole, *Literature and Heresy*, 151.

23. For discussions of the widespread belief that seeing the consecrated host, rather than ingesting it, was a form of eucharistic reception, see the following: Charles Caspers, "The Western Church during the Late Middle Ages: *Augenkommunion* or Popular Mysticism?" in *Bread of Heaven: Customs and Practices Surrounding Holy Communion*, ed. Caspers et al. (Kampen, NL: Kok Pharos, 1995), 83–98; Thomas Lentes, "'As far as the eye can see . . .': Rituals of Gazing in the Late Middle Ages," in *The Mind's Eye: Art and Theological Argument in the Middle Ages*, ed. Jeffrey F. Hamburger and Anne-Marie Bouché (Princeton, NJ: Department of Art and Archaeology, 2006), 360–73; Gary Macy, "The Eucharist and Popular Religiosity," in *Treasures from the Storeroom: Medieval Religion and the Eucharist* (Collegeville, MN: Liturgical Press, 1999), 172–95; Rubin, *Corpus Christi*, 49–82.

nouns all refer to human consciousness with varying degrees of emphasis on the relationship between the soul and the intellect, but Lydgate's use of all three reveals his investment in the believer's intellectual experience of Christ. Rather than seeing the intellect and figurative language as barriers to affective union with Christ, Lydgate works to show that such elements actually enhance and heighten the believer's spiritual experience. For Lydgate, the literary becomes the spiritual because poetic language, like the Eucharist, invites readers to participate actively in their own internal spiritual transformation.

THE SACRAMENTAL EPISTEMOLOGY OF LYDGATE'S *PILGRIMAGE*

It would be a mistake to consider Lydgate's emphasis on the reader's intellectual engagement with the Eucharist as a purely democratizing gesture; Lydgate does not remove the need for church mediation or clerical instruction when he describes the Eucharist as essentially literary. In his translation of Deguileville's *Le Pèlegrinage de la vie humaine*, *The Pilgrimage of the Life of Man*, in which a detailed discussion of eucharistic doctrine comprises roughly 3,000 lines of the almost 25,000-line poem, Lydgate draws on the Eucharist as a way of examining the religious authority of the poetic.[24] For Lydgate, the Eucharist reveals the spiritual superiority of figurative language and textually gained knowledge over visual or affective modes of devotion. The poem explicitly affirms the orthodoxy of transubstantiation, and it does so by emphasizing the importance of authority, both poetic and ecclesiastical, to what the poem presents as the correct interpretation of figurative signs. The Eucharist ultimately becomes essential to the poem's central project—the examination of how believers acquire knowledge of the divine through allegory—by showing how literary interpretation is modeled on the believer's interpretation of the Eucharist: both are intellectually challenging spiritual exercises that also demand the reader's recognition of and submission to authoritative meanings beyond the individual reader's subjective experience.[25]

---

24. Lydgate amplifies Deguileville's second recension from approximately 18,000 lines to almost 25,000. My reading of the *Pilgrimage* does not suggest that this attitude toward the Eucharist is distinct from that of Deguileville. Rather, I argue that, regardless of the poem's originality or lack thereof, the poem serves to develop what I consider to be representative of Lydgate's presentation of the Eucharist throughout his poetic corpus. Whether original or not, his presentation of the Eucharist is deliberate.

25. Lisa Cooper offers what is, to my knowledge, the only other in-depth scholarly examination of the Eucharist in Lydgate's poem. Although she also examines the Eucharist as a sign,

The ability of poetry to produce spiritual knowledge is the subject of both Lydgate's and Deguileville's poems; as several scholars have noted, the *Pilgrimage* is an allegory intently focused on examining the ways in which religious allegory functions.[26] As in other medieval personification allegories, throughout the poem, the pilgrim-dreamer encounters literalizations or visual signs of abstract concepts such as Reason, Grace, and Nature; religious personification allegory fulfills its didactic purpose by providing concrete images that aid the reader in learning and remembering abstract moral and theological concepts. The *Pilgrimage,* in particular, focuses on how allegory produces spiritual knowledge by presenting unusually difficult and often bizarre literalizations—what C. S. Lewis refers to as "monstrosities"—of concepts that cannot be literally understood.[27] The most famous example of such literalizations, and one that is central to the poem's depiction of the Eucharist, occurs when Grace Dieu informs the pilgrim that, in order to progress on his pilgrimage, he must remove his eyes and place them in his ears. The didactic point of this image, in simplest terms, is that the reader needs to be guided by the words of scripture rather than by physical sight. However, the grotesque nature of the image challenges readers because of the discrepancy between the visual image and the abstract idea it represents.

Early in the poem, the Eucharist becomes a focal point for the poem's examination of the disjunction between figure and truth in poetry. By insisting that the pilgrim understand the Eucharist as Christ's literal physical presence—both within and without the allegorical fiction of the poem itself—the poem complicates the relationship between linguistic representation and truth because with regard to the Eucharist, unlike the poem's other representations, there is no absolute divide between figure and truth. This understanding of transubstantiation is especially clear in Sapience's defence of the Eucharist against Aristotle's natural philosophy:

---

her primary focus is on how Lydgate utilizes discourses surrounding craft labor in its celebration of the sacrament. Cooper, "Markys ... off the workman."

26. Susan K. Hagen, *Allegorical Remembrance: A Study of* The Pilgrimage of the Life of Man *as a Medieval Treatise on Seeing and Remembering* (Athens: University of Georgia Press, 1990); Steiner, *Documentary Culture,* 17–46; Zeeman, "Medieval Religious Allegory."

27. C. S. Lewis, *The Allegory of Love* (Oxford: Oxford UP, 1936), 269. Nicolette Zeeman, for example, draws on Deguileville's text, which she regards as particularly highlighting a general principle at play in medieval religious allegory more generally: "If allegory always works by juxtaposing unlike terms, religious allegory seems especially often to foreground the unlikeness and the possible discrepancies between the terms it brings together." Zeeman, "Medieval Religious Allegory," 149.

The grettest good most sovereyn
Ys ther closyd in certeyn;
Nat only "ymaginatiue,"
Nouther "Representatiue,"
(Vnderstond now wel my lore,)
Nor "Virtualiter" with-oute more;
But ther yt ys put sothfastly,
(Yiff thow lyst lerne ffeythfully,)
Bothen "Corporaliter"
And also ek "Realiter;"
Both "Presencialiter"
And also ek "Veraciter;"
With-oute al symulacioun,
Deceyt, or any Ficcioun.
(6045–58)[28]

Sapience carefully uses Latin adverbs to describe the orthodox doctrine of transubstantiation and primarily uses vernacular literary words, such as "Representatiue" and "Ficcioun" to describe what she considers to be false and heretical views. It is heretical to view the Eucharist as an allegorical "Ficcioun" equivalent to the other fictions that the reader encounters.

When Lydgate describes the Eucharist in this poem, he presents it as a sign different than the other signs: everything in the poem is words transformed into flesh, but the Eucharist is literally the Word made flesh. The Eucharist is both truth and fiction. After the pilgrim has a rather typical miraculous vision of Christ's flesh in the Eucharist, Lydgate explains the vision's significance through personification allegory and historical figuration rather than a straightforward statement of doctrine. In this vision, Moses, a common prefiguration of the Christian priesthood, acts as a priest and, instead of providing manna, itself a frequent prefiguration of the Eucharist, he provides the Eucharist itself. Lydgate layers in further Old Testament figuration by explaining how the blood in the vision "sempte of a lambe" (3267), referring to the paschal lamb, a common prefiguration of Christ's crucifixion. This series of figurations is decidedly intellectual and textual rather than affective and visual, particularly because this last figuration presents an impossible image: lamb blood that is visually distinct from human blood. By combining personifica-

---

28. All in-text citations of the *Pilgrimage* are from John Lydgate, *The Pilgrimage of the Life of Man*, ed. F. J. Furnivall, EETS e.s. 77, 83, 92 (London: Kegan Paul, 1899, 1901, 1904).

tion and the exegetical practice of reading the Old Testament as prefiguring the events of the New Testament, Lydgate demands that readers interpret the text in two opposite ways. If patristic typological readings of the Old Testament require that readers take a literal historical narrative and interpret it as spiritually meaningful, personification allegory asks readers to imagine abstract spiritual ideals as if they were literal physical presences. Since the *Pilgrimage* operates under the explicit assumption that all readers and believers must necessarily accept the truth of transubstantiation, these contradictory modes of signification and interpretation reveal that the Eucharist is uniquely capable of absorbing all kinds of figurative discourses simultaneously.

The *Pilgrimage*'s insistence on the verbal over the visual—or ears over eyes—is a direct outgrowth of its presentation of the Eucharist as the fulfillment of figurative language. Grace Dieu insists that she must "bothe thyn Eyen take away, / And hem out off her place fette; / And in thyn Erys I shal hem sette" as a condition of continuing his pilgrimage and a prerequisite of eucharistic reception (6254–56). When the pilgrim objects to what he imagines to be a disfiguring process, Grace Dieu justifies the procedure by reminding him that he was initially unable to understand the spiritual efficacy of the Eucharist because "alle thy wyttys wer deceyved, / And lyede pleynly vn-to the, / What they felte or dyde se, / Saue the trouth (& thus yt stood) / With thyn Eryng style a-bood" (6292–96). The Eucharist is her primary evidence of the importance of the verbal over the visual because belief in the Eucharist necessitates accepting the priest's words rather than the physical appearance of bread. Likewise, in her earlier defence of the Eucharist against Nature's complaints, Grace Dieu tells the pilgrim that four of the senses are deceived with regard to the Eucharist, but the sense of hearing makes up for the others because hearing "more clerly in sentence / Haueth full intelligence" (5261–62). The understanding of the verbal over the visual is essential to the poem as a whole, enforcing its focus on language, intellect, and memory, but the starting point for its epistemology is the Eucharist.

The Eucharist is thus the test case that proves that readers ought to privilege language over vision more generally because the verbal holds a larger claim to the highest levels of truth and understanding. After giving her initial eucharistic defence of the importance of ears over eyes, Grace Dieu turns to figurative language, specifically historical figuration, in order to confirm that the verbal is more intellectually and spiritually authoritative than the visual. She claims that the Old Testament prefigures the importance of hearing in relation to the Eucharist when Jacob deceives his father, Isaac, by pretending to be Esau. As Grace Dieu tells it, Isaac is deceived because he erroneously rejects his own recognition of Jacob's voice in favor of the sense of touch: "But the handys that I fel, / The handys ben off Esau" (5308–9). Through this exemplum, which she calls a "fygure" (5317), Grace Dieu presents the moral lesson that the pilgrim ought to "abyde on heryng, and ther reste; / ffully truste to hys sentence; / Yiff feyth to hym, & ful credence; / ffor heryng shal, with-oute slouthe, / Teche to the, the pleyne trouthe" (5334–38). Through this exemplum, Lydgate emphasizes the truth of the verbal both with regard to the sacraments and to spiritual truths more generally. This logic applies to the Eucharist and to Lydgate's own poetry: what one sees can be significant, but words reach a higher spiritual and intellectual level of the soul. Through Lydgate's emphasis on hearing, the poetic becomes a powerful route to truth.

In the *Pilgrimage*, the importance of hearing stems from Lydgate's belief in the verbal, the textual, and the figurative language as essential to religious education. Grace Dieu's demand that the pilgrim place his eyes in his ears is a gloss on Saint Paul's letter to the Romans in which he states, "Faith comes from what is heard, and what is heard comes through the word of Christ" (Romans 10:17).[29] Both Grace Dieu and St. Paul equate "hearing" with an understanding of spiritual truth. For Lydgate's poem, "what is heard" refers to both oral preaching and written New Testament texts. Many of Lydgate's readers may have been unlikely to be able to read or have direct access to the Bible as a physical text; however, Lydgate emphasizes that believers need to understand that the truth of Christ is rooted in the verbal, both oral and written. When the pilgrim initially expresses horror at the idea of transplanting his eyes into his ears because he erroneously imagines the process to be a literal surgical procedure, Lydgate demonstrates that the movement of understanding from the visual to the verbal is also a shift from literal to figurative modes of reading. Lydgate draws on the figurative meaning of sight as understanding in order to then transfer that figurative meaning to hearing; he thereby emphasizes that figuration and textuality are essential to spiritual understanding itself.

Within the *Pilgrimage*, figurative texts provide readers with access to higher levels of spiritual understanding but this movement from eyes to ears comes at a cost: this movement necessarily means less interest in direct physical experiences of truth and an intellectual commitment to believing what one is told. By evoking the image of the surgical removal of the pilgrim's literal eyes, even as the poem insists on this transplantation as figurative, Lydgate also suggests that there is a virtue to a willfully chosen blindness to the external world. For Grace Dieu as for Lydgate, not all figurative language in and of itself is necessarily a guaranteed route to divine truth. The pilgrim and all

---

29. Hagen, *Allegorical Remembrance*, 67–68.

faithful believers need to listen to the correct sources of figurative language: voices of religious authority, including Lydgate's own clerical voice and the voice of the priest at Mass declaring "hoc est corpus meum." Verbal understanding may be more intellectually demanding for readers than affective images, but such understanding involves an increasing amount of obedience and subservience to divine authority, and in this poem, since the primacy of hearing is evidenced by transubstantiation, that obedience is also due to the voice of the institutional church.

Both allegorical interpretation and spiritual understanding necessarily involve submission to an external authority and a loss of immediate access to meaning. When Nature objects to Grace Dieu effecting transubstantiation, Grace Dieu accuses Nature of being too focused on the literal, physical world and failing to recognize that Nature herself falls under Grace Dieu's jurisdiction; Grace Dieu does not so much assert superior logic as superior authority. She encourages Nature to see that "with-oute me ye ha no thing" (3737) and compares Nature to a swine that only sees the food on the ground in front of it and "in hys swynys lawe, / Off hys rudnesse bestyal, / Ne kan no ferther se at al / Toward the hevene, nor the tre / Wher he receyveth hys plente/ That bar the frut for hys repast" (3718–23). Grace Dieu clearly draws on the figurative meaning of sight as understanding, but gives this understanding a peculiarly spatial dimension. The swine who only sees its food in front of it fails to understand because it chooses not to look at the world over any distance; it fails to see the spiritual truth that heaven provided the food, and fails to see even the physical tree from which the fruit fell because it was too far away. Spiritual understanding, in this analogy, demands an acknowledgment of power hierarchies and distant authorities. More than simply a rebuke to Nature, Grace Dieu's swine analogy is clear advice to both the reader and the pilgrim that nonliteral understanding necessitates a surrender to authority—in this case not only divine authority but the authority of the institutional church—and such a surrender involves acknowledging that to a certain extent understanding lies outside of the self.

The importance of authority to interpretation applies both to authorities outside the text and levels of figurative meaning within the allegory itself. After demonstrating the importance of hearing to the Eucharist, Grace Dieu explains the spiritual efficacy of the Eucharist through another allegory: Charity baking bread. It is clear that the baking process is an allegory for Christ's incarnation and resurrection when, for example, Grace Dieu explains that the grain was violently milled by stones fueled by scorn, envy, and derision. Before the crucifixion/milling and the baking/burial, Grace Dieu evokes the familiar patristic imagery of the shell and the kernel, for the literal meaning to be discarded and the hidden spiritual meaning hidden inside, respectively,[30] when she explains how Charity grew grain and collected it in her granary:

> Tyl the thressherys (with gret hete)
> Hadde this greyn ythrysshe & bete;
> And after fannyd yt so clene
> That ther was no chaff ysene,
> And the strawh yleyd a-syde;
> ffor ther ne myghte nat a-byde
> Husk nor chaff, but puryd greyn,
> Nor, no thing that was in veyn,
> Al mad nakyd off entent,
> Out off his olde vestement.
> (5411–20)

The process of threshing the grain refers to Christ beginning his public ministry and thereby both fulfilling and superseding the Old Testament. With Christ's coming, the "chaff" of the Old Law, or "olde vestement," is cast off to reveal the "puryd greyn" or naked meaning of Christ. By claiming that the institution of the Eucharist offers believers clarity because it removes Old Testament historical prefiguration even while asserting the importance of the Eucharist—itself understood as a figure—through an allegorical narrative, Grace Dieu shows that figuration is an essential part of understanding the sacrament. The veil cannot and should not be entirely lifted. By casting away the shell of the Old Testament through his institution of the Eucharist, Christ did not remove figuration; rather, he introduced more levels of figurative meaning. The incarnation of Christ is fulfilled in the Eucharist because it complicates rather than simplifies the available modes of figuration and signification. The challenge for believers is to recognize that certain kinds of figurative signification are more important than others; historical figuration of the Eucharist is less important than the full unification of figure and truth in the sacrament itself.

For Lydgate's *Pilgrimage*, the long parade of signifiers—both within the section on the Eucharist and the poem's long list of allegorical figures—suggests a richness of meaning and a poetic abundance that Lydgate sees as stemming from the sacramental and leading to the poetic. Lydgate praises the value of figurative language both because it places a hierarchy upon different levels of meaning and because it enables the overlap between these varying levels of

---

30. On the shell and kernel analogy, see David Aers, *Piers Plowman*.

signification. Even though one figure always leads to another figure and never to completely transparent spiritual enlightenment, the constant entangling of lines of signification provides readers with a sense of how Lydgate means to depict the transcendent and the true. Rather than leading to the collapse of signifier and signified, the Eucharist is the site of the multiplication of both, providing an abundance of language and an abundance of meaning. At the same time, the interpretive hierarchies the *Pilgrimage* proposes also suggest a social function to the Eucharist, particularly the clerical regulation of lay spirituality.

FIGURATION, COMMUNITY, AND *A PROCESSION OF CORPUS CHRISTI*

For Lydgate, poetry and the Eucharist share the social function of constructing the Christian community through spiritual and intellectual illumination. As he states in his *Fall of Princes*, "God sette wrytyng & lettres in sentence, / Ageyn the dullness of our infirmyte, / This world tenlumyne be craft of elloquence."[31] As Meyer-Lee explains, Lydgate regards poetry as "a mode of illuminating bestowed by God on writers so that they may make manifest eternal truths not otherwise available."[32] In *A Procession of Corpus Christi*, the focus of this final section, Lydgate makes his clearest case for poetic language as a reflection and outgrowth of eucharistic theology by showing how the Eucharist and figurative language are both instrumental in constructing the corporate body of Christ signified by the consecrated host. In this poem, Lydgate uses metonymy and historical prefiguration in order to demonstrate the way in which the Eucharist's figurative language makes religious community possible. In *Procession*, Lydgate effects a medieval Christian community centered on a salvation history made legible through a shared hermeneutics of figural interpretation.

This poem centers on the way in which historical figures have made and continue to make the Eucharist intelligible to medieval Christians through written texts. *Procession* is a poem that, as the title suggests, describes a dramatic procession to celebrate the feast of Corpus Christi, and like much of the literature surrounding the feast day, this poem focuses both on Christ's eucharistic presence and the Christian community as *corpus mysticum*, the corporate body of Christ. In the poem, Lydgate describes a procession that

---

31. John Lydgate, *Lydgate's Fall of Princes*, ed. Henry Bergen, EETS e.s. 121, 122, 123, 124 (London: Oxford UP, 1924–27), 4.29–31.

32. Meyer-Lee, "Lydgate's Laureate Pose," 43.

includes, in historical order, twenty-six historical biblical figures and theologians, beginning with Adam and concluding with Thomas Aquinas. There is no mention in the text itself that it is a script or performance record—although it is certainly a possibility—but Lydgate invites his reader to imagine it as a physical procession of important religious men who prefigure, write about, or develop complex theologies on the Eucharist.

By constructing a complex web of figurations and significations in order to explain the importance both of the Eucharist and of the Christian community, Lydgate deliberately examines the role of figurative interpretation in shaping medieval Christians' understanding of themselves as the corporate body of Christ.[33] The poem's first stanza demonstrates the interdependence of spirituality and figurative poetics. Lydgate introduces the procession, saying, "For now þis day al derkenesse tenlumyne, / In youre presence fette out of fygure, / Schal beo declared by many vnkouþe signe / Gracyous misteryes grounded in scripture" (5–8).[34] According to Lydgate, this dramatic procession is designed to explain the importance of the Eucharist and the feast of Corpus Christi itself. This illumination must occur through figures, meaning both human bodies and figurative signs, and "many vnkouþe signe." In other words, Lydgate intentionally presents the Eucharist in a way that is unfamiliar and intellectually challenging. The knowledge that readers are to gain about the feast and the sacrament comes necessarily through an intellectual process of disentangling known from unknown, truth from figure, and figure from sign. The immediacy of the physical procession, whether real or imagined, does not make spiritual knowledge more easily accessed; rather it makes interpretation more difficult because it demands that the Christian community view itself figuratively.

Through its use of a procession, the poem joins with writers such as William Langland and Margery Kempe by inviting readers to examine the complexity of the signifying relationship between *corpus Christi* and *corpus mysticum*.[35] Throughout the poem, Lydgate emphasizes the meaning of "figure" as "human body." On one level, the human body is important to the feast

---

33. I agree with James Simpson who contends that Lydgate's exploration of figuration in *Procession* indicates Lydgate's opposition to Lollard discourses: Lydgate's "stylistic pyrotechnics permit intellectually demanding, hermeneutically complex biblical variations. His style distinguishes an intellectually and poetically demanding practise from the plainness of Lollard discourse." Simpson, "John Lydgate," 215.

34. All in-text citations of *Procession* are from: John Lydgate, "A Procession of Corpus Christi," in *The Minor Poems of John Lydgate*, Part 1, 35–43.

35. On the relationship between *corpus mysticum* and *corpus Christi*, see de Lubac, *Corpus mysticum: L'Euchariste*. For an English translation see de Lubac, *Corpus Mysticum: The Eucharist*.

day because it celebrates the human body of Christ present in the Eucharist; however, the human "figure" is also important in this poem as the bodies of both performers and viewers constitute a human community metonymically signifying the corporate body of Christ. As scholars have shown, medieval celebrations of the feast of Corpus Christi often capitalize on the way in which the *corpus Christi* and *corpus mysticum* signify each other.[36] The more traditional Corpus Christi processions included both the consecrated host in a monstrance and representatives of a whole town's community; the corporate body of Christ processed alongside the sacramental body of Christ.[37] As the feast went on to develop in England, some municipalities produced more dramatic processions and less explicitly liturgical displays of devotion to the body of Christ. As Miri Rubin notes, the religious and social fraternity of the London skinners produced a dramatic procession involving *tableaux vivants*; she hypothesizes that Lydgate's *Procession* may be either a commentary on or a script for that particular performance.[38] Regardless of whether or not this particular procession was ever performed, Lydgate's poem certainly expects his audience to be familiar with this sort of physical procession and understand that he is describing physical human bodies, not simply abstract images. Thus, Lydgate challenges his audience to see how each physical human body signifies a historical person and that historical person signifies the Eucharist, which itself signifies both the corporate and historical bodies of Christ. The complex chain of signification begins and ends with a human body, but that body's meaning is not self-evident. Lydgate's audience must continually consider how body relates to body, how *corpus mysticum* has both a figurative and a physical relationship to *corpus Christi*. This relationship is one that involves multiple kinds of figuration that Lydgate sets out to interpret for his audience.

In order to make sense of the poem's series of historical figurations, Lydgate encourages readers to draw on a shared vocabulary of biblical prefiguration and salvation history, a salvation history that demands the audience's inward interpretation in order for it to be made legible. Particularly in the first half of the poem, historical prefiguration is central to Lydgate's understanding of the human body's relationship to Christ. By examining food imagery throughout the Old Testament, Lydgate creates both a history for the Eucharist and a shared history for the fifteenth-century English Christian community. The Eucharist is not merely an object or an opportunity for a one-on-one personal relationship with Christ's physical body; it is also an opportunity to

---

36. Beckwith, *Signifying God*; James, "Ritual"; Rubin, *Corpus Christi*, 213–87.

37. On Corpus Christi processions and their historical development, see: Rubin, *Corpus Christi*, 243–71.

38. Ibid., 238.

engage with a historical community. As a representative example, let us consider the poem's first figure, Adam:

> First, þat þis feste may more beo magnefyed,
> Seoþe and considerþe in youre ymaginatyf
> For Adams synne howe Cryst was crucefyed
> Vppon a crosse, to stinten al oure stryff.
> Fruyt celestyal hong on þe tree of lyff,
> Þe fruyt of fruytes, for shorte conclusyoun,
> Oure helpe, oure foode, and oure restoratyf
> And cheef repaste of oure redempcioun.
> (9–16)

While inviting his audience either to look on a physical performer or imagine one, Lydgate explains that the figure ought to remind the audience of a common historical prefiguration: the first man, Adam, prefigures the second Adam, Christ.[39] However, the way in which Lydgate asks his audience to make the connection between Adam and Christ is astonishingly swift and makes considerable demands on the reader. After spending only two lines explaining that Christ's crucifixion compensates for Adam's Original Sin, Lydgate goes on to compare the fruit of the tree of knowledge to the Eucharist, referring to the Eucharist as "þe fruyt of fruytes." The shift from one kind of fruit to another is swift and implicit, assuming that, by drawing on the conventional figurative relationship between Adam and Christ, readers will be able to make the leap from forbidden fruit to Eucharist through their own imaginative sight.

The interpretation in which Lydgate asks his audience to engage is fundamentally textual in nature, implying that the human community of the Christian church only becomes intelligible through textual representation. In large part, Lydgate creates this textual focus by presenting a procession of people whose identities are tied to writing: biblical characters, writers of books of the Bible, and writers of theology. In his description of Isaac, an ancestor of Mary, Lydgate praises the Virgin Mary, whom he explains is figured in the procession, not through a physical appearance but through an explicitly textual one. Mary's name, spelt "Marye," Lydgate tells us "is fygurde here with lettres five" (40). By excluding Mary physically from the procession, Lydgate is able to keep the entire procession male and thus maintain both the typical gender boundaries of traditional Corpus Christi processions as well as carefully dissociate this lone female figure from the priestly figures that otherwise

---

39. The biblical source for this prefiguration is 1 Corinthians 15.

populate the procession. More significantly, however, this emphasis on Mary's name highlights the importance of the written text to an understanding of the Christian community. Since many in Lydgate's audience—particularly if this poem was intended to be read aloud at a public performance—would be hearing rather than reading the poem, Lydgate's description of the number of letters of Mary's name is oddly distancing. Such a description, much like many of the biblical and theological texts that the poem invokes, asks readers to imagine a text that they are not physically reading. These methods of figuration, through procession or through physical writing, are certainly different, but both involve a level of linguistic and textual interpretation. Whether the medieval audience of the poem would have had access to biblical texts, theological texts, or the text of the poem itself, Lydgate posits that the very idea of Christian community is bound together by textuality, grounded in the interpretation of figurative language.

According to Lydgate, the Eucharist provides spiritual clarity to the Christian church by making figurative interpretation possible. Lydgate emphasizes the supersession of the New Testament by the Old Testament, but does not therefore dismiss the Old Testament figures or the importance of figuration itself.[40] After Lydgate concludes his description of Old Testament figures and writers, the word "figure" itself does not appear again until the concluding stanza of the poem. As he moves forward in history, Lydgate implies a degree of historical supersession such that Christian history fulfills and is therefore superior to Jewish history. Thus, the relationship between the figures in the procession is hierarchical with some figures more fully representing truth than others. In contrast to his description of Old Testament figures, Lydgate's description of Saint Luke is illustrative:

> Lucas confermeþe of þis hooly bloode,
> Tavoyde aweye al Ambeguytee,
> 'þis is my bodye þat schal for man beo ded,
> Him to delyver frome infernal powstee;
> To Jherusalem, þemperyal cite,
> Him to conduyte eternally tabyde,
> Adam oure fader and his posteritee,

---

40. My reading thus differs somewhat from Andrew Cole's reading insofar as I argue that there is a degree of figurative supersession at work in the poem, even if Lydgate does not believe that the figure is a concealment that is eventually removed. Cole argues that, for Lydgate, "there is no figurative supersession, no discarding of form for the sake of substance or meaning." Cole, *Literature and Heresy*, 151.

By Cryst þat suffred a spere to perce his syde.'
(145-52)

In his recounting of Luke's gospel account of the Last Supper, Lydgate returns to the prefiguration from the second stanza—the relationship between Adam and Christ—and clearly demonstrates how Christ's crucifixion is the solution to the problem of Original Sin created by Adam's disobedience. Unlike the Old Testament figures, whom he explicitly names as figures and likenesses, Lydgate depicts Luke as straightforward and literal about the Eucharist in order to avoid any "Ambeguytee." Of course, on many levels, this stanza about Luke does not in fact avoid ambiguity. If we are looking for a statement on or a response to contemporary discussions of transubstantiation and its alternatives, for example, we will not find answers here. Essentially, all this stanza reveals about the Eucharist is that the Eucharist is Christ's body and that this body has the power, through the crucifixion, to provide salvation to all of humankind. This stanza is simultaneously straightforward and surprisingly vague, given the complex doctrinal discussions circulating around the Eucharist during the fifteenth century. However, Lydgate claims that Luke dispels ambiguity insofar as he fulfills the prophecies and prefigurations of the Old Testament. In that sense, with the coming of Christ and the institution of the Eucharist, figurative language from the Old Testament is clearer because it now signifies the historical person of Christ, but the veil of figuration does not disappear altogether. Lydgate still uses figuration to describe those who lived and wrote after the coming of Christ, but he suggests that Christ's eucharistic presence makes such figuration intelligible.

As in the *Pilgrimage*, the figurative interpretation in which Lydgate asks readers to engage is essentially hierarchical, both with regard to the relationship between figure and truth and with regard to the ecclesiastical hierarchy of the institutional church. In order to demonstrate that the Eucharist is different in kind from other figures in the poem insofar as it unites figure and truth, Lydgate carefully draws distinctions between the terms "figure," "figure only," and "likeness" throughout the poem.[41] When describing Melchisedech's offering of bread and wine, Lydgate cautiously explains that this offering is "fygure oonly of þe sacrament" (19), indicating that there is a distinction between the Eucharist—which is both figure and truth—and other symbols that do not contain and effect what they signify. All the figures in the poem are like

---

41. In contrast, Cole argues that Lydgate does not make such a sharp distinction. While it is true, as Cole argues, that this poem does not go behind appearances in order to make a direct statement on the true form of Christ's sacramental body, I would argue that this interest in the figure is not a radical theological move. Cole, *Literature and Heresy*, 150.

the Eucharist insofar as they carry meaning across time; have a relationship to physical bodies, texts, and the body of Christ; and point to a divine truth, but not every figure operates in precisely the same way. When Lydgate uses the term "likeness," it has a much narrower range of meaning than "figure," suggesting primarily resemblance. So, for example, manna is both a "figure and liknesse" of the Eucharist because it both prefigures the Eucharist and, as bread, physically resembles the host (53). And Aaron is a "liknesse . . . Of trewe preesthode" because the way in which he performs priestly duties for the Israelites resembles the duties of medieval Christian priests (57; 59). Lydgate does not want his audience to equate manna with the Eucharist or to equate Aaron with Christian priests. Rather, he continually reminds his audience that there is a difference between different kinds of figuration and resemblance. The Eucharist makes possible an enfolding of figure and truth that is not fully possible outside of a sacramental context. Lydgate encourages readers to engage in poetic interpretation while recognizing that such interpretation has limits that have been defined by a wider church community and ecclesiastical hierarchy that extend beyond the individual reader's subjective experience.

Procession emphasizes how its own use of figurative language makes the social event of Corpus Christi legible as a feast that draws together a human Christian community across temporal boundaries. The poem's figurative language, modeled on the Eucharist itself, invites readers to see themselves as actively engaged in salvation history through poetic interpretation. In the closing stanza, Lydgate reintroduces the word "figure" in order to encourage readers to see how the Eucharist makes possible their own engagement in the history of figuration that the poem presents. He concludes:

> With þeos figures shewed in youre presence,
> By diuers liknesses you to doo plesaunce,
> Resceiueþe hem with devoute reverence,
> Þis bred of lyfe yee kepe in Remembraunce
> Oute of þis Egipte of worldely grevaunce,
> Youre restoratyff celestyal manna,
> Of which God graunt eternal suffysaunce
> Where aungels sing everlasting Osanna.
> (217–24)

He acknowledges that part of the function of figuration is to entertain readers and to provide them with aesthetic pleasure, and through this aesthetic pleasure, readers are meant to see how their own lives are also part of this figural history and web of significations. He refers to manna once again as a prefiguration of the Eucharist, but then suggests that the Exodus narrative is not only a prefiguration of Christ but also a tropological allegory prefiguring Christians' exile from the promised land of heaven. The readers themselves become figures in the poem, both drawing on and referring to the Eucharist. The Eucharist's multiple levels of figuration make it possible for readers to see themselves as participating in that figuration. Lydgate suggests that the community becomes intelligible as a manifestation of the *corpus mysticum* by engaging in the theological and poetic work of interpreting figures.

Throughout his poetic treatments of the Eucharist, Lydgate consistently challenges readers to regard the Eucharist and poetic language as mutually constituting; neither would be intelligible without the other. Both eucharistic devotion and poetic interpretation demand the reader's intellectual engagement and self-reflection, processes that Lydgate presents as leading to spiritual growth both of the individual and the wider Christian community. Instead of merely using figurative language to explain the Eucharist, Lydgate draws on the Eucharist to reveal the spiritual and social importance of figurative language. Thus, as a self-proclaimed authority on the Middle English poetic tradition, Lydgate engages with the vernacular tradition of eucharistic poetics in order to make a claim for the importance of his own highly figurative and intellectual poetic style. It is through eucharistic poetics—with its emphasis on the ways in which inscribed textual objects both invite and deny access to transcendent meaning—that believers can come to an understanding of both the historical and corporate bodies of Christ.

CONCLUSION

∽

However abstract and philosophical some of the late medieval debates surrounding eucharistic transformation may seem, at stake in these debates was the individual believer's hope for redemption. From the Latin language of the liturgy to the infrequency of lay eucharistic reception, the medieval ecclesiastical hierarchy in many ways seems to have designed the Mass to render individual believers impotent before power structures both wordly and divine. Within this social and political context, Middle English eucharistic poetics proved to be a powerful and pervasive discourse because it recognized believers' disempowerment and aimed to transform this alienated experience within the Christian church into a spiritual and poetic asset. Though the diverse authors in this study do not necessarily share the same social and political aims, they do share a belief in the transformative power of the Eucharist that arises from the frustratingly incomplete union with the divine it provides.

As John Lydgate clearly recognized, the eucharistic poetic tradition consistently enables Middle English writers to explore the intersections between the political and poetic. By employing self-consciously literary language that emphasizes communion with and alienation from transcendent meaning, Middle English writings on the Eucharist invite readers to consider the mediating nature of both the institutional church and language itself. For Robert Mannyng and the *Pearl*-poet, a belief in transubstantiation inspires a reflection on the ways in which lay readers can transform their spiritual states by recognizing that access to the divine is always to some extent figurative. William Langland and Margery Kempe draw on the the Eucharist's imperfect allegorical signification of the Christian community in order to argue that allegorical textual interpretation should cause spiritual and social change. Julian of Norwich and Nicholas Love establish the Eucharist as lying at the heart of lay reading practices: all spiritual meaning to some extent arises from the way in which the church's institution of the Eucharist as a sacrament transformed earthly models of signification. For all the writers in this study, the Eucharist provides a model for devotional reading practices as always predicated on distance and frustrated meaning. And all of them, to greater or lesser extents, invite readers to contemplate and question the necessity of the institutional church as mediator between Christ and humanity.

In this regard, the eucharistic poetic tradition is remarkably consistent across the later Middle Ages even though Middle English texts necessarily shifted their political and theological content in response to the increasingly restrictive political climate of the fifteenth century. As many scholars have demonstrated, the religious writings of the fifteenth century tended to be more strictly devotional rather than theological, with a focus on the production of genres such as hagiography, lives of Christ, pastoralia, and sermons. Despite this political climate, vernacular texts of the fifteenth century continue to investigate the Eucharist in both literal and figurative ways. Though the Ambrosian approach to the Eucharist—with its emphasis on the literal presence of Christ's flesh in the Eucharist—continued to dominate, the Augustinian focus on the Eucharist as an allegorical sign persisted even in such a self-consciously orthodox and Ambrosian text as *The Book of Margery Kempe*. A striking example of the intertwining of Ambrosian and Augustinian approaches throughout the later Middle Ages in England is the consistent use of Aquinas's *Pange Lingua* in Corpus Christi processions.[1] In that hymn, Aquinas specifically celebrates the relationship between linguistic sign and literal flesh: "Verbum caro, panem verum / Verbo carnem efficit" (The Word made flesh transforms true bread into flesh by a word).[2] In these two lines, "verbum" (word) is both subject and agent, and the synonyms "caro" and "carnis" (flesh) are both subject and object; Aquinas confuses the relationship

---

1. Rubin, *Corpus Christi*, 284; 246. It is worth noting that, in his discussion of the possibility of being saved through faith alone, Langland cites *Pangue Lingua*, "As clerkes in Corpus Christi feeste syngen and redden / That *sola fides sufficit* to save with lewed peple." William Langland, *The Vision of Piers Plowman*, XV.387–88.

2. Barbara R. Walters, Vincent Corrigan, and Peter T. Ricketts, eds., *The Feast of Corpus Christi* (University Park: Pennsylvania State UP, 2006), 395. Translation is my own.

between "word" and "flesh" both grammatically and logically. He stresses the verbal origin of the Incarnation alongside the verbal origin of the consecration in order to demonstrate that, in both mysteries, words and flesh are mysteriously related and mutually reinforcing. For Aquinas, the figure most closely associated with the highly Ambrosian doctrine of transubstantiation, as for many Middle English writers across the fourteenth and fifteenth centuries, the power of the Eucharist both maintains and confounds distinctions between figure and truth.

As a final vernacular example that demonstrates the historical and generic reach of eucharistic poetics, I want to turn briefly to a later fifteenth-century text that has primarily political rather than theological ambitions: the grail quest narrative from Thomas Malory's *Morte Darthur*. In his narrative, Malory shares many of the same concerns of the other texts in this study, particularly the alienated relationship between the human community, the individual believer, and Christ's body in the Eucharist.[3] In a manner akin to other Middle English texts that depict eucharistic encounters as fundamentally alienating, Malory intently focuses not on the knights who achieve the grail but on Lancelot, the knight who is *not quite* able to find it.[4] More than any of the other knights on the quest, Lancelot becomes increasingly sorrowful at his inability to interpret the allegorical signs immanent in the landscape. The list of Lancelot's misreadings and failures on the grail quest is extensive, including accidentally attacking his own son, being unable to enter a chapel because he cannot find a door, and wrongly attempting to help 250 black knights in battle, not realizing that the knights allegorically represent unconfessed sins. Through his encounter with an array of confusing representations, Lancelot is often uncomfortably caught between feeling that he is enjoying the direct presence of the divine and understanding that he has lost that very presence. Lancelot's frustration lies at the center of Malory's narrative.

When Lancelot finally accepts that he will not achieve the Grail, he is devastated, not because he is utterly barred from understanding holiness, but

---

3. Malory deliberately alters his sources in order to present the grail quest as a quest for Christ's body in the Eucharist. Sandra Ness Ihle, *Malory's Grail Quest: Invention and Adaptation in Medieval Prose Romance* (Madison: University of Wisconsin Press, 1983). On the indeterminacy of Grail symbolism, see Dhira B. Mahoney, "Introduction," *The Grail: A Casebook*, ed. Dhira B. Mahoney (New York: Garland, 2000), 1–100.

4. Scholars have generally agreed that Malory is primarily interested in the figure of Lancelot and encourages readers to empathize with him. See Stephen C. B. Atkinson, "Malory's Lancelot and the Quest of the Grail," in *Studies in Malory*, ed. James W. Spisak (Kalamazoo, MI: Medieval Institute Publications, 1985), 129–52; Raluca L. Radulescu, "Malory and the Quest for the Holy Grail," in *A Companion to Arthurian Literature*, ed. Helen Fulton (West Sussex: Wiley-Blackwell, 2009), 326–39.

because he has understood so very much. After he has a limited vision of the grail, Lancelot declares "A, Jesu Cryste, who myght be so blyssed that might se opynly Thy grete mervayles of secretenesse?"[5] Lancelot recognizes that he was able to see the divine, but he was not able to see it "opynly." When Lancelot puts on his hair shirt, he does so because he knows that the divine is not barred from him; he just experiences the divine *as if* it were separate from him. The pain and confusion that Lancelot feels at his apparent failure is because of the pain that there is no separation: truth and figure, body and soul are inextricably linked. The pain is that he has to live in a world in which those terms appear distinct and intelligible. For Malory, the state of isolation and alienation that the individual subject feels when faced with the possibility of transcendent meaning stems not from a lack of belief in the possibility of language to convey meaning; instead it stems from the certain belief that language and signs do connect the human community with the divine.

Like the fictional figure of Lancelot, mainstream believers were presented with a world that seemed constructed to prevent access to the divine. Through a eucharistic poetics that emphasizes both communion with and alienation from Christ's body, Middle English texts seek to empower readers by giving them a language for defining themselves in relation to social, ecclesiastical, and theological power structures. Instead of telling their readers that they will have an ecstatic moment of union with the divine, these texts frequently make meaning out of what was undoubtedly the most common experience of the Mass: listening to a priest speak in a foreign language and watching him lift a piece of bread above his head that never appears to be anything other than a piece of bread. Surprisingly, this potentially distancing liturgical experience becomes an opportunity for individual Christians to reform themselves and their communities. Eucharistic poetics was a discourse that sought to empower readers by inviting them to contemplate their own access to the divine through ritual and through poetic language. For writers of Middle English, the Eucharist and literary language itself provide vital access to transcendence, and that access comes because of, not in spite of, the limitations placed on the reader's experience of the divine.

---

5. Thomas Malory, *Complete Works*, ed. Eugene Vinaver, 2nd ed. (Oxford: Oxford UP, 1971), 597.

BIBLIOGRAPHY

Abbot, Christopher. *Julian of Norwich: Autobiography and Theology.* Cambridge: D. S. Brewer, 1999.

Ackerman, Robert W. "The Pearl-Maiden and the Penny." *Romance Philology* 17 (1964): 615– 23.

Adams, Robert. "Langland's Theology." In *A Companion to Piers Plowman,* edited by John A. Alford, 87–114. Berkeley: University of California Press, 1988.

Aers, David. "Christianity for Courtly Subjects: Reflections on the *Gawain*-Poet." In *A Companion to the Gawain-Poet,* edited by Derek Brewer and Jonathan Gibson, 91–101. Cambridge: D. S. Brewer, 1997.

———. *Piers Plowman and Christian Allegory.* London: Edward Arnold, 1975.

———. "The Sacrament of the Altar in *Piers Plowman* and Late Medieval England." In *Images, Idolatry and Iconoclasm in Late Medieval England: Textuality and the Visual Image,* edited by Jeremy Dimmick, James Simpson, and Nicolette Zeeman, 63–80. Oxford: Oxford University Press, 2002.

———. *Sanctifying Signs: Making Christian Tradition in Late Medieval England.* Notre Dame, IN: University of Notre Dame Press, 2004.

———. "The Self Mourning: Reflections on *Pearl*." *Speculum* 68 (1993): 54–73.

Aers, David, and Sarah Beckwith. "The Eucharist." In *Cultural Reformations: Medieval and Renaissance in Literary History,* edited by Brian Cummings and James Simpson, 153–65. Oxford: Oxford University Press, 2010.

Aers, David, and Lynn Staley. *The Powers of the Holy: Religion, Politics, and Gender in Late Medieval English Culture.* University Park: Pennsylvania State University Press, 1996.

Akbari, Suzanne Conklin. *Seeing through the Veil: Optical Theory and Medieval Allegory.* Toronto: University of Toronto Press, 2004.

Allen, Elizabeth. *False Fables and Exemplary Truth in Later Middle English Literature.* New York: Palgrave Macmillan, 2005.

Ambrose. "De Sacramentis." In *Sancti Ambrosii Opera,* Pars Septima, Corpus Scriptorum Ecclesiasticorum Latinorum, vol. 73, 13–85. Vienna, AT: Höelder-Pichler-Tempsky, 1955.

Anderson, J. J. *Language and Imagination in the* Gawain-*poems.* Manchester and New York: Manchester University Press, 2005.

Andrew, Malcolm, and Ronald Waldron, eds. *The Poems of the Pearl Manuscript: Pearl, Cleanness, Patience, Sir Gawain and the Green Knight.* 4th ed. Exeter: University of Exeter Press, 2002.

Aquinas, Thomas. *Summa Theologiae.* Blackfriars edition. New York and London: McGraw-Hill, 1964.

Arnold, John H. "Margery's Trials: Heresy, Lollardy and Dissent." In *A Companion to the Book of Margery Kempe,* edited by John H. Arnold and Katherine J. Lewis, 75–93. Cambridge: D. S. Brewer, 2004.

———. "The Materiality of Unbelief in Late Medieval England." In *The Unorthodox Imagination in Late Medieval England,* edited by Sophie Page, 65–95. Manchester: Manchester University Press, 2010.

Arnould, E. J. *Le Manuel des Péchés: Étude de Littérature Religieuse Anglo-Normande.* Paris: Libraire E. Droz, 1940.

Astell, Ann W. *Eating Beauty: The Eucharist and the Spiritual Arts of the Middle Ages.* Ithaca, NY, and London: Cornell University Press, 2006.

Aston, Margaret. *Lollards and Reformers: Images and Literacy in Late Medieval Religion.* London: Hambledon, 1984.

———. "Wyclif and the Vernacular." In *From Ockham to Wyclif,* edited by Anne Hudson and Michael Wilks, Studies in Church History, Subsidia 5, 281–330. Oxford: Blackwell, 1987.

Atkinson, Clarissa W. *Mystic and Pilgrim: The Book and the World of Margery Kempe.* Ithaca, NY: Cornell University Press, 1983.

Atkinson, Stephen C. B. "Malory's Lancelot and the Quest of the Grail." In *Studies in Malory,* edited by James W. Spisak, 129–52. Kalamazoo, MI: Medieval Institute Publications, 1985.

Audelay, John. *The Poems of John Audelay.* Edited by Ella Keats Whiting, EETS o.s. 184. London: Oxford University Press, 1931.

Augustine. *De Doctrina Christians. De Vera Religione.* Corpus Christianorum Series Latina, vol. 32. Turnhout, BE: Brepols, 1962.

———. *De Trinitate libri XV.* Corpus Christianorum Series Latina vol. 50. Turnhout, BE: Brepols, 1968.

———. *Enarrationes in Psalmos, LI-C.* Corpus Christianorum Series Latina, vol. 39. Turnhout, BE: Brepols, 1956.

———. *In Iohannis Evangelium Tractatus CXXIV.* Corpus Christianorum Series Latina, vol. 36. Turnhout, BE: Brepols, 1954.

———. *On Christian Doctrine.* Translated by D. W. Robertson, Jr. Indianapolis: Liberal Arts Press, 1958.

———. *Tractates on the Gospel of John.* Translated by John W. Rettig, The Fathers of the Church, A New Translation, vol. 79. Washington, DC: Catholic University of America Press, 1988.

Auerbach, Erich. "Figura." In *Scenes from the Drama of European Literature,* 11–76. Minneapolis: University of Minnesota Press, 1984.

Bahr, Arthur. "The Manifold Singularity of *Pearl.*" *ELH* 82 (2015): 729–58.

Bailey, Terence. *The Processions of Sarum and the Western Church.* Toronto: Pontifical Institute of Mediaeval Studies, 1971.

Baker, Denise N. *Julian of Norwich's "Showings": From Vision to Book.* Princeton, NJ: Princeton University Press, 1994.

———. "The Structure of the Soul and the 'Godly Wylle' in Julian of Norwich's *Showings.*" In *The Medieval Mystical Tradition in England: Exeter Symposium VII,* edited by E. A. Jones, 37–49. Cambridge: D. S. Brewer, 2004.

Barney, Stephen A. *The Penn Commentary on* Piers Plowman. Vol. 5. Philadelphia: University of Pennsylvania Press, 2006.

Barr, Helen. "*Pearl*—or 'The Jeweller's Tale.'" *Medium Ævum* 69 (2000): 59–79.

Barr, Jessica. *Willing to Know God: Dreamers and Visionaries in the Later Middle Ages.* Columbus: The Ohio State University Press, 2010.

Barratt, Alexandra. "'In the Lowest Part of Our Need': Julian and Medieval Gynecological Writing." In *Julian of Norwich: A Book of Essays,* edited by Sandra J. McEntire, 239–56. New York: Garland, 1998.

Bauerschmidt, Frederick Christian. *Julian of Norwich and the Mystical Body Politic of Christ.* Notre Dame, IN: University of Notre Dame Press, 1999.

Beadle, Richard. "'Devout ymaginacioun' and the Dramatic Sense in Love's *Mirror* and the N-Town Plays." In *Nicholas Love at Waseda,* edited by Shoichi Oguro, Richard Beadle, and Michael G. Sargent, 1–17. Cambridge: D. S. Brewer, 1997.

Beckwith, Sarah. *Christ's Body: Identity, Culture and Society in Late Medieval Writings.* Florence, KY: Routledge, 1996.

———. *Signifying God: Social Relation and Symbolic Act in the York Corpus Christi Plays.* Chicago: University of Chicago Press, 2001.

Besserman, Lawrence. *Chaucer's Biblical Poetics.* Norman: University of Oklahoma Press, 1998.

The Book of Vices and Virtues. Edited by W. Nelson Francis, EETS 217. London: Oxford University Press, 1942.

Bose, Mishtooni, and J. Patrick Hornbeck II, eds. *Wycliffite Controversies.* Turnhout, BE: Brepols, 2011.

Bossy, John. "Christian Life in the Later Middle Ages: Prayers." *Transactions of the Royal Historical Society* 6th series, 1 (1991): 137–48.

———. "The Mass as a Social Institution, 1200–1700." *Past and Present* 100 (1983): 29–61.

Bowers, John M. *The Crisis of Will in* Piers Plowman. Washington, DC: Catholic University of America Press, 1986.

———. *The Politics of* Pearl: *Court Poetry in the Age of Richard II.* Cambridge: D. S. Brewer, 2001.

Boyle, Leonard E., O. P. "The Fourth Lateran Council and Manuals of Popular Theology." In *The Popular Literature of Medieval England,* edited by Thomas J. Heffernan, 30–43. Knoxville: University of Tennessee Press, 1985.

Bradley, Christopher G. "Censorship and Cultural Continuity: Love's *Mirror,* the *Pore Caitif,* and Religious Experience before and after Arundel." In *After Arundel: Religious Writing in Fifteenth-Century England,* edited by Vincent Gillespie and Kantik Ghosh, 115–32. Turnhout, BE: Brepols, 2011.

Browe, Peter. *Die Eucharistichen Wunder des Mittelalters.* Breslau, PL: Verlag Müller & Seiffert, 1938.

Bryan, Jennifer. *Looking Inward: Devotional Reading and the Private Self in Late Medieval England.* Philadelphia: University of Pennsylvania Press, 2007.

Burr, David. *Eucharistic Presence and Conversion in Late Thirteenth-Century Franciscan Thought.* Philadelphia: American Philosophical Society, 1984.

Burrow, J. A. *Gestures and Looks in Medieval Narrative*. Cambridge: Cambridge University Press, 2002.

Bynum, Caroline Walker. "Did the Twelfth Century Discover the Individual?" In *Jesus as Mother: Studies in the Spirituality of the High Middle Ages*, 82–109. Berkeley: University of California Press, 1982.

———. *Holy Feast and Holy Fast: The Religious Significance of Food to Medieval Women*. Berkeley: University of California Press, 1987.

———. "Jesus as Mother and Abbot as Mother: Some Themes in Twelfth-Century Cistercian Writing," In *Jesus as Mother: Studies in the Spirituality of the High Middle Ages*, 110–69. Berkeley: University of California Press, 1982.

———. "Seeing and Seeing Beyond: The Mass of St. Gregory in the Fifteenth Century." In *The Mind's Eye: Art and Theological Argument in the Middle Ages*, edited by Jeffrey F. Hamburger and Anne-Marie Bouché, 208–40. Princeton, NJ: Department of Art and Archaeology and Princeton UP, 2006.

———. "Women Mystics and Eucharistic Devotion in the Thirteenth Century." In *Fragmentation and Redemption: Essays on Gender and the Human Body in Medieval Religion*, 119–50. New York: Zone Books, 1992.

———. *Wonderful Blood: Theology and Practice in Late Medieval Northern Germany and Beyond*. Philadelphia: University of Pennsylvania Press, 2007.

Cannon, Christopher. *The Grounds of English Literature*. Oxford: Oxford University Press, 2004.

Carruthers, Mary. *The Search for St. Truth: A Study of Meaning in Piers Plowman*. Evanston, IL: Northwestern University Press, 1973.

Caspers, Charles. "The Western Church during the Late Middle Ages: *Augenkommunion* or Popular Mysticism?" In *Bread of Heaven: Customs and Practices Surrounding Holy Communion*, edited by Charles Caspers, Gerard Lukken, Gerard Rouwhorst, and Louis P. Rogge, 83–98. Kampen, NL: Kok Pharos, 1995.

Catto, J. I. "John Wyclif and the Cult of the Eucharist." In *The Bible in the Medieval World: Essays in Memory of Beryl Smalley*, edited by Katherine Walsh and Diana Wood, Studies in Church History, Subsidia 4, 269–86. Oxford: Blackwell, 1985.

———. "Religion and the English Nobility in the Later Fourteenth Century." In *History and Imagination: Essays in Honour of H. R. Trevor-Roper*, edited by Hugh Lloyd-Jones, Valerie Pearl, and Blair Worden, 43–55. London: Duckworth, 1981.

Cervone, Cristina Maria. *Poetics of the Incarnation: Middle English Writing and the Leap of Love*. Philadelphia: University of Pennsylvania Press, 2012.

Chazelle, Celia. "Figure, Character, and the Glorified Body in the Carolingian Eucharistic Controversy." *Traditio* 47 (1992): 1–36.

Clark, Francis. *Eucharistic Sacrifice and the Reformation*. Westminster, MD: Newman Press, 1960.

Clopper, Lawrence M. "Langland and Allegory: A Proposition." *Yearbook of Langland Studies* 15 (2001): 35–42.

Cole, Andrew. *Literacy and Heresy in the Age of Chaucer*. Cambridge: Cambridge University Press, 2008.

Coleman, Joyce. "Handling Pilgrims: Robert Mannyng and the Gilbertine Cult." *Philological Quarterly* 81 (2002): 311–26.

Colish, Marcia L. *The Mirror of Language: A Study in the Medieval Theory of Knowledge*. Rev. ed. Lincoln: University of Nebraska Press, 1983.

———. *Peter Lombard.* Vol. 2. Leiden, NL: E. J. Brill, 1994.

Cooper, Lisa H. "'Markys . . . off the workman': Heresy, Hagiography, and the Heavens in *The Pilgrimage of the Life of Man.*" In *Lydgate Matters: Poetry and Material Culture in the Fifteenth Century,* edited by Lisa H. Cooper and Andrea Denny-Brown, 89–111. New York: Palgrave Macmillan, 2008.

Cooper, Lisa H., and Andrea Denny-Brown, eds. *Lydgate Matters: Poetry and Material Culture in the Fifteenth Century.* New York: Palgrave Macmillan, 2008.

Cooper-Rompato, Christine F. *The Gift of Tongues: Women's Xenoglossia in the Later Middle Ages.* University Park: Pennsylvania State University Press, 2010.

Copeland, Rita. *Pedagogy, Intellectuals, and Dissent in the Later Middle Ages: Lollardy and Ideas of Learning.* Cambridge: Cambridge University Press, 2001.

Crane, Susan. *The Performance of Self: Ritual, Clothing, and Identity During the Hundred Years War.* Philadelphia: University of Pennsylvania Press, 2002.

Craun, Edwin D. "*Fama* and Pastoral Constraints on Rebuking Sinners: *The Book of Margery Kempe.*" In *Fama: The Politics of Talk and Reputation in Medieval Europe,* edited by Thelma Fenster and Daniel Lord Smail, 187–209. Ithaca, NY: Cornell University Press, 2003.

Crosby, Ruth. "Robert Mannyng of Brunne: A New Biography." *PMLA* 57 (1942): 15–28.

Davidson, Clifford, ed. *Gesture in Medieval Drama and Art.* Kalamazoo, MI: Medieval Institute Publications, 2001.

de Lubac, Henri. *Corpus Mysticum: The Eucharist and the Church in the Middle Ages.* Translated by Gemma Simmonds with Richard Price and Christopher Stephens. Edited by Laurence Paul Hemming and Susan Frank Parsons. London: SCM Press, 2006.

———. *Corpus Mysticum: L'euchariste et L'église au Moyen Age.* 2nd ed., rev. Paris: Aubier, 1949.

de Man, Paul. "The Rhetoric of Temporality." In *Blindness and Insight: Essays in the Rhetoric of Contemporary Criticism.* 2nd ed., rev. 187–228. Minneapolis: University of Minnesota Press, 1983.

Despres, Denise Louise. *Ghostly Sights: Visual Meditation in Late-Medieval Literature.* Norman, OK: Pilgrim Books, 1989.

Dinshaw, Carolyn. *Getting Medieval: Sexualities and Communities, Pre- and Postmodern.* Durham: Duke University Press, 1999.

Duffy, Eamon. *Marking the Hours: English People and Their Prayers 1240–1570.* New Haven, CT: Yale University Press, 2006.

———. *The Stripping of the Altars: Traditional Religion in England c. 1400–c. 1580.* New Haven, CT: Yale University Press, 1992.

Duggan, H. N. "Meter, Stanza, Vocabulary, Dialect." In *A Companion to the* Gawain-*Poet,* edited by Derek Brewer and Jonathan Gibson, 221–42. Cambridge: D. S. Brewer, 1997.

Edmondson, George. "*Pearl:* The Shadow of the Object, the Shape of the Law." *Studies in the Age of Chaucer* 26 (2004): 29–63.

Finke, Laurie A. "Truth's Treasure: Allegory and Meaning in *Piers Plowman.*" In *Medieval Texts and Contemporary Readers,* edited by Laurie A. Finke and Martin B. Shichtman, 51–68. Ithaca, NY: Cornell University Press, 1987.

Fitzpatrick, P. J. *In Breaking of Bread: The Eucharist and Ritual.* Cambridge: Cambridge University Press, 1993.

———. "On Eucharistic Sacrifice in the Middle Ages." In *Sacrifice and Redemption: Durham Essays in Theology*, edited by S. W. Sykes, 129–56. Cambridge: Cambridge University Press, 1990.

Fradenburg, Louise O. "'Be not far from me': Psychoanalysis, Medieval Studies and the Subject of Religion." *Exemplaria* 7 (1995): 41–54.

Freud, Sigmund. "Mourning and Melancholia." In *The Standard Edition of the Complete Psychological Works of Sigmund Freud*, translated by James Strachey, vol. 14, 243–58. London: Hogarth Press, 1957.

Fulton, Rachel. *From Judgment to Passion: Devotion to Christ and the Virgin Mary, 800–1200*. New York: Columbia University Press, 2002.

Furnivall, F. J., ed. *The Minor Poems of the Vernon Manuscript*. Part 2. EETS o.s. 117. London: Kegan Paul, 1901.

Fuss, Diana. *Identification Papers*. New York: Routledge, 1995.

Ganim, John M. "The Devil's Writing Lesson." In *Oral Poetics in Middle English Poetry*, edited by Mark C. Amodio with Sarah Gray Miller, 109–23. New York: Garland, 1994.

Garrett, Robert Max. *The Pearl: An Interpretation*. Seattle: University of Washington, 1918.

Gasse, Rosanne. "Langland's 'Lewed Vicory' Reconsidered." *Journal of English and Germanic Philology* 95 (1996): 322–35.

Gatta, John, Jr. "Transformation Symbolism and the Liturgy of the Mass in *Pearl*." *Modern Philology* 71 (1974): 243–56.

Gayk, Shannon. *Image, Text, and Religious Reform in Fifteenth-Century England*. Cambridge: Cambridge University Press, 2010.

Gayk, Shannon, and Robyn Malo. "The Sacred Object." *Journal of Medieval and Early Modern Studies* 44.3 (2014): 457–67.

Gayk, Shannon, and Kathleen Tonry, eds. *Form and Reform: Reading across the Fifteenth Century*. Columbus: The Ohio State University Press, 2011.

Ghosh, Kantik. *The Wycliffite Heresy: Authority and the Interpretation of Texts*. Cambridge: Cambridge University Press, 2002.

Gibson, Gail McMurray. *The Theater of Devotion: East Anglian Drama and Society in the Late Middle Ages*. Chicago: University of Chicago Press, 1989.

Gillespie, Vincent, and Kantik Ghosh, eds. *After Arundel: Religious Writing in Fifteenth-Century England*. Turnhout, BE: Brepols, 2011.

Godden, Malcolm. *The Making of Piers Plowman*. London: Longman, 1990.

Goering, Joseph. "The Invention of Transubstantiation." *Traditio* 46 (1991): 147–70.

Graves, Pamela C. "Social Space in the English Medieval Parish Church." *Economy and Society* 18 (1989): 297–322.

Greenspan, Kate. "Lessons for the Priest, Lessons for the People: Robert Mannyng of Brunne's Audiences for Handlyng Synne." *Essays in Medieval Studies* 21 (2005): 109–21.

Griffiths, Lavinia. *Personification in Piers Plowman*. Cambridge: D. S. Brewer, 1985.

Grisdale, D. M., ed. *Three Middle English Sermons from the Worcester Chapter Manuscript F.10*. Kendal, UK: Titus Wilson, 1939.

Hagen, Susan K. *Allegorical Remembrance: A Study of* The Pilgrimage of the Life of Man *as a Medieval Treatise on Seeing and Remembering*. Athens: University of Georgia Press, 1990.

Hanna, Ralph. *London Literature, 1300–1380*. Cambridge: Cambridge University Press, 2005.

Haren, Michael. "Confession, Social Ethics and Social Discipline in the *Memoriale presbitorum*." In *Handling Sin: Confession in the Middle Ages*, edited by Peter Biller and A. J. Minnis, 109–22. York: University of York Press, 1998.

Hardman, Phillipa. "Lydgate's Uneasy Syntax." In *John Lydgate: Poetry, Culture, and Lancastrian England*, edited by Larry Scanlon and James Simpson, 12–35. Notre Dame, IN: University of Notre Dame Press, 2006.

Harper, John. *The Forms and Orders of Western Liturgy: From the Tenth to the Eighteenth Century*. Oxford: Clarendon Press, 1991.

Hewett-Smith, Kathleen M. "Allegory on the Half-Acre: The Demands of History." *Yearbook of Langland Studies* 10 (1996): 1–22.

———. "'Nede ne hath no lawe': Poverty and the De-stabilization of Allegory in the Final Visions of *Piers Plowman*." In *William Langland's* Piers Plowman: *A Book of Essays*, edited by Kathleen M. Hewett-Smith, 233–53. New York: Routledge, 2001.

Holloway, Julia Bolton. "Bride, Margery, Julian, and Alice: Bridget of Sweden's Textual Community in Medieval England." In *Margery Kempe: A Book of Essays*, edited by Sandra J. McEntire, 203–22. New York: Garland, 1992.

Holsinger, Bruce, ed. "Literary History and the Religious Turn." *English Language Notes* 44.1 (2006): 1–302.

Horstmann, Carl, ed. *The Minor Poems of the Vernon Manuscript*. Part 1. EETS o.s. 98. London: Kegan Paul, 1892.

"How to Hear Mass." In *The Minor Poems of the Vernon Manuscript*, edited by F. J. Furnivall, 493–511. Part 2. EETS o.s. 117. London: Kegan Paul, 1901.

Hudson, Anne. *The Premature Reformation: Wycliffite Texts and Lollard History*. Oxford: Clarendon Press, 1988.

Hugh of St. Victor. *De sacramentis chrisianae fidei*. In *Patrologia Latina, cursus completus* edited by J. P Migne, 176, Col. 173–618. 1844–55.

———. *On the Sacraments of the Christian Faith (De Sacramentis)*. Translated by Roy J. Deferrari. Cambridge, MA: Mediaeval Academy of America, 1951.

Ihle, Sandra Ness. *Malory's Grail Quest: Invention and Adaptation in Medieval Prose Romance*. Madison: University of Wisconsin Press, 1983.

James, Mervyn. "Ritual, Drama and Social Body in the Late Medieval English Town." *Past and Present* 98 (1983): 3–29.

Jenkins, Jacqueline. "Reading and *The Book of Margery Kempe*." In *A Companion to the Book of Margery Kempe*, edited by John H. Arnold and Katherine J. Lewis, 113–28. Cambridge: D. S. Brewer, 2004.

Jenkins, Priscilla. "Conscience: The Frustration of Allegory." In *Piers Plowman: Critical Approaches*, edited by S. S. Hussey, 125–42. London: Methuen, 1969.

Johnson, Ian. "The Non-Dissenting Vernacular and the Middle English Life of Christ: The Case of Love's *Mirror*." In *The Medieval Translator: Lost in Translation?* edited by Denis Renevey and Christiania Whitehead, 223–36. Turnhout, BE: Brepols, 2009.

Julian of Norwich. *The Writings of Julian of Norwich: "A Vision Showed to a Devout Woman" and "A Revelation of Love*." Edited by Nicholas Watson and Jacqueline Jenkins. University Park: Pennsylvania State University Press, 2005.

Jungmann, Joseph A. *The Mass of the Roman Rite: Its Origins and Development*. Translated by Francis A. Brunner. Dublin: Four Courts Press, 1951.

Justice, Steven. "Eucharistic Miracle and Eucharistic Doubt." *Journal of Medieval and Early Modern Studies* 42 (2012): 308–32.

Karnes, Michelle. "Julian of Norwich's Art of Interpretation." *Journal of Medieval and Early Modern Studies* 42 (2012): 333–63.

———. "Nicholas Love and Medieval Meditations on Christ." *Speculum* 82 (2007): 380–408.

Kemmler, Fritz. *'Exempla' in Context: A Historical and Critical Study of Robert Mannyng of Brunne's 'Handlyng Synne.'* Tübingen, DE: Narr, 1984.

Kempe, Margery. *The Book of Margery Kempe*, edited by Barry Windeatt. Woodbridge, UK: D. S. Brewer, 2004.

Kennedy, V. L. "The Moment of Consecration and the Elevation of the Host." *Medieval Studies* 6 (1944): 121–50.

Knox, Ronald. "Finding the Law: Developments in Canon Law during the Gregorian Reform." *Studi Gregoriani* 9 (1972): 419–66.

Krug, Rebecca. "The Fifteen Oes." In *Cultures of Piety: Medieval English Devotional Literature in Translation,* edited by Anne Clark Bartlett and Thomas H. Bestul, 107–17. Ithaca, NY: Cornell University Press, 1999.

———. "Margery Kempe." In *The Cambridge Companion to Medieval English Literature 1100–1500,* edited by Larry Scanlon, 217–28. Cambridge: Cambridge University Press, 2009.

Langland, William. *The Vision of Piers Plowman.* Edited by A. V. C. Schmidt. 2nd ed. London: Dent/Everyman, 1995.

Lawton, David. "Dullness and the Fifteenth Century." *ELH* 54 (1987): 761–99.

———. "Voice, Authority, and Blasphemy in *The Book of Margery Kempe*." In *Margery Kempe: A Book of Essays,* edited by Sandra J. McEntire, 93–115. New York: Garland, 1992.

Lay Folks Mass Book. Edited by Thomas Frederick Simmons, EETS o.s. 71. London: Oxford University Press, 1968.

Leclercq, Jean. *The Love of Learning and the Desire for God.* Translated by Catharine Misrahi. New York: Fordham University Press, 1961.

Lentes, Thomas. "'As far as the eye can see . . .': Rituals of Gazing in the Late Middle Ages." In *The Mind's Eye: Art and Theological Argument in the Middle Ages,* edited by Jeffrey F. Hamburger and Anne-Marie Bouché, 360–73. Princeton, NJ: Department of Art and Archaeology and Princeton UP, 2006.

Levy, Ian Christopher. *John Wyclif: Scriptural Logic, Real Presence, and the Parameters of Orthodoxy.* Milwaukee, WI: Marquette University Press, 2003.

Lewis, C. S. *The Allegory of Love.* Oxford: Oxford University Press, 1936.

Lichtmann, Maria R. "'God fulfilled my bodye': Body, Self, and God in Julian of Norwich." In *Gender and Text in the Later Middle Ages,* edited by Jane Chance, 263–78. Gainesville: University Press of Florida, 1996.

Lindahl, Carl. "The Re-Oralized Legends of Robert Mannyng's *Handlyng Synne.*" *Contemporary Legend* 2 (1999): 34–62.

Little, Katherine C. *Confession and Resistance: Defining the Self in Late Medieval England.* Notre Dame, IN: University of Notre Dame Press, 2006.

Lochrie, Karma. *Covert Operations: The Medieval Uses of Secrecy.* Philadelphia: University of Pennsylvania Press, 1999.

———. *Margery Kempe and Translations of the Flesh.* Philadelphia: University of Pennsylvania Press, 1991.

Love, Nicholas. *The Mirror of the Blessed Life of Jesus Christ. A Full Critical Edition.* Edited by Michael G. Sargent. Exeter: University of Exeter Press, 2005.

Ložar, Paula. "The Prologue to the Ordinances of the York Corpus Christi Guild." *Allegorica* 1 (1976): 94–113.

Lydgate, John. "Exposition of the Pater Noster." In *The Minor Poems of John Lydgate*, edited by Henry Noble MacCracken, 60–71. EETS e.s. 107. London: Oxford University Press, 1911.

———. "Fifteen Oes of Christ." In *The Minor Poems of John Lydgate*, edited by Henry Noble MacCracken, 238–50. EETS e.s. 107. London: Oxford University Press, 1911.

———. *Lydgate's Fall of Princes.* Edited by Henry Bergen. EETS e.s. 121, 122, 123, 124. London: Oxford University Press, 1924–27.

———. *The Minor Poems of John Lydgate.* Edited by Henry Noble MacCracken. EETS e.s. 107. London: Oxford University Press, 1911.

———. *The Pilgrimage of the Life of Man.* Edited by F. J. Furnivall. EETS e.s. 77, 83, 92. London: Kegan Paul, 1899, 1901, 1904.

———. "Virtues of the Mass." In *The Minor Poems of John Lydgate*, edited by Henry Noble MacCracken, 87–115. EETS e.s. 107. London: Oxford University Press, 1911.

Macy, Gary. "The 'Dogma of Transubstantiation' in the Middle Ages." In *Treasures from the Storeroom: Medieval Religion and the Eucharist*, 81–120. Collegeville, MN: Liturgical Press, 1999. Originally published in *Journal of Ecclesiastical History* 45 (1994): 11–41.

———. "The Eucharist and Popular Religiosity." In *Treasures from the Storeroom: Medieval Religion and the Eucharist*, 172–95. Collegeville, MN: Liturgical Press, 1999.

———. "The Theological Fate of Berengar's Oath of 1059: Interpreting a Blunder Become Tradition." In *Treasures from the Storeroom: Medieval Religion and the Eucharist*, 36–58. Collegeville, MN: Liturgical Press, 1999. Originally published in *Interpreting Tradition: The Art of Theological Reflection*, edited by Jane Kopas, 27–38. Chico, CA: Scholars Press, 1984.

———. *The Theologies of the Eucharist in the Early Scholastic Period: A Study of the Salvific Function of the Sacrament According to the Theologians c. 1080–c. 1220.* Oxford: Clarendon Press, 1984.

Magill, Kevin J. *Julian of Norwich: Mystic or Visionary?* London: Routledge, 2006.

Mahoney, Dhira B. "Introduction." In *The Grail: A Casebook*, edited by Dhira B. Mahoney, 1–100. New York: Garland, 2000.

Mailloux, Steven. "Hermeneutics, Deconstruction, Allegory." In *The Cambridge Companion to Allegory*, edited by Rita Copeland and Peter T. Struck, 254–65. Cambridge: Cambridge University Press, 2010.

Malory, Thomas. *Complete Works.* Edited by Eugene Vinaver. 2nd ed. Oxford: Oxford University Press, 1971.

Mann, Jill. *Langland and Allegory.* Morton W. Bloomfield Lectures on Medieval English Literature, II. Kalamazoo, MI: Medieval Institute Publications, 1992.

Mannyng, Robert. *The Chronicle.* Edited by Idelle Sullens. Binghamton, NY: Medieval & Renaissance Texts & Studies, 1996.

———. *Handlyng Synne.* Edited by Idelle Sullens. Binghamton, NY: Medieval & Renaissance Texts & Studies, 1983.

Manter, Lisa. "The Savior of Her Desire: Margery Kempe's Passionate Gaze." *Exemplaria* 13 (2001): 39–66.

Manuel des Pechiez. British Library MS Harley 273.

———. British Library MS Harley 4657.

Masson, Cynthea. "The Point of Coincidence: Rhetoric and the Apophatic in Julian of Norwich's Showings." In *Julian of Norwich: A Book of Essays*, edited by Sandra J. McEntire, 153–81. New York: Garland, 1998.

McAvoy, Liz Herbert. *Authority and the Female Body in the Writings of Julian of Norwich and Margery Kempe*. Cambridge: D. S. Brewer, 2004.

McCue, James F. "The Doctrine of Transubstantiation from Berengar through Trent: The Point at Issue." *Harvard Theological Review* 61 (1968): 385–430.

McEntire, Sandra J. "The Likeness of God and the Restoration of Humanity in Julian of Norwich's Showings." In *Julian of Norwich: A Book of Essays*, edited by Sandra J. McEntire, 3–33. New York: Garland, 1998.

McNamer, Sarah. *Affective Meditation and the Invention of Medieval Compassion*. Philadelphia: University of Pennsylvania Press, 2010.

Meditations on the Supper of our Lord, and the Hours of the Passion. Edited by J. Meadows Cowper. EETS o.s. 60. London: N. Trübner & Co., 1875.

Meyer-Lee, Robert J. "Lydgate's Laureate Pose." In *John Lydgate: Poetry, Culture, and Lancastrian England*, edited by Larry Scanlon and James Simpson, 36–60. Notre Dame, IN: University of Notre Dame Press, 2006.

Middle English Dictionary Online. University of Michigan. http://quod.lib.umich.edu/m/med/.

Migne, J. P., ed. *Patrologia Latina, cursus completus*. 1844–55.

Miller, Mark. "Displaced Souls, Idle Talk, Spectacular Scenes: Handlyng Synne and the Perspective of Agency." *Speculum* 71 (1996): 606–32.

Minnis, Alastair. "1215–1349: Culture and History." In *The Cambridge Companion to Medieval English Mysticism*, edited by Vincent Gillespie and Samuel Fanous, 69–89. Cambridge: Cambridge University Press, 2011.

Mirk, John. "De Solempnitate Corporis Cristi." In *Mirk's Festial: A Collection of Homilies*, edited by Theodor Erbe, 168–75. EETS e.s. 96. London: Kegan Paul, 1905.

———. *Mirk's Festial: A Collection of Homilies*. Edited by Theodor Erbe, EETS e.s. 96. London: Kegan Paul, 1905.

Mitchell, Nathan. *Cult and Controversy: The Worship of the Eucharist Outside Mass*. New York: Pueblo, 1982.

Netzley, Ryan. *Reading, Desire, and the Eucharist in Early Modern Religious Poetry*. Toronto: University of Toronto Press, 2011.

Newman, Barbara. *God and the Goddesses: Vision, Poetry, and Belief in the Middle Ages*. Philadelphia: University of Pennsylvania Press, 2003.

———. "What Did It Mean to Say "I Saw"? The Clash between Theory and Practice in Medieval Visionary Culture." *Speculum* 80 (2005): 1–43.

Nissé, Ruth. "'Was it not Routhe to Se?': Lydgate and the Styles of Martyrdom." In *John Lydgate: Poetry, Culture, and Lancastrian England*, edited by Larry Scanlon and James Simpson, 279–98. Notre Dame, IN: University of Notre Dame Press, 2006.

Nolan, Maura. *John Lydgate and the Making of Public Culture*. Cambridge: Cambridge UP, 2005.

———. "Lydgate's Worst Poem." In *Lydgate Matters: Poetry and Material Culture in the Fifteenth Century*, edited by Lisa H. Cooper and Andrea Denny-Brown, 71–87. New York: Palgrave Macmillan, 2008.

Noonan, Sarah. "'Bycause the redyng shold not turne hem to enoye': Reading, Selectivity, and *Pietatis Affectum* in Late Medieval England." *New Medieval Literatures* 15 (2013): 225–54.

Patterson, Lee. *Chaucer and the Subject of History*. Madison: University of Wisconsin Press, 1991.

Paxson, James J. "Inventing the Subject and the Personification of Will in *Piers Plowman*: Rhetorical, Erotic, and Ideological Origins and Limits in Langland's Allegorical Poetics." In *William Langland's* Piers Plowman: *A Book of Essays*, edited by Kathleen M. Hewett-Smith, 195–231. New York: Routledge, 2001.

Pearl. Edited by Sarah Stanbury. Kalamazoo, MI: Medieval Institute Publications, 2001.

Pearsall, Derek. *Old English and Middle English Poetry*. London: Routledge, 1977.

Phillips, Heather. "The Eucharistic Allusions of Pearl." *Mediaeval Studies* 47 (1985): 474–86.

Phillips, Susan E. *Transforming Talk: The Problem with Gossip in Late Medieval England*. University Park: Pennsylvania State University Press, 2007.

Pickstock, Catherine. "Thomas Aquinas and the Quest for the Eucharist." In *Catholicism and Catholicity: Eucharistic Communities in Historical and Contemporary Perspectives*, edited by Sarah Beckwith, 47–68. Oxford: Blackwell, 1999.

Plamper, Jan. "The History of Emotions: An Interview with William Reddy, Barbara Rosenwein, and Peter Stearns." *History and Theory* 49 (2010): 237–65.

"A Prayer to the Sacrament of the Altar." In *Medieval English Lyrics: A Critical Anthology*, edited by R. T. Davies, 115. London: Northwestern University Press, 1963.

Quilligan, Maureen. "Langland's Literal Allegory." *Essays in Criticism* 28 (1978): 95–111.

———. *The Language of Allegory: Defining the Genre*. Ithaca, NY: Cornell University Press, 1979.

Raabe, Pamela. *Imitating God: The Allegory of Faith in* Piers Plowman B. Athens: University of Georgia Press, 1990.

Radbertus, Paschasius. *De Corpore et Sanguine Domini*. Edited by Bede Paulus, Corpus Christianorum, Continuatio Mediaevalis XVI. Turnhout, BE: Brepols, 1969.

Radulescu, Raluca L. "Malory and the Quest for the Holy Grail." In *A Companion to Arthurian Literature*, edited by Helen Fulton, 326–39. West Sussex: Wiley-Blackwell, 2009.

Ratramnus. *De Corpore et Sanguine Domini*. Edited by J. N. Bakhuizen van den Brink. Amsterdam: North-Holland Publishing Company, 1954.

Raymo, Robert R. "Works of Religious and Philosophical Instruction." In *A Manual of the Writings in Middle English*. Ed. Albert E. Hartung. Vol. 7. New Haven: Connecticut Academy, 1986.

Reading, Amity. "'The Ende of Alle Kynez Flesch': Ritual Sacrifice and Feasting in *Cleanness*." *Exemplaria* 21 (2009): 274–95.

Rice, Nicole R. *Lay Piety and Religious Discipline in Middle English Literature*. Cambridge: Cambridge University Press, 2008.

Richmond, Colin. "Margins and Marginality: English Devotion in the Later Middle Ages." In *England in the Fifteenth Century: Proceedings of the 1992 Harlaxton Symposium*, edited by Nicholas Rogers, 242–52. Stamford, CA: Paul Watkins, 1994.

———. "Religion and the Fifteenth-Century English Gentleman." In *The Church, Politics and Patronage in the Fifteenth Century*, edited by Barrie Dobson, 193–203. Gloucester: Alan Sutton, 1984.

Riddy, Felicity. "Text and Self in *The Book of Margery Kempe.*" In *Voices in Dialogue: Reading Women in the Middle Ages,* edited by Linda Olson and Kathryn Kerby-Fulton, 435–53. Notre Dame, IN: University of Notre Dame Press, 2005.

Robbins, Rossell Hope. "Levation Prayers in Middle English Verse." *Modern Philology* 39 (1942): 131–46.

———. "Popular Prayers in Middle English Verse." *Modern Philology* 36 (1939): 337–50.

Robertson, D. W., Jr. "The Cultural Tradition of Handlyng Synne." *Speculum* 22 (1947): 162–85.

Robertson, D. W., Jr., and Bernard F. Huppé. *Piers Plowman and the Scriptural Tradition.* Princeton, NJ: Princeton University Press, 1951.

Robertson, Elizabeth. "Medieval Medical Views of Women and Female Spirituality in the *Ancrene Wisse* and Julian of Norwich's *Showings.*" In *Feminist Approaches to the Body in Medieval Literature,* edited by Linda Lomperis and Sarah Stanbury, 142–67. Philadelphia: University of Pennsylvania Press, 1993.

Ross, Woodburn O., ed. *Middle English Sermons.* EETS o.s. 209. London: Oxford University Press, 1940.

Rubin, Miri. *Corpus Christi: The Eucharist in Late Medieval Culture.* Cambridge: Cambridge University Press, 1991.

Salih, Sarah. "Margery's Bodies: Piety, Work and Penance." In *A Companion to the Book of Margery Kempe,* edited by John H. Arnold and Katherine J. Lewis, 161–76. Cambridge: D. S. Brewer, 2004.

———. *Versions of Virginity in Late Medieval England.* Cambridge: D. S. Brewer, 2001.

Sanok, Catherine. *Her Life Historical: Exemplarity and Female Saints' Lives in Late Medieval England.* Philadelphia: University of Pennsylvania Press, 2007.

Scanlon, Larry. "Lydgate's Poetics: Laureation and Domesticity in the *Temple of Glass.*" In *John Lydgate: Poetry, Culture, and Lancastrian England,* edited by Larry Scanlon and James Simpson, 61–97. Notre Dame, IN: University of Notre Dame Press, 2006.

———. *Narrative, Authority, and Power: The Medieval Exemplum and the Chaucerian Tradition.* Cambridge: Cambridge University Press, 1994.

Scanlon, Larry, and James Simpson, eds. *John Lydgate: Poetry, Culture, and Lancastrian England.* Notre Dame, IN: University of Notre Dame Press, 2006.

Schwartz, Regina Mara. *Sacramental Poetics at the Dawn of Secularism: When God Left the World.* Stanford, CA: Stanford University Press, 2008.

Scott, Anne M. "'For lewed men y vndyr toke on englyssh tonge to make this boke': *Handlyng Synne* and English Didactic Writing for the Laity." In *What Nature Does Not Teach: Didactic Literature in the Medieval and Early Modern Periods,* edited by Juanita Feros Ruys, 377–400. Turnhout, BE: Brepols, 2008.

Shickler, Jon. "The Cross and the Citadel: Reconciling Apophatic and Cataphatic Traditions in the *Showings.*" *Studia Mystica* 21 (2000): 95–125.

Shklar, Ruth. "Cobham's Daughter: *The Book of Margery Kempe* and the Power of Heterodox Thinking." *Modern Language Quarterly* 56 (1995): 277–304.

Shoaf, R. A. "'Mutatio Amoris': 'Penitentia' and the Form of the Book of the Duchess." *Genre* 14 (1981): 163–89.

Simpson, James. "John Lydgate." In *The Cambridge Companion to Medieval English Literature, 1100–1500,* edited by Larry Scanlon, 205–16. Cambridge: Cambridge University Press, 2009.

———. *Piers Plowman: An Introduction*. 2nd rev. ed. Exeter: University of Exeter Press, 2007.

Smith, D. Vance. "Medieval *Forma*: The Logic of the Work." In *Reading for Form*, edited by Susan Wolfson and Marshall Brown, 66–79. Seattle and London: University of Washington Press, 2006.

Somerset, Fiona. *Feeling Like Saints: Lollard Writings after Wyclif*. Ithaca, NY: Cornell University Press, 2014.

———. "'Hard is with seyntis for to make affray': Lydgate the 'Poet-Propagandist' as Hagiographer." In *John Lydgate: Poetry, Culture, and Lancastrian England*, edited by Larry Scanlon and James Simpson, 258–78. Notre Dame, IN: University of Notre Dame Press, 2006.

Somerset, Fiona, Jill C. Havens, and Derrick G. Pitard, eds. *Lollards and Their Influence in Late Medieval England*. Woodbridge: Boydell Press, 2003.

Sponsler, Claire. "Drama and Piety: Margery Kempe." In *A Companion to the Book of Margery Kempe*, edited by John H. Arnold and Katherine J. Lewis, 129–43. Cambridge: D. S. Brewer, 2004.

The Southern Passion. Edited by Beatrice Daw Brown, EETS o.s. 169. London: Oxford University Press, 1927.

Staley, Lynn. *Margery Kempe's Dissenting Fictions*. University Park: Pennsylvania State University Press, 1994.

———. "*Pearl* and the Contingencies of Love and Piety." In *Medieval Literature and Historical Inquiry: Essays in Honor of Derek Pearsall*, edited by David Aers, 83–114. Cambridge: D. S. Brewer, 2000.

Stanbury, Sarah. "The Body and the City in *Pearl*." *Representations* 48 (1994): 30–47.

———. "Introduction." In *Pearl* edited by Sarah Stanbury, 1–30. Kalamazoo, MI: Medieval Institute Publications, 2001.

———. *Seeing the* Gawain-*Poet: Description and the Act of Perception*. Philadelphia: University of Pennsylvania Press, 1991.

———. *The Visual Object of Desire in Late Medieval England*. Philadelphia: University of Pennsylvania Press, 2008.

Steiner, Emily. *Documentary Culture and the Making of Medieval English Literature*. Cambridge: Cambridge University Press, 2003.

Stock, Lorraine Kochanske. "Parable, Allegory, History, and *Piers Plowman*." *Yearbook in Langland Studies* 5 (1991): 143–64.

Sullens, Idelle. "Introduction." In *The Chronicle*, edited by Idelle Sullens, 1–89. Binghamton, NY: Medieval & Renaissance Texts & Studies, 1996. 17

Swanson, R. N. "Passion and Practice: The Social and Ecclesiastical Implications of Passion Devotion in the Late Middle Ages." In *The Broken Body: Passion Devotion in Late-Medieval Culture*, edited by A. A. MacDonald et al., 1–30. Groningen, NL: Egbert Forsten, 1998.

Tanner, Norman P. *The Church in Late Medieval Norwich, 1370–1532*. Toronto: Pontifical Institute of Mediaeval Studies, 1984.

———, ed. *Heresy Trials in the Diocese of Norwich, 1482–31*. London: Royal Historical Society, 1977.

Tentler, Thomas N. *Sin and Confession on the Eve of the Reformation*. Princeton, NJ: Princeton University Press, 1977.

Tomasch, Sylvia. "A *Pearl* Punnology." *Journal of English and Germanic Philology* 88 (1989): 1–20.

Tonry, Kathleen. "Introduction: The 'Sotil Fourmes' of the Fifteenth Century." In *Form and Reform: Reading Across the Fifteenth Century*, edited by Shannon Gayk and Kathleen Tonry, 1–15. Columbus: The Ohio State University Press, 2011.

Torti, Anna. *The Glass of Form: Mirroring Structures from Chaucer to Skelton*. Cambridge: D. S. Brewer, 1991.

Tubach, Frederic C. *Index Exemplorum: A Handbook of Medieval Religious Tales*. Helsinki: Suomalainene Tiedeakatemia, 1969.

Voaden, Rosalynn, ed. *Prophets Abroad: The Reception of Continental Holy Women in Late-Medieval England*. Cambridge: D. S. Brewer, 1996.

Walters, Barbara R., Vincent Corrigan, and Peter T. Ricketts, eds. *The Feast of Corpus Christi*. University Park: Pennsylvania State University Press, 2006.

Walton, Audrey. "The Mendicant Margery: Margery Kempe, Mary Magdalene, and the *Noli Me Tangere*." *Mystics Quarterly* 35 (2009): 1–29.

Watkins, John. "'Sengeley in synglere': *Pearl* and Late Medieval Individualism." *Chaucer Yearbook* 2 (1995): 117–36.

Watson, Nicholas. "Censorship and Cultural Change in Late-Medieval England: Vernacular Theology, the Oxford Translation Debate, and Arundel's Constitutions of 1409." *Speculum* 70 (1995): 822–64.

———. "The Composition of Julian of Norwich's *Revelation of Love*." *Speculum* 68 (1993): 637–83.

———. "The *Gawain*-Poet as a Vernacular Theologian." In *A Companion to the Gawain-Poet*, edited by Derek Brewer and Jonathan Gibson, 293–313. Cambridge: D. S. Brewer, 1997.

———. "The Making of *The Book of Margery Kempe*." In *Voices in Dialogue: Reading Women in the Middle Ages*, edited by Linda Olson and Kathryn Kerby-Fulton, 395–434. Notre Dame, IN: University of Notre Dame Press, 2005.

———. "Visions of Inclusion: Universal Salvation and Vernacular Theology in Pre-Reformation England." *Journal of Medieval and Early Modern Studies* 27 (1997): 145–87.

———. "'Yf women be double naturelly': Remaking 'Woman' in Julian of Norwich's Revelation of Love." *Exemplaria* 8 (1996): 1–34.

Watson, Nicholas, and Jocelyn Wogan-Browne. "The French of England: The *Compileison, Ancrene Wisse*, and the Idea of Anglo-Norman." *Journal of Romance Studies* 4 (2004): 35–58.

Webb, Diana. "Domestic Space and Devotion in the Middle Ages." In *Defining the Holy: Sacred Space in Medieval and Early Modern Europe*, edited by Andrew Spicer and Sarah Hamilton, 27–47. Aldershot: Ashgate, 2005.

———. *Privacy and Solitude in the Middle Ages*. London: Hambledon Continuum, 2007.

Wenzel, Siegfried, ed. *Verses in Sermons: Fasciculus morum and its Middle English Poems*. Cambridge, MA: Medieval Academy, 1978.

William of Shoreham. "De Septem Sacramentis." In *The Poems of William of Shoreham*, edited by M. Konrath, EETS e.s. 86, 1–78. London: Kegan Paul, 1902.

Williams, Tara. "Manipulating Mary: Maternal, Sexual, and Textual Authority in *The Book of Margery Kempe*." *Modern Philology* 107 (2010): 528–55.

Wogan-Browne, Jocelyn, Nicholas Watson, Andrew Taylor, and Ruth Evans, eds. *The Idea of the Vernacular: An Anthology of Middle English Literary Theory, 1280–1520*. University Park: Pennsylvania State University Press, 1999.

Wyclif, John. *De Eucharistia Tractatus Maior.* Edited by Iohann Loserth. London: Trübner & Co., 1892.

Zeeman, Nicolette. "Medieval Religious Allegory: French and English." In *Cambridge Companion to Allegory,* edited by Rita Copeland and Peter T. Struck, 148–61. Cambridge: Cambridge University Press, 2010.

INDEX

Abbot, Christopher, 109
Ackerman, Robert W., 75n33
Adams, Robert, 81n1
Aers, David, 5n7, 52n2, 53n3, 57, 67n31, 81–82, 88, 100n32, 101n34, 108n8, 109n10, 111n16, 116nn20–21, 137n11, 140n18, 173n30
affective piety, 7–9, 32, 34, 107–8, 115, 116, 125, 132–43, 154, 157, 166
Akbari, Suzanne Conklin, 116n20
allegory, 2, 3, 5, 9, 15, 16, 80, 183–84; as feature of eucharistic theology, 9–14; in *Book of Margery Kempe,* 144, 146, 158; in Lydgate's writings, 160, 164–65, 167–74, 181; in *Pearl,* 63, 72; in *Piers Plowman,* 81–103; in *A Revelation of Love,* 106, 115–22, 126–27, 129. See also *corpus mysticum*
Allen, Elizabeth, 37
Ambrose, 10–12, 49
Ambrosian approaches to the Eucharist, 10–15, 26, 28, 30, 47, 80–81, 183, 184. See also *corpus Christi*
Anderson, J. J., 52n2
Aquinas, Thomas, 12, 14, 27–30, 33–34, 76n34, 98n29, 100n32, 128, 141, 175, 183–84
Aristotle, 12, 28, 140, 168
Arnold, John H., 8n19, 145, 146n34, 150n37, 153n44
Arnould, E. J., 24n10
Astell, Ann W., 5n7, 98n29
Aston, Margaret, 5n6, 20n3, 110n15
Atkinson, Clarissa W., 144n29, 151n39

Atkinson, Stephen C. B., 184n4
Audelay, John, 54n9
Auerbach, Erich, 39
Augustine, 10–15, 28, 30, 81, 84, 94, 111n17, 116n20, 120n26
Augustinian approaches to the Eucharist, 10–15, 80, 81, 183. See also *corpus mysticum*

Bahr, Arthur, 52n3
Bailey, Terence, 77n36
Baker, Denise N., 106n3, 111n17, 114n18
baking, as eucharistic image, 162, 172
Barney, Stephen A., ix, 94n26, 98n28, 102n36, 103n37
Barr, Helen, 53n3
Barr, Jessica, 8n18, 154
Barratt, Alexandra, 106n3
Bauerschmidt, Frederick Christian, 111n16
Beadle, Richard, 137n14
Beckwith, Sarah, 5–6, 76n34, 88n20, 137n11, 143n27, 176n36
Berengar of Tours, 11–13, 26–28
Besserman, Lawrence, 55n15
Book of Margery Kempe. See Kempe, Margery
Book of Vice and Virtues, 75
books of hours, 32, 55, 133
Bose, Mishtooni, and J. Patrick Hornbeck II, 5n6
Bossy, John, 31n33, 34, 55n12, 55n13, 55n17
Bowers, John M., 52n2, 90n23

• 203 •

Boyle, Leonard E., O. P., 20n2
Bradley, Christopher G., 144n28
Bridget of Sweden, 107–8, 135, 147, 150
Browe, Peter, 32n37
Bryan, Jennifer, 8n18, 133n1, 142n26
Burr, David, 29n27
Burrow, J. A., 57n24
Bynum, Caroline Walker, 5n7, 8n17, 31n36, 34n46, 47n58, 53n4, 56n22, 76n34, 89n22, 105, 107–8, 120n25, 138n15, 156n48

cannibalism, 2, 10, 11, 26, 35, 49
Cannon, Christopher, 6–7
Carruthers, Mary, 82n4, 83n5
Caspers, Charles, 166n23
Catto, J. I., 31n34, 55n12, 56n21, 110n15
Cervone, Cristina Maria, 8
Chazelle, Celia, 85n9
child, eucharistic images of, 1, 28, 37n50, 44–50, 89, 148
Chronicle. See Mannyng, Robert
Clark, Francis, 33n44
Cleanness. See *Pearl*-poet
Clopper, Lawrence M., 83n6
Cole, Andrew, ix, 5n6, 160, 162n8, 166n22, 178n40, 179n41
Coleman, Joyce, 19n1, 23n9
Colish, Marcia L., 84n7, 86, 99n30
confession, 20, 24, 46n57, 56, 99–104, 144, 159n2
Constitutions (1401), 4
Cooper, Lisa H., 160n2, 167n25
Cooper-Rompato, Christine F., 150n36
Copeland, Rita, 5n6, 117nn23–24
corporate body of Christ. See *corpus mysticum*
corpus Christi (as distinct from *corpus mysticum*), 13, 14, 87, 88, 143, 149, 151–52, 175–76. *See also* Real Presence
Corpus Christi (feast day), 1, 5, 88, 146, 148, 174–81, 183
corpus mysticum, 13–16, 82–83, 87–92, 97–98, 101–3, 133, 143–49, 150–53, 158, 161, 174–76, 181
Crane, Susan, 57
Craun, Edwin D., 152n42
Crosby, Ruth, 23n9

crucifixion, as eucharistic imagery, 32; and *Handlyng Synne*, 19, 38–41, 43, 46–47; and Julian of Norwich, 113; and Love's *Mirror*, 142; and Lydgate, 164, 169, 177, 179; and Margery Kempe, 146–47, 154–55; and *Piers Plowman*, 91. *See also* Passion, Christ's

Davidson, Clifford, 57n24
Deguileville, 167–68
De Heretico Cumburendo (1401), 4
de Lubac, Henri, 13, 175n35
de Man, Paul, 9
Despres, Denise Louise, 52n2
Dinshaw, Carolyn, 145n32, 157
Doubting Thomas, 48–49, 97
Duffy, Eamon, 5n7, 54n10, 55nn11–13, 55n17
Duggan, H. N., 78n37

Easter, 24, 31, 82, 90–91, 100
Edmondson, George, 67n31
elevation of the host, 31, 32, 54, 108, 134n5, 141, 143, 165–66
exempla, 1–2, 11, 15, 19–24, 33, 34–50, 89, 142, 151–53, 171

figura and *veritas* (figure and truth), 13, 81, 84–88, 184–85
Finke, Laurie A., 83n5
Fitzpatrick, P. J., 13n33, 33n44, 47n58
Fradenburg, Louise O., 67n31
Freud, Sigmund, 67n31
Fulton, Rachel, 11n27
Furnivall, F. J., 20n3, 54n8, 169n28
Fuss, Diana, 67n31

Ganim, John M., 20n1
Garrett, Robert Max, 52n2
Gasse, Rosanne, 102n35
Gatta, John, Jr., 52n2
Gawain-poet. See *Pearl*-poet
Gayk, Shannon, ix, 6, 160nn2–3, 161n5, 162n8, 163
Ghosh, Kantik, 4n5, 5n6, 8n18, 139n16, 144n28
Gibson, Gail McMurray, 136n10, 150n36, 154n46
Gillespie, Vincent, 4n5, 8n18, 144n28

INDEX   205

Godden, Malcolm, 90n24
Goering, Joseph, 12n30, 27n18
grail, 184–85
grain imagery, 63–64, 98–99, 172–73
Graves, Pamela C., 55n16
Greenspan, Kate, 23n9
Griffiths, Lavinia, 82n4, 83n5
Grisdale, D. M., 88n19

Hagen, Susan K., 168n26, 171n29
Handlyng Synne. *See* Mannyng, Robert
Hanna, Ralph, 23
Hardman, Phillipa, 161n6
Haren, Michael, 58n27
Harper, John, 31n30, 31n33, 54nn5–6
heresy, 5, 107, 110, 136, 145, 160. *See also* Lollards
Hewett-Smith, Kathleen M., 83
Hilton, Walter, 135, 138, 141
Holloway, Julia Bolton, 150n36
Holsinger, Bruce, 7n16
Horstmann, Carl, 1n2, 33n41
"How to Hear Mass," 20n3, 54
Hudson, Anne, 5n6, 20n3, 110n13
Hugh of St. Victor, 76n35, 86, 98

identification, 1, 4, 8–9, 15–16; and *Handlyng Synne*, 19, 21, 30, 32, 34, 37–50; and Julian of Norwich, 105, 108, 110, 112–13, 117, 126; and Love's *Mirror*, 138, 142; and Margery Kempe, 146–47, 150, 153–55; and *Pearl*, 52, 62, 67–71, 77, 80
Ihle, Sandra Ness, 184n3
Incarnation, 7, 8n20, 84, 95, 119, 120, 162, 172–73, 184; as Word made flesh, 3, 7, 84, 183–84
interpretation, 73, 83, 96, 106, 115–18, 122, 129, 160, 170–72, 174–81, 183; of the Eucharist as a text, 7, 13, 18, 50, 51, 80, 87, 102, 104, 138–40, 164–67, 170–72; refusal of, 3, 51, 138–40

James, Mervyn, 5, 88n20, 176n36
Jenkins, Jacqueline, 105n2, 150n37
Jenkins, Priscilla, 102n36
Johnson, Ian, 137n11
Julian of Norwich, 3, 15–17, 104–31, 138, 183
Jungmann, Joseph A., 31n30, 33n44, 54n5

Justice, Steven, 29

Karnes, Michelle, 111n16, 115–16, 121n27, 137n11
Kemmler, Fritz, 19n1
Kempe, Margery, 2, 9, 15, 17, 105, 131–36, 143–58, 164, 175, 183
Kennedy, V. L., 31n35
Knox, Ronald, 25n11
Krug, Rebecca, 135, 144, 163n12

lamb imagery, 3, 63, 66, 68–72, 76–78, 166, 169
Lanfranc of Bec, 11
Langland, William, 2, 9, 15–16, 57, 81–104, 106, 109, 117, 143, 149, 175, 183n1
Last Supper, 26, 35, 136–39, 162, 179
Lateran Council, Fourth (1215), 20, 27–30
Lawton, David, 145n33, 159n2
Lay Folks Mass Book, 20n3, 32, 54, 134n5
Leclercq, Jean, 135n6
Lentes, Thomas, 166n23
Levy, Ian Christopher, 10n22, 11nn26–27, 12n28, 26n14, 27n19, 28n20, 29n27, 85n9, 86n12
Lewis, C. S., 168
Lichtmann, Maria R., 111n16
Lindahl, Carl, 20n1, 23n9
Little, Katherine C., 7n16, 46n57
liturgy. *See* Mass
Lochrie, Karma, 46n57, 144n29, 145n32
Lollards, 5, 20n3, 83, 110, 136, 139–40, 151, 152n41, 175n33. *See also* Wyclif
Love, Nicholas, 15, 17, 131–44, 150, 154–55, 157–58, 165, 183
Ložar, Paula, 88n18
Lydgate, John, 15, 17, 141, 159–82; *Exposition of the Pater Noster*, 162; *Fall of Princes*, 174; *Fifteen Oes*, 162–64; *Pilgrimage of the Life of Man*, 160, 167–74, 179; *Procession of Corpus Christi*, 160, 174–81; *Virtues of the Mass*, 162n9, 164–67

Macy, Gary, 10n22, 11n27, 12nn29–30, 26n15, 27nn17–18, 30n29, 85n9, 166n23
Magill, Kevin J., 111n16
Mahoney, Dhira B., 184n3
Mailloux, Steven, 117n23

Malory, Thomas, 184–85
Mann, Jill, 82n4
Mannyng, Robert: *Chronicle*, 23; *Handlyng Synne*, 15, 19–25, 32, 34–51, 54, 80–81, 90n23, 109, 138, 164, 182
Man of Sorrows, 148, 162
Manter, Lisa, 154n46
Manuel des Pechiez, 20n1, 22, 24
Mary (mother of Jesus), 11, 44–46, 96, 112–13, 115, 123, 154–55, 166, 177–78
Mary Magdalene, 156–57
Mass, 3, 7, 16, 20n3, 24, 26, 29–37, 50, 53–63, 74–80, 82, 89–93, 108, 132–44, 145, 151, 164–66, 172, 182, 185; as exemplum setting, 1–2, 47–50; practice of purchasing Masses, 21n4, 24, 34, 56. *See also* elevation of the host; processions
Masson, Cynthea, 111n16
materiality, 2–4, 6–7, 83
McAvoy, Liz Herbert, 154n46, 155, 156n47
McCue, James F., 10n22, 29nn26–27, 30nn28–30
McEntire, Sandra J., 106n3, 111n16, 114n18, 145n33, 150n36
McNamer, Sarah, 8n18, 134, 137n12, 142n24, 142n26, 166n21
Meditations on the Supper of our Lord, 20n3
metaphor, 3, 11, 15–17, 51, 84; and Julian of Norwich, 122–23; and Lydgate, 160, 162–64; and Margery Kempe, 153, 156–57; and *Pearl*, 51, 62–74, 76, 79–80; and *Piers Plowman*, 92, 103
Meyer-Lee, Robert J., 159n1, 174
Miller, Mark, 37, 20n1
Minnis, Alastair, 20n2, 58n27
miracles, eucharistic, 29, 32–33, 41, 47–49, 89n22, 142, 145–46, 169. *See also* exempla
Mirk, John, 33, 88n19, 100n33
Mirror of the Blessed Life of Jesus Christ. See Love, Nicholas
Mitchell, Nathan, 11n27, 25n11, 31n31
mystical body of Christ. *See corpus mysticum*
mystics, 5, 8n17, 17, 105–31, 143–58

Netzley, Ryan, 3n4
Newman, Barbara, 120n25, 151n38
Nissé, Ruth, 160n2
Nolan, Maura, 6, 7n12, 161nn5–7

Noonan, Sarah, 135n9

paradox, 2, 14, 24–25, 76n34, 81, 124, 137, 140, 142
Passion, Christ's, 20n3, 32n38, 35, 38, 40, 43, 47, 54n10, 89, 112–13, 134, 139, 154–55, 162–64. *See also* crucifixion; Last Supper
Patience. *See Pearl*-poet
Patterson, Lee, 46n57
pax, 55, 75
Paxson, James J., 83n5
Pearl-poet, 16, 50, 51–80, 109, 141, 182; *Cleanness*, 16, 58–62, 63, 80; *Patience*, 16, 58–59, 63, 80; *Pearl*, 15–16, 50–53, 58–59, 62–81; *Sir Gawain and the Green Knight*, 16, 59, 61, 63, 80
Pearsall, Derek, 19n1
penance. *See* confession
Pentecost, 88, 91–92, 98, 103, 149
Phillips, Heather, 52n2
Phillips, Susan E., 37
Pickstock, Catherine, 76n34
Piers Plowman. See Langland, William
Plamper, Jan, 142n23
poetics, 2–9, 15, 17, 50, 105, 106, 109, 159–60, 175, 181, 182, 184–85
"Prayer to the Sacrament of the Altar," 54n9
prefiguration, 162, 165–66, 169–70, 173–77, 179–81
processions, 77, 145, 148–49, 174–81, 183

Quilligan, Maureen, 82n4, 83n5, 116n20, 117n22

Raabe, Pamela, 82n4, 83n6
Radbertus, Paschasius, 85–86
Radulescu, Raluca L., 184n4
Ratramnus, 85
Reading, Amity, 59n29
Real Presence, 21, 25–29, 31, 36, 49, 52n2, 82, 84–85, 89, 100, 164
reception of the Eucharist, 2, 16, 30–31, 36, 47, 55, 75, 82, 87–91, 99–104, 130, 132, 146–47, 166n23, 170, 182
resurrection, 48, 63–64, 68, 86, 90–91, 95, 97, 127, 157, 162, 172. *See also* Easter
Revelation of Love. See Julian of Norwich
Rice, Nicole R., 8n18, 133n1

Richmond, Colin, 55n16, 57n25
Riddy, Felicity, 145n33, 153n44
Robbins, Rossell Hope, 20n3, 32n41, 33n41, 54n9
Robertson, D. W., Jr., 19n1, 82n4, 102n36
Robertson, Elizabeth, 7n16, 106n3
Rolle, Richard, 135, 141
Ross, Woodburn, O., 88n19, 100n33
Rubin, Miri, 1n1, 5, 7n15, 11n27, 31nn31–32, 33nn41–42, 44n54, 55n14, 88n20, 89n22, 98n29, 162n10, 163n13, 164n16, 166n23, 176, 183n1

sacrament, 28–29, 33, 47, 83–88, 128–30, 146, 161, 166, 173, 183; sacramental actions, 60, 77–80, 100; seven sacraments, 98, 106–10, 114, 121–25, 128–30, 151–52, 171; 161, 166, 171
sacrifice, 21, 32–37, 40–41, 44–49, 59n29, 77, 89, 120, 141, 156n48, 166
Salih, Sarah, 144n31, 153n44
Sanok, Catherine, 37, 146n35, 150n36
Scanlon, Larry, 37–38, 135n8, 159n1, 160nn2–3
Schwartz, Regina Mara, 3n4
Scott, Ann M., 20n1, 22n5
Scotus, Duns, 29–30, 34n46
Shickler, Jon, 111n16
Shklar, Ruth, 145n32
Shoaf, R. A., 20n1
Simpson, James, 5n7, 7n16, 82n2, 90n24, 159n1, 160nn2–3, 175n33
Sir Gawain and the Green Knight. See Pearl-poet
Smith, D. Vance, 7n12
Somerset, Fiona, 5n6, 8n18, 160n2
Southern Passion, 20n3

Sponsler, Claire, 145n32
Staley, Lynn, 7n16, 53n3, 108n8, 109n10, 111n16, 144n29, 144n31, 145n32, 151n40
Stanbury, Sarah, 52nn1–2, 56n18, 67n31, 79, 106n3, 137, 142nn25–26
Steiner, Emily, 163n13, 168n26
Stock, Lorraine Kochanske, 99n31
Sullens, Idelle, 22n6, 23nn8–9
Swanson, R. N., 32n38

Tanner, Norman P., 107n4, 152n41
Tentler, Thomas N., 20n2
Tomasch, Sylvia, 71n32
Tonry, Kathleen, 6, 7n13
Torti, Anna, 134n3, 165n19
transubstantiation, 1–6, 8n17, 12–13, 25–30, 31, 35–36, 84, 93, 106, 110, 125, 136–41, 145, 152n41, 162, 167–70, 172, 179, 182, 184
Tubach, Frederic C., 37n50

vernacular theology, 4, 8
Voaden, Rosalynn, 107n4

Walton, Audrey, 157n49
Watkins, John, 53n3
Watson, Nicholas, 4n5, 7n16, 22n5, 56n23, 57, 105n2, 106n3, 107nn4–5, 110n12, 114n18, 137n11, 151n38, 153n43
Webb, Diana, 55n15, 56nn19–20
Wenzel, Siegfried, 33n41
William of Shoreham, 20n3, 21n3, 32, 87
Williams, Tara, 154n46
Word made flesh. *See* Incarnation
Wyclif, John, 20n3, 83, 110. *See also* Lollards

Zeeman, Nicolette, 82n2, 117, 168nn26–27

INTERVENTIONS: NEW STUDIES IN MEDIEVAL CULTURE
Ethan Knapp, Series Editor

Interventions: New Studies in Medieval Culture publishes theoretically informed work in medieval literary and cultural studies. We are interested both in studies of medieval culture and in work on the continuing importance of medieval tropes and topics in contemporary intellectual life.

Challenging Communion: The Eucharist and Middle English Literature
    JENNIFER GARRISON

Chaucer on Screen: Absence, Presence, and Adapting the Canterbury Tales
    EDITED BY KATHLEEN COYNE KELLY AND TISON PUGH

Chaucer, Gower, and the Affect of Invention
    STEELE NOWLIN

Fragments for a History of a Vanishing Humanism
    EDITED BY MYRA SEAMAN AND EILEEN A. JOY

The Medieval Risk-Reward Society: Courts, Adventure, and Love in the European Middle Ages
    WILL HASTY

The Politics of Ecology: Land, Life, and Law in Medieval Britain
    EDITED BY RANDY P. SCHIFF AND JOSEPH TAYLOR

The Art of Vision: Ekphrasis in Medieval Literature and Culture
    EDITED BY ANDREW JAMES JOHNSTON, ETHAN KNAPP, AND MARGITTA ROUSE

Desire in the Canterbury Tales
    ELIZABETH SCALA

Imagining the Parish in Late Medieval England
    ELLEN K. RENTZ

Truth and Tales: Cultural Mobility and Medieval Media
    EDITED BY FIONA SOMERSET AND NICHOLAS WATSON

Eschatological Subjects: Divine and Literary Judgment in Fourteenth-Century French Poetry
    J. M. MOREAU

Chaucer's (Anti-)Eroticisms and the Queer Middle Ages
    TISON PUGH

Trading Tongues: Merchants, Multilingualism, and Medieval Literature
    JONATHAN HSY

Translating Troy: Provincial Politics in Alliterative Romance
    ALEX MUELLER

Fictions of Evidence: Witnessing, Literature, and Community in the Late Middle Ages
    JAMIE K. TAYLOR

Answerable Style: The Idea of the Literary in Medieval England
    EDITED BY FRANK GRADY AND ANDREW GALLOWAY

Scribal Authorship and the Writing of History in Medieval England
    MATTHEW FISHER

Fashioning Change: The Trope of Clothing in High- and Late-Medieval England
    ANDREA DENNY-BROWN

Form and Reform: Reading across the Fifteenth Century
    EDITED BY SHANNON GAYK AND KATHLEEN TONRY

How to Make a Human: Animals and Violence in the Middle Ages
    KARL STEEL

Revivalist Fantasy: Alliterative Verse and Nationalist Literary History
    RANDY P. SCHIFF

Inventing Womanhood: Gender and Language in Later Middle English Writing
    TARA WILLIAMS

Body Against Soul: Gender and Sowlehele *in Middle English Allegory*
    MASHA RASKOLNIKOV

www.ingramcontent.com/pod-product-compliance
Lightning Source LLC
Chambersburg PA
CBHW030111010526
44116CB00005B/194